Forum Italicum
Filibrary Series
No. 21

The Italian Jewish Experience

**Edited by
Honorable Thomas P. DiNapoli**

**Forum Italicum Publishing
Stony Brook, New York**

Library of Congress Cataloging-in-Publication Data

Thomas P. DiNapoli, *The Italian Jewish Experience*

p. cm.
1. Jews in Italy   2. Holocaust
3. Jews and social problems
4. Italy: Ethnic relations
I. Title.   II. Series.

ISBN   1-893127-21-4

FORUM ITALICUM
Center for Italian Studies
State University of New York at Stony Brook
Stony Brook, NY 11794-3358
USA
http:// www.italianstudies.org

Copyright © 2000 by *Forum Italicum, Inc.*
All Rights Reserved
Printed in the United States of America

TABLE OF CONTENTS

Preface vii

A Map to the World's First Ghetto
    Steve Siporin 1

The Jew Rediscovered
    Fabio Della Seta 15

An Historical Perspective
    Gastone Ortona Orefice 39

The Jews in Sicily
    Gaetano Cipolla 51

La Lumia and the Story of the Sicilian Jews
    Salvatore G. Rotella 65

Devils Without Horns: The Festa dei Giudei
    Salvatore Salerno 83

Identity of a Jewish Community in a Provincial Town: Ancona
    Davide Stimili 97

The Jewish Risorgimento and the Questione Romana
    Roberto Maria Dainotto 107

Reflections on the Priebke Affair on Massacres, Trials, History and Memory
    Stanislao G. Pugliese 117

Risking All for Brotherhood
    Maria Lombardo 127

Mussolini and Fascist Anti-Semitism: Turning Point of a Regime
    Philip V. Cannistraro 133

Nationalisms and Internationalism: The Response of Italian Jews to Fascism
    James Walston 141

Child of the Ghetto
    Edda Servi-Machlin 155

Racial laws and internment in Natalia Ginzburg's *La strada che va in città* and *Tutti i nostri ieri*
    Claudia Nocentini 163

Jews, Catholics, and Pope Pius XII
    Sister Margherita Marchione 177

Judaism and Manhood in the Novels of Giorgio Bassani
    Lucienne Kroha 185

Italy: A Fond Remembrance
    Harry Kaufmann 199

The Coherence of Memory
    M. Sofia Casnedi 207

Contemporary Jewish Memorialists in Italy: The Reasons of a Recent Literary Phenomenon
    Fabio Girelli-Carasi 213

The Garden of Arturo Vivante
    Carolyn Feleppa Balducci 225

Index 241

Preface

The history of the Jewish people is one of triumph and tragedy. An important and often overlooked chapter in this history is the story of the Jewish community in Italy. It is a story that tells of an enduring relationship between this land and this people. The Jewish presence on the Italian peninsula extends to ancient time, two millenniums before the founding of a modern unified Italy and even predating Christianity. Like any lasting relationship, it is a story laced with intimacy and stress, beauty and darkness, ease and contradiction. Above all it is a story of lasting significance, worthy of a full exploration of all its complexities, many high points and even the low points.

The State University of New York at Stony Brook's renown Center for Italian Studies delved into this story by presenting a symposium entitled "The Italian Jewish Experience" on October 24-25, 1998. The program included photo exhibits, a film presentation, a reception and scholarly presentations depicting the full range of topics related to the Italian Jewish saga. This volume includes some of the papers presented at the symposium. It is an important contribution to the continuing examination of the Italian Jewish experience in both historical and contemporary analysis.

I was privileged to chair one of the sessions and I was struck by the response from the local community to this symposium as evidenced by the large audience that turned out to witness the proceedings. Without question, the interest can be attributed to the strong connection and shared experiences of the Long Island Jewish and Italian American communities.

As Americans, their immigrant histories have been interwoven for over one hundred years from the days when these two groups constituted a major proportion of the people coming to the United States during the period of great immigration at the start of the twentieth century. As New Yorkers, their personal stories of struggle and success occupy the same time, space and place. Beyond sharing the geography of the city, the county, the neighborhood and the block, it is often observed that Jews and Italians have a commonality in values with regard to such priorities as family, faith, and food and possess an abiding belief in the American Dream. One point in evidence, though anecdotal, but to which any New Yorker can readily and happily attest, is the striking similarity among Jewish and Italian grandmothers!

That the modern, American associations between these peoples have powerful parallels and precedents in the history of the Italian Jewish experience is a remarkable reminder of this topic's relevance to us. It helps us to understand the relative ease in relations between American Jews and Italians. It helps us to appreciate the longevity of the Jewish presence in the larger Italian community. It helps us to value the emotions that motivated many non-Jewish Italians to defy official policy in protecting Jews during the Nazi occupation. The pages of this volume chronicle the breadth and depth of the Italian Jewish experience in a way that is meaningful to us as Americans.

A Map to the World's First Ghetto by Steve Siporin describes the neighborhood in Venice in which Jews created their own community within a community. Though the ghetto represents a negative treatment, it also serves as a reminder and preserver of identity. Fabio Della Seta's The Jew Rediscovered provides a comprehensive review of Jewish life in the city of Rome throughout history. As an Italian Jew, Della Seta's insights are rooted in a self-exploration of his Jewish identity. His witness to the years of the racial laws and the Nazi occupation, including his own story of being hidden with the help of Italian church officials, offers a powerful narrative. Similarly, Gastone Ortona Orefice presents a compelling description of his experiences as an Italian Jew surviving the tragic days of the Fascist regime and the Nazis. Orefice's An Historical Perspective surveys the course of Jewish history on the Italian peninsula from the era of ancient Rome to modern Italy and is punctuated with telling observations

The history of Sicily and of the Sicilian Jews receives considerable analysis in The Jews in Sicily by Gaetano Cipolla and in La Lumia and the Story of the Sicilian Jews by Salvatore Rotella. Both Cipolla and Rotella illuminate Jewish life on Sicily throughout the ever-changing dominance and governance of the island by successive conquerors, culminating with the Spanish edict of 1492 which led to conversion or expulsion. Devils Without Horn,: The Festa dei Giudei by Salvatore Salerno describes an odd and old custom included in the holy week celebrations that take place in the small Sicilian mountain town of San Fratello. Salerno speculates on the mysterious origins of the curious, carnival-like "Feast of the Jews" that is an integral part of the town's Easter observance. The focus on communities continues in Identity of a Jewish Community in a Provincial Town: Ancona by Davide Stimili. Utilizing descriptions found in novels, Stimili paints the picture of Jewish life in this community on the shore of the Adriatic.

The Italian Jewish community felt the impact of historical events in ways that were at times the same as the larger Italian community and sometimes in ways that were distinctly, and tragically, linked to their Jewish identity. The events of the Risorgimento and the unification of Italy had great effect on all Italians. In The Jewish Risorgimento and the Questione Romana, Roberto Maria Dainotto examines the anticipation with which the Jewish community of Rome awaited Garibaldi's liberation of the city from the Pope's armies. The agony Rome's Jewish community suffered as some of the victims in the notorious 1944 Nazi massacre of Italian citizens in the Ardeatine Caves is considered in Reflections on the Priebke Affair on Massacres, Trials, History and Memory by Stanislao G. Pugliese. Nationalisms and Internationalism: The Response of Italian Jews to Fascism by James Watson outlines how Italian Jews generally supported Italian unification and goes on to discuss the community's response to Fascism, Anti-Fascism and Zionism. In an intriguing point about the early days of the Fascist movement, Watson identifies Jewish participation in the founding of the party, thus underscoring how most Italian Jews have been generally supportive of the mainstream of Italian public opinion.

Italian Jews were not spared the tragedy, dislocation and devastation of the Holocaust. Though a far greater proportion of the Italian Jewish community survived this most inhuman chapter in human history as compared to most other European Jewish populations, the story of the Italian Jews includes the horrors of this period. In Racial Laws and Internment in Natalia Ginzburg's *La strada che va in città* and *Tutti i nostri ieri*, Claudia Nocentini discusses the writer's experience of internment and its impact on her literary works. Sister Margherita Marchione's Jews, Catholics and Pope Pius XII provides a sympathetic view on the efforts of the Roman Catholic Church and Pope Pius XII to protect the Jewish people.

Lucienne Kroha further examines the Italian Jewish experience through a literary perspective in Judaism and Manhood in the Novels of Giorgio Bassani, Three novels, the best known of which was popularized in the film version of The Garden of the Finzi-Continis, take place in the author's hometown of Ferrara and poignantly reflect Bassani's own life experience as Jew before and during the enactment of the racial laws in 1938. Italy: A Fond Remembrance may seem an unexpected title for the story of a Jewish family's life in Austria, Croatia and Italy during the years of World War II. But Harry Kaufmann's personal history is indeed a story of compassion and humanity. The bittersweet expressions in The Coherence of Memory by M. Sofia Casnedi reflect a contrasting recollection.

Fabio Girelli-Carasi, in Contemporary Jewish Memorialists in Italy: The Reasons of a Recent Literary Phenomenon, analyzes the vitality of Jewish expression in Italian publishing today as a positive sign of accepted diversity. The insight to be gleaned from the literature of Italian Jewish writers is exemplified in The Garden of Arturo Vivante by Carolyn Feleppa Balducci. Vivante's writing captures a broad range of experience, including the writer's internment as an Italian national in camps in Britain and Canada.

As the reader will see, this volume is a varied and evocative survey of a subject worthy of continued research. It is sure to be a significant addition to the evolving scholarship on the Italian Jewish experience. We all owe a debt of gratitude to the Center for Italian Studies for convening a symposium that produced such thought provoking and insightful presentations.

The Center for Italian Studies at SUNY Stony Brook is a premier institution in its field and is widely respected in the United States as well as in Italy for its work. Inspired by the dynamic leadership of its Director, Professor Mario Mignone, the Center effectively promotes scholarship and research on Italian language, culture and history and in Italian American studies. The success of the Center is a tribute to the dedicated efforts of Mario Mignone and the invaluable assistance he receives from the Center's staff including Executive Director Jo Fusco, the Executive

Council, and the Advisory Council. New York State Senator Kenneth LaValle, Chairman of the Advisory Council, has been an especially ardent supporter. The Center's many achievements would not be possible without the generous support provided by the University's administration, led by SUNY Stony Brook's highly regarded President, Dr. Shirley Strum Kenny.

On a personal note, I would like to express my deep appreciation to Mario Mignone for inviting me to participate in the preparation of this publication. I admire Mario for his academic accomplishments and I value the warm friendship extended by him and his extraordinary wife, Dr. Lois Mignone, to me over many years.

I invite you to read the pages that follow to explore the fascinating story of The Italian Jewish Experience.

HONORABLE THOMAS P. DiNAPOLI
Great Neck, Long Island, New York
April 2000

A Map to the World's First Ghetto

The Jewish community of Venice, Italy, small as it has become at the end of the twentieth century, still maintains a direct connection with its historic past through an informal, folk map of the ghetto, an ironic sense of place that is passed along orally within a religious/ethnic group. The contents of that map and the importance the ghetto still holds for Jewish Venetian identity is the topic of this article.

A brief, outline history of how and why Jews came to occupy their small corner of Venice will provide the reader with a context in which to understand the data I have gathered here.

In 1516, the world's first ghetto was created in Venice, Italy. Jews, like other minorities with a strong sense of community (then and now) often clustered together in their own neighborhoods or streets, their own quarters within cities. But this practice had oftentimes been partly voluntary, had not necessarily included all the Jews in a given city, and had never been so extreme. In Venice, the Jewish quarter was to be walled-off, closed, guarded, and patrolled — virtually sealed-off like a prison each night from sunset to sunrise — with the Jews locked in.[1]

The Venetian authorities, like other rulers in Christian Europe, did not want to allow Jews — the "leaven of disbelief" — to live permanently in their city. Jews were seen as bearing something like an infectious disease — they were dangerous, they might "contaminate" Christians, and their very existence seemed to represent a challenge and an insult to Christianity.[2]

But, on the other hand, the Venetian state (and other Italian city-states as well) did not want to forego the economic advantage that the Jews brought — particularly the low-interest loans they provided the urban poor through pawnshops. The city did not have to subsidize the poor through loans when Jewish pawnshops could be required by law to provide low-interest loans instead. Not only that — the city could tax Jews for the right to perform this service *and* make it one of the few legal occupations allowed Jews besides.[3]

But these economic advantages flew in the face of religious and racial fear of the Jews. Their presence was desirable, yet it was felt to be threatening and dangerous. Still, the power of the Venetian state was built on trade, and its authorities were much too sanguine and mercenary to let go of the Jews.

The invention of the ghetto was the perfect solution. Keep the Jews in the city for the money they saved the state, tax them for the right to live in Venice, but imprison them, seal them off, keep them from "infecting" the rest of the city. (And in the early sixteenth century their options for going elsewhere were extremely limited.) Venetians could avail themselves of the benefits of Jewish loan banks while minimizing the "danger" of being influenced by Jews.

In 1516 the Serenissima found a place for the segregation of the Jews that was far from the geographic, political, and spiritual center of the city, Piazza San Marco. The choice of location itself appears to have been a symbolic statement, conscious or not — an objective correlative of the alien, "infectious" status of the Jews. "We will allow you space here, but you do not belong," the statement read. "We consign you to the margins."[4] The authorities in the Doge's Palace chose a peripheral area — a tiny island called "the new foundry" because of the iron foundry that previously existed there. "New foundry" in Italian was "*ghetto nuovo*" — a fateful name not just for Jews in Venice but for other minorities ever since.[5]

The New Foundry, the Ghetto Nuovo, was ideal for the government's purpose because it was a self-contained, walled island, easily sealed-off and monitored. At the same time, it was physically part of the city of Venice (not isolated out in the lagoon) and thus easily accessible by foot to the urban poor who needed the services of loan banks. The outer windows were to be bricked-in so Jews couldn't even *see* out. (Was there an evil-eye notion in this restriction?) Access would be controlled through two entrances. The Jews would pay the salaries of the guards, their keepers, stationed at those two entrances. The pawnshops would be located inside the ghetto, and Christians could go there for business during daylight hours. Jews, marked by identifying badges, could circulate throughout the city during the day.

When the Ghetto Nuovo, the New Foundry, became a site of forced residence in 1516, the term ghetto did not yet have the meaning it has today in Venice or in the rest of the world. Even in 1541, when the ghetto expanded to include the adjoining "old foundry" or "ghetto vecchio," the current meaning of the word evidently had not yet developed. (Notice that the "New Ghetto" is actually the old one and the "Old Ghetto" is the new addition — revealing that *ghetto* still meant "foundry" in 1541.) However, a third addition to the ghetto was made in 1633, and it was called the "Ghetto Nuovissimo" — the "Newest Ghetto." This area had never been a foundry, and it is clear that by this date, at least in Venice, the term "ghetto" had acquired a good deal of its modern meaning.[6]

More than two hundred years ago, in 1797, Napoleon's troops liberated the entire ghetto of Venice. Most Venetian Jews at that time did not have the means to move out of this poverty-stricken corner of Venice — in fact a census taken at the time confirms the impoverishment that the decline of the Serenissima and nearly three hundred years in the ghetto had created.[7] Even up to World War Two, many Venetian Jews remained in the ghetto and its vicinity. A few are still there today.

In 1946, Cecil Roth, then the leading historian of Italian Jewry, wrote that the "folklore of the Italian ghetto has never been collected and it is now, unhappily, too late."[8] As reasonable as Roth's remark sounds — after all, the ghetto had been liberated 150 years earlier — it was not completely true, not even in 1978, when I was doing fieldwork in Venice. I heard and saw not only "folklore *of* the Italian ghetto" but folklore *about* the ghetto — folklore in the form of a shared, unwritten, informally communicated map of the ghetto that still expresses and embodies a sense of place for Venetian Jews today.

Ghetto folklore is esoteric folklore — folklore that circulates mainly within a particular group, in this case among Venetian Jews. Other Venetians no longer know what the ghetto was, or even where it is, as Giovannina Sullam Rheinisch, a Venetian Jew, remarked in 1978:

> If one asks a Venetian where the ghetto is, it can often happen that the response will be he doesn't know. And it's probably right there, a few hundred meters away....It is as if a psychological segregation continues, a cancellation from the memory, in perfectly good faith...[9]

Most Venetians don't possess the traditional knowledge that is necessary to recognize certain elements in their city, like the ghetto and its details. For them the ghetto is just another *campo* (*piazza* or "square"). But among Venetian Jews, a mental map of the ghetto has been passed on orally — and it has more to it than just recognizing the location of the historic ghetto; it is a map made up of intimate details — specific peculiarities that record and recall human interaction in this urban landscape.[10] (See figure 1.)

1. Ghetto Vecchio entrance, Rio di Carnareggio

2. Guard station at Ghetto Vecchio entrance, showing bricked-in windows.

3. Guard station at Ghetto Vecchio entrance, showing holes for gate fittings.

4. Guard stations at Ghetto Nuovo entrance, Fondamenta dei Ormesini.

One of the entrances to the Ghetto Vecchio is marked for tourists with signage in both Italian and Hebrew. But the sign for Venetian Jews is subtler and says more with less. Venetian Jews "remember" that this entrance was guarded, and the bricked-in openings are recognized and recalled as the windows of the guard station where officials monitored the comings and goings of their ancestors (figure 2).

A Map to the World's First Ghetto

Seemingly innocuous holes in the same entranceway register with insiders as the fittings for gates that locked the ghetto each night and all day on Easter (figure 3). History — unmediated by historians or their books — is engraved in place and creates a sense of place for those who have the traditional knowledge (folklore) to read the engraving. Jewish Venetians who pointed out these gate fittings to me did so with an immediacy of emotion almost suggesting that they themselves had suffered the humiliation of being locked in the ghetto.

An entrance at the opposite end of the ghetto is flanked by two small, apparently insignificant buildings (figure 4). On the unwritten Jewish map of Venice, these buildings are not insignificant — they are recollected as guard posts, and thus they are seen, symbolically, always from *inside* the ghetto where their meaning is still nourished by folk memory.

The point, of course, is not that I noticed these physical details of the ghetto and then did research to confirm their historical accuracy, proving that they were indeed what "the natives" claimed they were. The point is that today's Venetian Jews, not scholars, identified them and told me what they meant to them.

A small groove in a doorway is usually meaningless and probably would not be noticed by most people (figure 5). But to Jewish eyes, this groove — at this specific angle, at this particular height, on the right hand side as one enters a building — is an unmistakable sign of a Jewish presence. It conforms precisely to one of the most basic Jewish obligations — to place a *mezzuzah* (an amulet containing particular biblical passages) on the doorposts of one's dwelling.

For Venetian Jews, this mere groove in a doorway to a house inside the ghetto delivers a powerful, if ironic sense of ownership that goes beyond religious observance. It confirms history; it testifies materially. It says, "We were here. We didn't stop being us in spite of what happened to us. We are still here." For Venetian Jews, the small groove of the mezzuzah communicates in a way intentionally created monuments, on a grand scale, can never really aspire to. It is a folk monument and speaks to insiders with the power of folklore.

Within the relatively large, open space of the original ghetto lies another folk monument, decodable by Venetian Jews. Under a portico used by local kids as soccer goal posts and shade from the sun is a barely visible marble sign from one of the three pawn shops that operated in the ghetto nuovo in ghetto times. It reads "Banco Rosso" — Red Bank (figure 6).

5. Niche on doorpost for a mezzuzah, Ghetto Nuovissimo.

6. "Banco Rosso," Campo di Ghetto Nuovo.

7. Midrash Leone da Modena, Ghetto Vecchio

8. Ark protruding from synagogue, Ghetto Nuovo

Pawn tickets were color-coded — thus the Red Bank, the Green Bank, and the Black or Yellow Bank. Two of my non-Jewish, Venetian friends who grew up and have lived most of their lives within a hundred yards of this folk monument were completely unaware of it. Since it wasn't part of their sense of place, why would it register with them? For Venetian Jews, however, the Banco Rosso sign has remained meaningful and thus visible as an uncertified public monument.

The building known unofficially among Venetian Jews as the "House of Study of Leone da Modena" (figure 7) displays a typical facade along a typical *calle*, as the streets in Venice are called — except that this calle is the main thoroughfare of the Ghetto Vecchio.

In 1978 it was being used as a small warehouse, and there was no sign identifying it as special in any way. Insiders, nevertheless, recognized the building as once having been the *Bet-HaMidrash Leone da Modena* — a house of study named for the most famous of Venetian Rabbis. It matters little whether the building really was a study house or whether it was the study house of a seventeenth century genius; believing it to be such creates place out of space, connecting the individual to his/her surroundings in a meaningful way.[11]

There is a strange protrusion on the outer wall of a building that also happens to be the outer wall of the Ghetto Nuovo (figure 8). Most Venetians can't tell you what this is, if they even take note of it; but all Jewish Venetians probably can. It is one of several such bulges, and they all are parts of the synagogues that were originally built to blend modestly into Venice's urban architecture and avoid calling attention to themselves or the people who frequented them. The protrusions are the holy arks that house torah scrolls, the most sacred feature in a synagogue. Today these odd rectangular features remind Venetian Jews of the premium put on space when the ghetto of Venice was the most densely populated area in Europe. They are one more of a series of reminders of the uniqueness of their heritage in this particular place.

Venetian Jews will also point to stacked, jumbled buildings in the ghetto and say, ironically-proudly, "We built the world's first skyscrapers" (figure 9). Although the ghetto expanded twice as the population grew (adding the Ghetto Vecchio and the Ghetto Nuovissimo), Jews usually could add more space only by building upwards; obviously, they couldn't move out. The skyscraper claim is "ironically proud" since unsupported, top-heavy structures in the ghetto periodically collapsed, with injury and loss of life. More than once, this happened at wedding parties, when too many people gathered in an upper story room.[12]

At least one more physical feature is worth mentioning. This one is an official monument, one that was constructed long after the ghetto ended. It consists of the roll of Jewish soldiers from the ghetto who died in World War One (figure 10). The monument appears on the outside (public) wall of the *Tempio Levantino*, the Levantine Synagogue, in the Ghetto Vecchio, one of two synagogues in use today. (The Tempio Levantino was built in the late sixteenth century.)

9. "Skyscrapers," Ghetto Nuovo

10. Monument to Venetian Jewish soldiers who died in W.W. I, Tempio Levantino, Ghetto Vecchio

The names of the soldiers themselves are interesting, but what is also notable is that this monument follows the same pattern found in each Catholic parish in Venice and probably throughout Italy: a permanent posting of the young men from the neighborhood who died in "the Great War," engraved in stone on the outer wall of the parish church. In following this pattern, Venetian Jews were, as late as right after World War One, 120 years after the end of the ghetto, still claiming the ghetto as their "neighborhood," their bit of Italian soil, the place to make a statement about their contribution to the nation — in exactly same way that Catholics did so in their neighborhoods. The formula is the same, but the contents are different.[13]

Throughout northern Italy, as Jews moved out of the ghetto and its humiliation over the course of the nineteenth century, they were anxious to forget the ghetto and put it behind them. A Jewish newspaper article from 1863 celebrates the destruction of the ghetto of Florence:

> The transfer of the capital of Italy to Florence is favorable to the Jews. Requiring space for the new buildings, the ugly ghetto, in which the Jews used to be confined, will disappear quickly, and thus the last trace of intolerance will be canceled.[14]
>
> (Would that it were so — that intolerance could be razed as easily as stone.)

A Map to the World's First Ghetto

It is not surprising that this negative attitude toward the ghetto pervaded late nineteenth century Italian Jewish culture: it was time to get out of the ghetto, forget it, and eradicate it if possible.[15] Magnificent new synagogues on a monumental scale were being constructed in Milan, Rome, Trieste, Florence, and other Italian Jewish centers. Surely a new age was dawning — or so most Italian Jews thought.

Venice, however, is not readily dismantled, and the old synagogues in the ghetto continued to house the central activities of communal religious life — although religious life itself was greatly diminished from ghetto days. But class now divided Venetian Jews culturally — and spatially. By the twentieth century, many Venetian Jews had escaped the poverty of the ghetto and lived throughout the city, even in *palazzi* along the Grand Canal. Others, less well-off economically and often more traditional religiously, continued to live in the ghetto area.

Venetians, not just Venetian Jews, carry around a mental map of the city, too. On this unwritten map, Venice is divided between "*so*" and "*xo*" which is Venetian dialect for standard Italian "*su*" and "*giù*" or "up" and "down," in English. It signifies something like what "uptown" and "downtown" mean in New York.

But the model in Venice is a circle rather than the linear rectangle of Manhattan. "So" means "up" and refers to the center of town (Piazza San Marco and Rialto); "Xo" means down and away from the center — i.e., places on the periphery, like the ghetto. "So" and "xo" also refer to the conventional distinction between "high and low" class — those of "so," living near the center, were upper class while those living in the ghetto, those of "xo," were lower class.

In the first part of the twentieth century, the Jewish community offices and the women's organization (A.d.e.i.: *Associazione donne ebraiche italiane*) were to be found near the center of Venice, not in the ghetto. Those of "so," the upper class, ran the community; and although they came to the ghetto for religious services in the synagogues, they were trying to identify the center of Venice as their identity center — which was no longer the ghetto. The Jewish community was divided into an elite living away from the ghetto and middle and lower classes often living in or near the ghetto. Class difference was manifested spatially, as religious difference once had been.

The Holocaust made this distinction absurd. Venetian Jews were sent directly to Auschwitz by the German occupiers regardless of class.[16] The

Holocaust also led Venetian Jews to realize that even though the ghetto symbolized their mistreatment at the hands of Christians, it also contained their history and symbolized core aspects of their identity. In other words, the ghetto had positive as well as negative features. A reclaiming of the ghetto began.

A large, group, Passover Seder — the major festival of the community — was returned from "so" to "xo," to the building in the ghetto in which it had originated in the 1890s.[17] The *mazzah* oven continues to bake mazzah (unleavened bread) for Passover each year in the old "*calle del forno*" of the Ghetto Vecchio. The offices of the community were relocated within the ghetto in 1973, and the rabbi's official residence is once again inside the ghetto. The renewal of customs such as gathering in the *sukkah* on the holiday of *Sukkot* takes place in the ghetto. In 1978, a couple of Venetian origin returned from Israel not just to visit Venice but to have their wedding in the ghetto itself. Why in the ghetto, besides the fact that the synagogues are here? Because the sense of identity is strongest in the ghetto, and thus the possibility of renewal is most strongly, if paradoxically, felt.

Recently (in 1995 and 1997) a biennial festival celebrating Venetian Jewish culture was staged in the ghetto, and proposals to create an international Jewish studies center within the ghetto of Venice have been gaining support.[18]

The change of heart that came in the latter half of the twentieth century was not foreseeable two centuries ago when newly liberated Venetian Jews and their compatriots hacked and burned the ghetto gates, danced joyously around a Tree of Liberty, and renamed the ghetto the "*Contrada dell'Unione*"[19] — or even over a century ago when progressive Italian Jews, eager to assimilate, sought to forget and erase the ghetto era of their past. In reality it was the humblest members of the community who, in their folklore, maintained the sense of place that has become a resource of identity for all Venetian Jews in the late twentieth and early twenty-first centuries.

STEVE SIPORIN

Utah State University

---

[1] The capsule historical narrative, unless otherwise noted, is derived from Roth, Cecil, *History of the Jews in Venice* (Philadelphia: Jewish Publication Society, 1975).

A MAP TO THE WORLD'S FIRST GHETTO

Jewish quarters existed in Islamic countries and Southern Italy in medieval times. Roth *(The History of the Jews of Italy* [Philadelphia: Jewish Publication Society, 1946]) cites Benjamin of Tudela, the well known twelfth century Spanish Jewish traveler, who described a Jewish population of 600 in Salerno, "living mainly in the Jewish quarter *(judaica)*...which we find mentioned repeatedly from the year 1004 — the oldest specific reference in medieval history to a section of a town reserved for Jewish residents; there is, however, no suggestion of compulsory concentration or of its being walled off from the outside world — the characteristics of the later Ghetto" (79).

Venice itself contains the enigma of the island called *Giudecca* (*Zudega* in Venetian), a name that antedates the ghetto and seems to indicate an even older Jewish quarter; but there is no strong documentary evidence that the Giudecca was ever inhabited by Jews. See Ravid, Benjamin, "The Jewish Mercantile Settlement of Twelfth and Thirteenth Century Venice: Reality or Conjecture?," *Association for Jewish Studies Review* 2 (1977): 201-226.

[2] Roth, *Venice*, 49, uses the term "contaminate" in this context. Perhaps Venice, as the "true heir" to the Roman Empire, retained some of the ancient sense of the stranger "defiling" the city (Fustel de Coulanges, Numa-Denys, "The Ancient City," *Reader in Comparative Religion: An Anthropological Approach*, ed. William A. Lessa and Evon Z. Vogt (New York: Harper and Row, 1972) 55.

[3] For the argument regarding the economic role and position of the Jews in Venice, see Pullen, Brian, *Rich and Poor in Renaissance Venice: The Social Institutions of a Catholic State to 1620* (Cambridge: Harvard University Press, 1971).

[4] German Jewish quarters were also located in peripheral or inferior parts of cities. See Pollack, Herman, *Jewish Folkways in Germanic Lands (1648-1806): Studies in Aspects of Daily Life* (Cambridge: M.I.T. Press, 1971).

[5] There is an fascinating literature about the origin of the term "ghetto" to designate an imposed Jewish quarter in a city, but today there is little doubt that the term originated in Venice. See Roth, Cecil, "The Origin of *Ghetto*: A Final Word," *Romania* 60 (1934): 67-76, and Ravid.

[6] Other cities in Italy, beginning with Rome in 1555, followed Venice's lead in creating separated Jewish quarters and calling them ghettos.

[7] Luzzatto, Gino, "Un'anagrafe degli Ebrei di Venezia del Settembre 1797," *Scritti in memoria di Sally Mayer* (Jerusalem and Milan: Sally Mayer Foundation, 1956), 194-198.

[8] Roth, Cecil, *Italy*, 389.

[9] "Tra le pietre del ghetto," *L'Europeo* May 1978: 57.

[10] A good example from another ghetto, that of Casale Monferrato, was recorded in Augusto Segre's memoir, *Memorie di vita ebraica: Casale Monterrato-Roma-Gerusalemme, 1918-1960* (Roma: Bonacci, 1979) 21:

Il *sur* Elia ricordava molto bene che un suo vecchio parente, noto per le sue stranezze, quand'egli era ancora un ragazzo, gli aveva fatto osservare alcuni gradini e un angolo sporgente della parete, dove c'erano certi segni, che secondo lui, erano colpi di spada; più in basso poi macchie molto scure, che i più dicevano essere semplicemente opera dell'umidità, erano invece per quel vecchio parente macchie di sangue: 'tanto ce n'era,' così sosteneva, che la parete l'aveva bevuto, per così dire, a sorsate e conservato assumendo poi col passar del tempo quel colore così scuro."

[Sur Elia remembered very well that when he was still a boy one of his old relatives (noted for his quirks) had shown him some steps and a corner jutting-out from the wall where there were certain marks which, according to him, were sword strokes. Lower down were very dark stains, which almost everyone said were simply the work of humidity, but which were, for that old relative, blood stains: "There was so much," or so he maintained, "that the wall had drunk it up, so to speak, in gulps and preserved it, taking on that very dark color with the passing of time."]

[11] For Leone da Modena's remarkable life and a contemporary view of late sixteenth and early seventeenth century Venice, see Cohen, Mark R., ed. and trans. *The Autobiography of a Seventeenth-Century Venetian Rabbi: Leon Modena's Life of Judah* (Princeton: Princeton UP, 1988).

[12] Roth, *Venice*, 107-108.

[13] I believe that this was the same cultural solution that Italian Jews expressed through their cuisine — Jewish contents (dishes) fit into an Italian meal formula (antipasto, primo piatto, secondo piatto, etc.). This is another example of an Italian formula or pattern with Jewish contents — a neat resolution of dual identity. See Siporin, Steve, "From *Kashrut* to *Cucina Ebraica*: The Recasting of Italian Jewish Foodways," *Journal of American Folklore* 107 (1994): 268-281.

[14] *Il Corriere Israelitico* 2 (1863): 285.

[15] For assessments of the Jewish Italian political and cultural predicament in the nineteenth century, see Bernardini, Paolo, "The Jews in Nineteenth-Century Italy: Towards a Reappraisal," *Journal of Modern Italian Studies* 1 (1996): 292-310; Canepa, Andrew, "Emancipation and Jewish Response in Mid-Nineteenth-Century Italy," *European History Quarterly* 16 (1986): 403-439; and Voghera, Gadi Luzzatto, *Il prezzo dell'eguaglianza. Il dibattito sull'emancipazione degli ebrei in Italia (1781-1848)* (Milan: Franco Angeli, 1997).

[16] For the events leading up to and including the deportation of Venetian Jews during the Holocaust, see Fano, Letizia Morpurgo, *Diario: Ricordi di Prigionia*, Venice: n.p., n.d.

[17] Steve Siporin, "Passover, Shavuot, and Simhat Torah in Venice: Elite Innovations and Their Acceptance by the Folk," *Rassegna Mensile di Israel* 50 (1984): 23-41, and "'To Hold High Their Glorious Origins': The Jewish Festivals in Venice," *Shofar: An Interdisciplinary Journal of Jewish Studies* 8 (1989): 30-46.

[18] The idea was first offered in print by David Cassuto in *Ricerche sulle cinque sinagoghe (scuole) di Venezia: Suggerimenti per il loro ripristino* (Jerusalem: n.p., 1978).

[19] The contrada ("street" or "district") of union — i.e., no longer of separation, as the ghetto had been.

Works Cited

Bernardini, Paolo. "The Jews in Nineteenth-Century Italy: Towards a Reappraisal." *Journal of Modern Italian Studies* 1 (1996): 292-310.

Canepa, Andrew. "Emancipation and Jewish Response in Mid-Nineteenth-Century Italy." *European History Quarterly* 16 (1986): 403-439.

Cassuto, David. *Ricerche sulle cinque sinagoghe (scuole) di Venezia: Suggerimenti per il loro ripristino*. Jerusalem: n.p., 1978.

Cohen, Mark R., ed. and trans. *The Autobiography of a Seventeenth-Century Venetian Rabbi: Leon Modena's Life of Judah*. Princeton: Princeton University Press, 1988.

Il Corriere Israelitico 2 (1863): 285.

Fano, Letizia Morpurgo. *Diario: Ricordi di Prigionia*. Venice: n.p., n.d.

Fustel de Coulanges, Numa-Denys. "The Ancient City." *Reader in Comparative Religion: An Anthropological Approach*. Ed. William A. Lessa and Evon Z. Vogt. New York: Harper and Row, 1972. 52-62.

Luzzatto, Gino. "Un'anagrafe degli Ebrei di Venezia del Settembre 1797." *Scritti in memoria di Sally Mayer*. Jerusalem and Milan: Sally Mayer Foundation, 1956. 194-198.

Pollack, Herman. *Jewish Folkways in Germanic Lands (1648-1806): Studies in Aspects of Daily Life*. Cambridge: The M.I.T. Press, 1971.

Pullen, Brian. *Rich and Poor in Renaissance Venice: The Social Institutions of a Catholic State to 1620*. Cambridge: Harvard University Press, 1971.

Ravid, Benjamin. "The Jewish Mercantile Settlement of Twelfth and Thirteenth Century Venice: Reality or Conjecture?" *Association for Jewish Studies Review* 2 (1977): 201-226.

Roth, Cecil. *History of the Jews in Venice*. Philadelphia: Jewish Publication Society, 1975.

———. *The History of the Jews of Italy*. Philadelphia: Jewish Publication Society, 1946.

———. "The Origin of *Ghetto*: A Final Word." *Romania* 60 (1934): 67-76.

Segre, Augusto. *Memorie di vita ebraica: Casale Monferrato-Roma-Gerusalemme, 1918-1960*. Roma: Bonacci, 1979.

Siporin, Steve. "From *Kashrut* to *Cucina Ebraica*: The Recasting of Italian Jewish Foodways." *Journal of American Folklore* 107 (1994): 268-281.

———. "Passover, Shavuot, and Simhat Torah in Venice: Elite Innovations and Their Acceptance by the Folk." *Rassegna Mensile di Israel* 50 (1984): 23-41.

———. "'To Hold High Their Glorious Origins': The Jewish Festivals in Venice." *Shofar: An Interdisciplinary Journal of Jewish Studies* 8 (1989): 30-46.

"Tra le pietre del ghetto." *L'Europeo* May 1978: 57.

Voghera, Gadi Luzzatto. *Il prezzo dell'eguaglianza. Il dibattito sull'emancipazione degli ebrei in Italia (1781-1848)*. Milan: Franco Angeli, 1997.

The Jew Rediscovered

I am not a professional historian and, in a sense, I am a Jew "malgré soi" — something I hope to clarify during the course of my presentation. I intend linking this presentation to my own experiences and to those of my family: this is what I know best and I hope that through them I may in some way contribute to the development and success of this meeting.

According to Attilio Milano, a historian specialized in Italian Jewish history, my family's Roman roots date back to the end of the 16th century. Meir di Gabriel Magino was a Venetian Jew who bred silk worms. He marketed his personal breeding method which was apparently so successful it doubled silk production.

He exported his method to various cities — Milan, Turin, Florence — until he reached Rome where he won the favor of the reigning pontiff, a former Capuchin monk by the name of Peretti, who ascended the Throne of Peter under the name, Sixtus V.

The city that welcomed Magino was the Rome of the Counter Reformation which, in 1555, by decree of Pope Paul IV, had confined the Jews to the cramped quarters of the ghetto.

But Sixtus V was a Pope who longed to transform the sleepy lifestyle of his tiny State's capital. He planned to make it more modern, encouraging industry — like the kind Magino described to him. The Pope agreed to help him get started, according him extremely unusual privileges, like being exempt from living inside the ghetto and controlling his own monopoly.

The Pope even went so far as to find him suitable business premises in the neighborhood of his sister Camilla's villa, near the Basilica of St Mary Major. Ironically, Camilla Peretti became the business partner of the enterprising Venetian Jew.[1]

Obviously, there are families in Rome whose historical ties to the city go back a lot further than those of my own presumed ancestor. In 161 BC, around 151 BC and again in 139 BC, those in power in Rome received Jewish delegations: the first was sent by Judas Maccabee, the others by his brothers, the Asmonean family which was embroiled in a struggle against the Syriac dynasty of the Seleucides and needed powerful allies. We know that during the third ambassadorial visit, the small group of Jews that had settled in Rome was involved in an obscure episode of proselytizing that almost got them expelled. The names of four of those families are still remembered in Rome today. The surname of one of them can be found in the city's onomatology, together with other typically Roman names. Alongside the Massimo's and the Savelli's — descendants of the Massima and the Sabella families — are the Anav or Anavim, the "peaceful ones," with all their Italian and Spanish variations: Delli Mansi, or Almansi, or Umani, or the more common Piattelli, not to mention the Levi's and Coen's which — together with their subsequent litany of translations and adaptations — are among the oldest names in the world.

We don't know whether to attribute to fact or fancy the account found in the "Mirabilia Urbis" describing a large bronze tablet inscribed with a friendship treaty sealed between Romans and Jews and still visible, according to the aforesaid source, in the Church of St Basil. This touching testimony was said to have been signed thirteen centuries earlier.

In reality, relations between Romans and Jews weren't always idyllic. Julius Caesar was obliged to take account of their notable presence and of their relations with other communities in the Mediterranean, Egypt, Syria and Asia Minor. Their friendship would be useful to him in undermining the authority of his rival, Pompey. As a mark of respect for their religious beliefs, Caesar exempted them from military service. He also accorded them several privileges when it came to the distribution of rations.

Tradition has it that when Caesar was murdered the Jews wept over his body more bitterly than the other citizens of Rome. The favorable treatment of the Roman Jews was confirmed by his successor, Augustus, and again by Tiberius. It was this Emperor's favorite, Sejanus, who suggested expelling from Rome a great number of eastern religious sects — among these the Jews — whom he considered too numerous. Four thousand young Jews were deported to Sardinia where most of them were killed by brigands or malaria. The Senate decreed that those who remained should have their property confiscated or face expulsion, unless they renounced their religious beliefs.

The death of Sejanus marked the return of the former tolerant regime of Tiberius. But his successor, Caligula, demanded that his statue be erected inside every temple in the Empire — including Jerusalem: an irreparable break between the Jewish community and the Roman State seemed inevitable.

As the ancient world's greatest power, the Roman Empire had to consider a series of factors while maintaining the balance in its complex play of alliances and friendships: one of these was the beliefs and traditions of the various peoples with whom it came in contact. Besides the demands of its "realpolitik," the Roman world, in its component parts, had different reactions in its dealings with foreign peoples — whether they had been recently conquered or were temporary allies. In both cases, slaves and allies came to Rome and bustled through the streets of what was certainly the most cosmopolitan city in the world (rather like modern-day New York).

It was quite common for upper class Roman society to demonstrate its curiosity over some new religion. It appears that one of Nero's wives, Poppea, was extremely interested in the Jewish religion. On the one hand there are examples of this kind of intellectual snob curiosity, and on the other the attitude of poets and writers like Horace, who criticized a religion he considered based on pure superstition; or Tacitus who wrote of "absurd and ridiculous customs" (*mos absurdus sordidusque*), adding: "Among the Jews all things are profane that we hold sacred; on the other hand they regard as permissible what seems to us immoral" (Histories, 5, 2-6).

In the year 49 of the Christian calendar, Suetonius writes how the Jews were stirred up by a certain Christ (*impulsore Chresto*), creating such disorder that the Emperor Claudius was obliged to expel them. The comment indicates how Suetonius, along with his fellow Roman citizens, was still unable to distinguish Jews of the old observance from disciples of the new word being proclaimed by the Nazarene. It could also mean that the entire community was already split by quarrels between the traditionalists and those who would soon be known as Christians. About ten years later two apostles called Peter and Paul arrived in Rome and the distinction was finally clarified — the split became definitive.

Another ten years passed and the destruction of the Second Temple by the legionaries of Titus brought the national autonomy of the Jewish people to an end. From then on — in the words of the historian, Dubnov — Israel's home would be the world and the Temple the heart of every Jew. From that date on, the new history of the Jewish Diaspora began — lasting for two millennia and stretching into our own day.

Eminent figures like Joseph of Mattatia, better known as Joseph Flavius and the Alexandrine philosopher, Philo, struggled to communicate the basis of Jewish history and thought.

The entire Roman world, meanwhile, was absorbing the new word, preached by the tireless Paul: a word that was open to the beliefs and expectations of pagan cultures and thus more and more detached from the ancient roots from which it sprang.

Constantine's edict sanctioned a situation that had been developing and consolidating itself for some time. Christianity achieved dominant status, especially in relation to the religion from which it had taken root. Constantine and his successors drew ever stronger dividing lines between the two: anyone who converted to Judaism risked having his property confiscated; no Jew could possess Christian slaves — and in time, not even pagan slaves (who converted from Judaism to Christianity and thus had to be freed); no Jew could marry a Christian, under pain of death for both; Jews could not assume public office, work in the legal profession, perform military service or build new synagogues (old ones could be maintained but not embellished). The Jew was thus effectively demoted to the rank of second-class citizen.

The removal of his rights became even more apparent from the fourth century on when Jews were attributed with every kind of vile infamy and denounced in the sermons and writings of the Church Fathers, the clergy and Christian authors.

We know very little about the High Middle Ages and even less about the relationships that came to be established between the Christian majority and the Jewish communities scattered around the entire Mediterranean basin, Italy in particular. A partial guide is offered by the papal Bull, *Sicut Judaeis*, promulgated during the pontificate of Gregory the Great (590 - 604).

The Pope appears to have been guided by two principles: not to change Church rules regarding the Jews, nor to admit that some people twisted these rules to their own advantage; to remain steadfast in upholding principles while applying them with as much flexibility as possible. Jews could live according to Roman common law and fully enjoy the right to property and possessions. Only the ban on Christian slaves remained intact. Threats and violence were to be avoided when attempting to convert Jews — patience and flattery were preferable.

There follow four centuries of almost total silence regarding relationships between the small Roman Jewish community of probably no more than a hundred individuals, and their Christian counterparts. We suppose they must have been times of ups and downs, with Jews occasionally being victims of intolerance and misunderstanding. But they were also times that gave rise to important characters like Nathan of Jechiel of the house of Anav, author of *Aruch* ("The Ordained") — an imposing work that reads like a dictionary of post-biblical literature and an encyclopedia of the Talmud. Or like Baruch, who converted and changed his name to Benedictus. He married a nobleman's daughter, a Frangipane, from whom he had a son who was baptized by Leo IX and named after the Pope Leo (Leone in Italian) had his own son, Pietro, from whom the family got its name: Petrus Leonis, or Pierleoni in the vulgate. In 1120 one of his sons, also named Pietro, was made a cardinal and ten years later was elected pope. For all eight years of his pontificate Anacletus II had to struggle against his rival, Innocent II. He was eventually denounced as the Anti-pope — and there is little doubt his Jewish origins weighed heavily against him.

A precise account of the flourishing condition of Rome's Jewish community and of the high intellectual level of some of its members is provided by Benjamin di Jona da Tudela, a Spanish merchant who visited several countries and came to Rome between 1159 and 1167. In Rome he was impressed by the "eighty palaces of the eighty emperors" as well as by the statues and ancient ruins. He also wrote about the Jews he met in Rome: two hundred families, all respected and exempt from paying any special tax. Among the personalities he met were Jechiel, grandson of the previously mentioned Nathan, whom he described as "a good-looking, intelligent and cultured young man" who freely entered the pontifical palace (Alexander III, 1159-1181) insofar as he administered "the papal house and everything in it."

As I said at the beginning of this presentation, I am not a historian but simply a Jew who, as a result of the race laws, discovered a connection between himself, his origins and his Jewish identity.

I have no intention of following the various vicissitudes of the Middle Ages and Renaissance which saw sizeable Jewish communities living side by side with a progressively triumphant Christianity — even if torn by schisms and violent theological debates throughout Italy, the Papal States and Rome, residence of the successors of Peter. The events that marked these centuries are already well known and chronicled. I refer to episodes of intolerance: the Crusades, wearing distinguishing marks, the burning of books on Jewish doctrine, the Talmud especially, the recurrent accusation of ritual murder, the walling in of the ghettos, and the Inquisition. But I also refer to proofs of the opposite: the humane and tolerant attitude of certain popes, the respect shown towards scientists, doctors and men of letters, the mediating role of the Jews with regard to the Islamic civilization. This proved to be the bridge that allowed the recovery of the values inherent in the great tradition of classical thought, Aristotelian thought in particular. So it becomes important to remember that when the thriving Jewish community in Spain was expelled, it was the Sultans of the Ottoman Empire who opened their doors to the refugees, and the wisely political Medici who did the same in Florence, aiding the commercial expansion of their town of Leghorn. Pope Alexander VI also intervened decreeing that the Rome Jewish community should absorb at least some of the refugees from Spain and Sicily.[2]

Among the eminent Jewish figures that shine on the Italian cultural horizon is that of Immanuel Romano, precursor or imitator of Dante, as well as translators, copiers and commentators of biblical texts and ancient classical writings. There is a whole series of physicians starting with Gaius, or Isaac of Mordechai who was personal physician to popes Nicholas IV and Boniface VIII and the first in a long line of medical luminaries who performed their services at the papal court.

Another source of Jewish pride during the Renaissance regards the spread of the art of printing, newly arrived from Germany, which allowed a much greater distribution of rare texts in both Latin, Hebrew and the vulgate (it also reignited the age-old discussion concerning specific texts, the Talmud especially). Trading and commerce was also flourishing along with the demand for financing and this meant new activity in the economic field. Alongside the major powers of the era — and the name of the Medici stands out — it was clear that some kind of secure banking system was needed. The Jews frequently lent money because they were not subject to the limitations placed on monetary transactions by the Catholic Church. There wasn't a single Lord who did not boast the presence of one or more Jewish money-lenders in his feudal state. On the other hand there were those who believed the invectives spread by certain preachers (the most famous being Giovanni da Capistrano and later, Bernardino da Feltre) and revoked their concessions — naturally, after confiscating their property.

This was a time of great advances in trade, the arts and sciences. But it was also a time of great intellectual renewal, a time when the Church

THE JEW REDISCOVERED

found itself facing one of the most dramatic crises in its history — one that has still not been completely resolved. The debates and passionate arguments surrounding the ideas of the monk, Martin Luther, rapidly divided Italy as well. More tolerant popes, like Martin V, Leo X and Clement VII followed with concern the heated discussions that were taking place in Rome and that involved some of the greatest minds of the time. Participating in the debate were strange individuals like David Reubeni' who rode around the city on a white horse followed by a train of Jews and Christians. He claimed to be the brother and messenger of Josef, king of the tribe of Reuben — one of the ten of which nothing had been known for centuries but which, he said, were now nomads in Tartar lands. He declared he was ready to organize an army of Jews who, if provided with weapons, could conquer the Muslims, free Jerusalem from the infidel and thus fulfill the great dream of both Jews and Christians. His most influential patron was Pope Clement VII who put him up in the papal palace. His fiercest enemy was the Jewish doctor, Jacob Mantino, an intelligent and powerful man who had the ear of both the Doge of Venice and the Roman Curia. Reubeni' was eventually condemned to death by the Inquisition but the Pope saved him at the last moment by sending to the stake an unfortunate individual who looked just like him. Reubeni' fled to Germany and tried to win the favor of Charles V, without success. He disappeared and probably ended up being burned at the stake anyway or rotting away in some prison.

The story of David Reubeni' shows how the age still drew a very uncertain line between sincere research and outright roguery. It also explains why the majority within the Church began their long struggle known as the Counter Reformation. While the followers of Martin Luther worked towards a definitive schism, the Church of Roberto Bellarmino, Ignatius of Loyola and his powerful Society of Jesus, battled to promote the Council of Trent. It was a battle against all forms of heresy and one that would inevitably involve the Jews as well.

Paul III (1534-1549) was the Pope of the change that was so slow and imperceptible the Jews didn't even notice it at first. This was the Pope who recognized the Society of Jesus (1540), who brought the Inquisition to Rome and gave it the name of the Holy Office (1542) while convening the Council of Trent that same year. The start of his pontificate had also seen the opening in Rome of the first Monte di Pietà (official pawn-brokering), an institution that already existed all over Italy and that openly clashed with a typically Jewish business activity.

Paul IV was the Pope of the encyclical *Cum nimis absurdum* (July 12, 1555), the first lines of which give a clear indication of the fate awaiting the Rome Jewish community:

> "Since it is utterly absurd and unbecoming that the Jews, condemned through their own fault to eternal slavery, should, with the excuse of being protected by Christian charity and tolerated to live among Christians, show such ingratitude towards them as to insult them in exchange for the mercy received and presume to dominate them instead of serving them as they should..."

The immediate effect of this encyclical was that the Jews were again confined to the walled-in ghetto where they were locked in at dusk and kept apart from the rest of the city. They were obliged to wear a distinguishing mark on their clothing and forbidden to exercise any kind of free profession or trade except that of selling used clothes ("sola arte strazzariae seu cenciariae, ut vulgo dicitur, contenti"). Obviously all previous concessions and privileges accorded individual Jews or the Jewish community as a whole, were summarily revoked.

The encyclical *Cum nimis absurdum* heralds the long night of Roman Judaism and for most of Italy. Meanwhile the Church began its struggle with the schism that was to challenge its very existence. The night lasted for nearly three centuries, relieved by brief moments of reprieve and darkened again by fearsome reactions. The last papal decree reaffirming the previous bans is signed by Pope Pius VI and bears the date of April 5th 1775, just before the outbreak of the French Revolution — that cleansing turmoil which was to claim the Pope himself as one of its victims.

It would take too long to describe the abuses to which the surviving Jewish communities were subjected, squeezed into the unhealthy confines of their ghettos and forced to lead the most miserable existences. Aside from the recurrent accusation of ritual murder, they had to run in the races at Carnival time, listen to endless sermons and submit to forced conversions. Accepting to be baptized didn't protect them from persecution either: the adult who was accused of falsely converting was condemned to death and burned at the stake.

The Jew Rediscovered

This long and painful chapter closed on February 15th 1798 when the victorious French army declared the end of the Pope's temporal power and the beginning of the Roman Republic. That same day, the Jews ripped off the hated sign that distinguished them from the other citizens of Rome. On February 17th the tree of freedom was planted in the ghetto. On July 19th of the same year all citizens of Rome were declared equal before the law: "Considering that, according to the principles expressed in the constitution of the Roman Republic, the law must be generally and equally applied to all citizens of Rome, the following law is promulgated: that Jews who answer the conditions permitting them to be Roman Citizens shall be subject to the law common to all Roman Citizens and that, consequently, all other special rules pertaining to Jews are heretofore abolished as of today."[3]

Obviously, all of the above predates my own personal experiences and memories. Like the rest of my fellow Jews and Italians, I was born into a completely different world, at a very different moment in history.

In most areas of what constitutes modern-day Italy, especially the north, Jewish emancipation really took place early in the last century. Jews played an active and important role in events surrounding the Italian *Risorgimento*, both because they understood the advantages it could bring and because many of them were personally and sincerely motivated. A significant number of them fought in the battles for independence, especially those led by Garibaldi. The new-born Italian State acknowledged their contribution and included them in the state structures that were beginning to take shape. Industrial growth meant the population, Jews included, was beginning to converge on the major cities.

Generally-speaking, a 19th century Jew living in the region of Piedmont or Lombardy could be described as a law-abiding Italian citizen of the Hebrew religion. As such, Jews were fully integrated into the new society that was being created and could aspire to the highest social levels.[4]

This process took somewhat longer in Rome. The end of the Napoleonic adventure had brought with it the restoration of papal temporal power, a situation that lasted until 1870 when Rome was annexed to the new Italian State. Up until then, the gates of the ghetto were left open and living conditions inside were a lot less grim. There were still painful episodes, like the Mortara case. A child was separated from his family (with the complicity of a Christian servant girl) and taken to a religious house: an innocent soul to be freed from original sin and set on the road to Christian redemption.

My grandparents, on both my father's and my mother's side, were born in Rome on the eve of Italian occupation of the city, or in the years immediately following. They were born free, citizens of the new Italian State. Yet, in the stories they told me, I caught a glimpse of tales passed on by word of mouth from their parents. From my own childhood memories, I can recall the story of one Don Felice, a Catholic priest, who would visit their home. He had been one of those Jewish children, taken from their families, baptized and instructed in what his kidnappers believed to be the true faith. Times and attitudes changed and so the child, now grown to manhood, could again make contact with his family. But the slow, sure process of Christian indoctrination had done its work and there was little chance of his returning to any previous heresy: on the contrary, there was always the unmentionable hope that his presence and witness might serve to lead his relations along the road to conversion.

New stories were always being added to these old tales of the ghetto. My grandmother told me another anecdote about the excitement surrounding the first performance of Verdi's *Il Trovatore*, which was performed in Rome on January 19th 1853.

As had happened during *Nabucco* and *I Lombardi alla Prima Crociata*, the first night of *Il Trovatore* was an opportunity for impassioned outpourings of patriotism. At the beginning of Act III the bodyguard of Conte di Luna precedes its attack by singing, in the original words of the libretto: "The trumpet of war has sounded, it is a call to arms, to fight, to attack...." Such was the spectators' enthusiasm that they called for an encore, only this time they changed the words (enraging the papal police present): "If we should raise our flag in victory over the Capitoline Hill...." Several members of the audience at that performance, an ancestor of mine among them, spent the rest of the night in a papal prison.

During the previous three centuries, the Rome ghetto had been one of the most disturbing expressions of Jewish degradation. Yet it largely reflected its surroundings: papal Rome was a sleepy town that lived mainly off tourism and the sale of souvenirs. Aside from a few notable exceptions, the small Jewish community was a copy of the larger Roman one in terms of illiteracy, poverty, and lack of culture. Even if, on certain levels of the social scale, the process of integration into the new reality of the Italian state, was extremely rapid. Another sign of the times could be read in the celebration of family name-days. My great grandparents had typically Jewish names. But my grandmothers bore the very Roman names of Giulia and Italia, respectively. Two of Giulia's daughters were named Margherita and Elena, like the first two queens of Italy. Another branch of the family with the same surname, turned to the classics for inspiration and came up with Alceste, Alexander, Aeschylus and Clytemnestra. This branch gave birth to several important personalities: a parliamentarian, a famous physician and a world-renowned archeologist.[5]

The long list of eminent personalities of Jewish origin who distinguished themselves in the various cultural fields of Italian public life — politics, the armed forces, university professors, scientists, journalists, artists and writers — shows how quickly and how well the small Jewish community integrated itself into its surroundings.

During those years no Jew needed to refer to his or her religious or ethnic origins. They were simply Italian citizens who were making their own, often considerable, contribution to the common good. The small Italian Jewish community, perhaps with the exception of the old Rome ghetto, occupied an important position in promoting the civil progress of the nation.

In my book, "The Tiber Afire," I found myself trying to describe what it meant for an adolescent of my age to be a Jew just before the outbreak of the Second World War. My life was exactly like that of my peers. Only two things m arked a ny k ind o f dif ference: I did no t p articipate in r eligion classes at school, and once a year I was taken to Rome's Main Synagogue for the celebration of Yom Kippur. It was a ceremony I found totally incomprehensible: a crush of people, shouts and smells. The crowning point of the festivity was a somewhat out-of-the-ordinary meal comprising dishes that recalled age-old traditions, mainly linked to Spain. The family atmosphere was generally one of total indifference to all these traditions. A grandfather of mine frequented a small Spanish oratory and I think he knew the ritual prayers, although certainly not what they meant. A few phrases and words survived in the family banter: they recalled Spanish or Hebrew and were used mostly when one didn't want to be understood by some Christian neighbor, or in colloquial family chit-chat. They included terms that were really very clever and that couldn't possibly be understood by our Christian fellow-citizens. For example, Jesus is referred to as "Caròvve" — which could be translated as "that relative of ours." "Esav," the biblical Esau, is a term used to describe Christianity itself and means a bullying and arrogant brother.[6]

This small Jewish world, peacefully inserted into the wider national — but equally peaceful — world, was to be shaken then shattered by the events of 1938 and 1940.

There was a fleeting moment of excitement, felt as much by the Jews as by their fellow nationals, when Italy invaded Ethiopia. It was short-lived and the young adolescent who attended a local school should already have recognized the signs of the coming storm. Taking their places beside him on the school benches were new students recently arrived from other countries. They were Jewish refugees from Germany. But their presence was interpreted as yet another demonstration of the equilibrium and wisdom exercised by the regime personified by Benito Mussolini.

The first outpourings of the racist campaign that inundated the press in the summer of 1938 were greeted as signs of intolerance that would blow away as soon as the wind changed. The general air of security was fanned by a recently published book by a Jewish journalist, Emil Ludwig, entitled "Interviews with Mussolini." Openly contradicting his German counterpart, the fascist "Duce" energetically affirmed there never had been a Jewish question in Italy — nor would there ever be one.

The Racist Manifesto, signed by important figures in Italian cultural life, and the so-called racial defence legislation that followed in the fall, hit the small Italian Jewish community like a ton of bricks. The legislation included several death blows that threatened the very existence of the Jewish community: Jews were banned from holding public office or having jobs in the legal profession, the armed forces, schools and universities. Jews were also excluded from holding state jobs, subjected to other major or minor harassments and forbidden to attend state schools and (following clarification) even private schools.

In a single day the trust Jewish citizens had placed in the document which laid the basis for the Kingdom of Italy — and which the King, like his predecessors, had sworn to respect — was betrayed.[7] Article 24 of that Statute solemnly proclaims:

> "All subjects regardless of their title or position are equal before the law. All enjoy civil and political rights equally and may hold civil and military offices, apart from those exceptions which the law shall determine."

Jewish reactions were varied. All of them were systematically ignored by the press. Brave officials returned their decorations to the King, several others chose suicide: the most famous at the time was that of a newspaper editor, Formiggini, who threw himself off the famous Ghirlandina tower in Modena, proclaiming his devotion to his Italian homeland.

Some families that had already split from their Jewish origins, chose to convert; numerous others who had the means to obtain an entry visa to another country and to face a completely new life, chose exile. A handful left for Palestine. Others still set sail for distant shores, mostly for Latin America.[8]

The aged stayed, along with those who couldn't afford to do otherwise or those whose families were too numerous for them to consider emigrating anywhere. The Jews prepared to save whatever they could: they had few means at their disposal — and not much spiritual guidance either. The more knowledgeable among them understood the gravity of the coming catastrophe and had already transformed it into a return to Zion which, until then, had been only a utopian dream.

The first reaction was to make sure young people could continue their studies: this has been the principal preoccupation for dispersed Jewry always and everywhere. The Fascist regime neither encouraged nor opposed the initiative. Wherever they could, Jewish communities organized schools of every academic level. The largest and most important was the Rome school. Its tireless organizer was a certain Guido Coen: a man with no previous teaching experience, the new legislation had left him unemployed. The teachers were those who had lost their jobs in the state schools and, it is fair to say, were some of the best in the field.

In my book "The Tiber Afire" (which was well-received overseas), I tried hard to recreate the atmosphere inside those special schools. At first afraid and disoriented, it didn't take long for the children to create an atmosphere that was anything but special, although different from anything experienced in other Italian schools at the time.

All credit goes to the teachers and to one of them in particular: Enzo Monferini, a teacher of history and philosophy. Thanks to him especially, Rome's Jewish Middle School turned into a hive of free discussion — and anti-Fascism. Later, Monferini's pupils discovered that their beloved teacher had been following the lead given by another great figure in Italian education, Professor Augusto Monti of Turin. Long before the race laws, during the Africa campaign, he had laid the ground-rules for a new Italy — a more civil and democratically-minded nation. His pupils included some of the greatest minds Italy was yet to know: Leone Ginzburg, Massimo Mila, Cesare Pavese, Carlo Levi, and many others.[9]

Monferini and the other teachers created the right atmosphere for learning and discovery. But the pupils did their part too. I hope I succeeded in describing that contribution in "The Tiber Afire."

As we watched the storm clouds gathering overhead, we couldn't helping asking ourselves: they persecute us because we are Jewish — but what does being Jewish mean for us?

The children attending the Rome Jewish school were determined to get in touch with the roots of those Jewish origins. We started by turning to the most official source we could at the time: Rome's Chief Rabbi. He was an eminent figure in the field of semitic philology but seemed little inclined to encourage our youthful enthusiasm. He had already changed his name and surname once to align himself with the new Italian elite, and he would do so again when the conflict was over.

Monferini did all he could to assist us when it came to encouragement through the exercise of a healthy dialectic on the ideas that formed the basis of his own convictions. But when it came to researching their Jewish roots, Monferini's pupils had to rely on their own intuition and resources.

Giorgio Piperno, who had a special talent when it came to scientific research and showed exceptional promise in the mathematical field, decided he would take the lead. His ingenuous young fellow researchers dragged a whole host of names into the discussion on Judaism — from Marx and Einstein, Kafka and Chaplin, to Freud and Spinoza (often on the basis of their names alone) — while he offered a more serious reflection based on ancient biblical and rabbinical sources. Sacrifice and patient research eventually led Giorgio Piperno and his friends to come up with a handful of the greatest names in Jewish history: often by way of translations or vague summaries — whatever they could get their hands on.

The memory of the students of that period is not a sad one. On the contrary: it was often a period of great discovery and joy. Animated discussions and heated arguments alternated with moments of carefree playfulness: whether playing sport or preparing to stage a review as part of an evening's entertainment. The war seemed so far away. A sad parenthesis which would generate a new nation and a better lifestyle when it was over.

Of course, there was still the problem of those young people who had finished their high school studies and needed to continue at university level. Some of them managed to enter the Catholic Lateran Atheneum where they could start studying law. Others who wanted to deepen their knowledge of the sciences could follow an engineering course in collaboration with the Swiss University of Freibourg. Promoters of the latter were two of the greatest mathematical minds of the moment: Guido Castelnuovo and Federigo Enriquez, two Jewish professors who had lost their jobs at the State universities and who attracted vast numbers of non-Jewish pupils. Thus, everyday exchanges overturned exactly what the regime had tried to enforce — the fraternization of the persecuted minority with the rest of the community. Soon the winds of war would put men and principles to the test.

The bombing of Rome, the fall of Fascism, the proclamation of the armistice, the German occupation of the city — these were highpoints of excitement and terror that marked that event-filled 1943 (all of which are explored in greater detail in "The Tiber Afire"). The adolescents and young adults of the time, lived these moments alongside their Christian fellow citizens, often finding leadership in members of the militant anti-fascist movement who had just been released from prison or brought back from the islands where they had been interned.

Many of them remember a leaflet being distributed with a title that was way ahead of its time: it was called "European Unity."

Monferini's pupils received it from Eugenio Colorni, a Jewish intellectual who had known both prison and confinement and who was shot by the fascists on the eve of the liberation of Rome.

The long night of 1943 began with the shameful flight of the King, Supreme Commander of the Armed Forces, who abandoned the city without leaving orders for the troops left to defend Rome. The sacrifice of these few troops and the groups of volunteers — Colorni among them — that joined them, couldn't stop the armored German divisions from entering the city.

One of the first measures taken by the occupying forces was to demand that the Jewish community pay a toll of fifty kilos of gold within a very short time. It was an alarm bell and many Jews fled their homes in search of whatever refuge they could find. Not so the incurable optimists, or the poor, or the aged. Why would the Germans be bothered with them? On the 16th of October 1943 over two thousand Jews, including my own paternal grandparents were forced aboard a train bound for Auschwitz on a journey of no return.

They were not deported immediately. For three days they were held in the courtyard of Palazzo Salviati, on the right bank of the River Tiber, a few hundred yards from the walls of the Vatican. The Germans hesitated before deporting them, fearing some kind of reaction from the Pope. But no reaction came. Only a generic declaration in which the Pope expressed solidarity with all those who suffer: such a bland declaration that, as the German ambassador noted, most people wouldn't even notice it.[10]

And here we must comment on the highly controversial attitude assumed by the Catholic Church with regard to the persecution of the Jews.

Pope Pius XI had vigorously condemned the aberration of the pseudodoctrine called Nazism. His successor, Pius XII, on the contrary, adopted a position of extreme prudence. He was a politician: he had been Apostolic Nuncio in Munich during the turbulent years of the revolts and was subsequently appointed Vatican Secretary of State. He was influenced by political considerations rather than by humanitarian concerns. A clamorous gesture on his part in the days following the rounding up of the Rome Jews could very probably have avoided their deportation. The resolute position of the King of Denmark had avoided his subjects having the yellow mark imposed on them and provided the basis for saving most of them. But Pope Pacelli was not a man for that kind of gesture.

Having said this, it is important to note how much the Catholic Church and its finest members did do during those dramatic months to save persecuted Jews.

During the fearful hours that followed the demand for the gold, Jewish leaders received an offer whereby the Vatican proposed making a concrete contribution. The offer was turned down because the contribution proved to be unnecessary — but the moral value of the gesture remains. The doors of convents and religious houses opened to hide hunted Jews and most of them found protection there.

I myself, together with my family, found refuge in the international College of St Alessio Falconieri of the Servants of Mary on the Janiculum Hill. Previously we had stayed with the families of friends but the anonymous grapevine got word to us that we were in grave danger. The same happened when we were staying in the convent: the Rome Vicariate announced the arrival of a group of fascist thugs. Those staying at the convent

— mostly military officials and Jews — fled. My brother and I were the last to leave and we were caught by the fascists. The landing of the Allied Forces at Anzio twenty days later facilitated our liberation which was negotiated by some wonderful priests, Fr Raffaello Taucci, in particular, whom I recall with gratitude even today.

We could conclude our reflection on this issue by remembering that the Church is governed by men — with all their virtues and vices: men of very different characters and personalities which cause them to act very differently.

The times that followed this period of such tragedy and horror have seen popes working sincerely to cancel the misunderstandings and injustices of past centuries: popes like John XXIII who, when papal Nuncio in Turkey during the war, worked to save persecuted Jews in neighboring Bulgaria. The same John XXIII who called the Second Vatican Council which set the stage for so many memorable events in our own time — the most important being Pope John Paul II's visit to the Rome Synagogue and his historical embrace with Rabbi Elio Toaff whom he greeted as a brother, an elder brother.

Which brings us to the present day with Italy's slow but sure return to normality, along with that of its energetic Jewish community which — as we have seen — can boast over twenty centuries of historical presence here.

The community was decimated during the war years: over one third of its members were deported, converted, or emigrated to far away lands. As soon as the conflict abated, some of its finest minds left Italy: that group of young people the persecution had stimulated to seek the roots of Judaism, set out in search of a radical social renewal, fired by a renewed religious tension.[11] But the community was also enriched by many non-Italians who had found refuge in the country and now wanted to stay.

In each of the survivors there was an awareness of the enormity of the tragedy they had lived through — an awareness linked to their pride in the vicissitudes of the newly created State of Israel, which was coming into being with a sizeable contribution from the original Italian Jewish community.

Those who remained in Italy, and the few who returned, wasted no time in reintegrating themselves into the fabric of Italian society and the State which was already on the road to reconstruction and democracy. The small community that had given so much during the *Risorgimento* and had continued to do so under Fascism (the Treves, Modigliani, Terracini, Levi, Foa, Sereni) and who would give even more in the years to come — including several Nobel Prize winners, one of whom, Franco Modigliani, was of Roman origin — now hurried to make their contribution to the work of reconstruction. They also set about documenting their recent past in the hopes it might serve as a lesson for future generations.

The best known examples of this contribution in terms of first-hand testimonies can be found in two literary masterpieces: "Christ Stopped at Eboli," by Carlo Levi and "If This is a Man," by Primo Levi. The former evokes the era of political persecution and focusses on the traditions, problems and anxieties of Italy's deep south. The latter offers a testimony, in its infinitely touching detached style, of life in the hell of the Nazi death camps. Both books have spoken to the entire world about the history of our time.

Clearly they are not the only testimonies of what took place during those years; I have already had occasion to mention my own book, "The Tiber Afire," in which I recount the characters and events at the center of the small Rome Jewish community.

I am one of the survivors of the Holocaust with my share of personal tragedy: my paternal grandparents were lost in the hell of Auschwitz, a beloved cousin was killed when not yet twenty as he flung himself against the German lines. Notwithstanding, I have enjoyed a normal and satisfying career alongside brave colleagues, working for what was once my country's most important information and entertainment organization — the RAI (Radiotelevisione Italiana) Italian State Radio and Television.

My experiences, the fact of having enjoyed such an amazing scholastic adventure, the contact I had with so many avant-garde ideas and, later, with people so different from those my own parents had known, undoubtedly conditioned the latter part of my life and career.

Post-war Rome saw the Jewish community enlivened by two new factors: the presence of soldiers of the "Jewish Brigade" and the influx of important groups of Jews coming from other European countries.

The Palestinian soldiers, who proudly wore the "Maghen David," organized and stimulated debates in youth circles. They spread a new and concrete language that included words like "social dialectic" and "organization of democracy." They created the first youth groups and with their assistance the first modern Italian-Hebrew dictionary was printed. This latter task was undertaken by a Hungarian refugee by the name of Nicola Erdely who claimed to know eighty languages: he certainly knew several.

He also circulated a pamphlet wherein he extolled the finest virtues of the Italian people and expressed his gratitude for the hospitality he had received.

He wasn't an isolated case. Meetings and exchanges of ideas revealed incredible stories of what Italy and Italians had done to assist those persecuted under Hitler's regime. There was the story about the Ferramonti internment camp in southern Calabria where thousands of "enemy" families were reunited and received material, religious and even academic assistance. Jewish organizations were behind such assistance but Italian authorities had done whatever they could, within the limitations of the time, to guarantee the survival of the internees. There was the case of Croatia where the Second Armed Division refused point blank to participate in Nazi-sponsored acts of genocide. There was also the incredible story linked to the part of France under Italian occupation: tens of thousands of Jews converged there in response to a mysteriously circulated rumor claiming Italians didn't persecute Jewish refugees. The main characters in this story quickly became legendary — like the Jewish banker, Angelo Donati or the Capuchin priest, Benedetto Maria. Just before the armistice a brave attempt was made to transport these thousands of derelicts across the sea to Tunisia: all with the active assistance of the Italian military and civil authorities and, safe from Vatican constraints, by the American and British ambassadors.[12]

There were several conflicting reasons behind this attitude, which was certainly unusual in a Europe dominated by Nazi Germany: the naturally tolerant and humane approach that has always distinguished Italians; the Armed Forces' refusal to harm helpless civilians; concern in certain diplomatic circles over the consequences of a different approach in the event of a defeat, which appeared inevitable; a growing intolerance towards aggressive behavior in general and contempt towards their Nazi allies in particular. All these were undoubtedly determining factors that penetrated every level, up to the highest spheres within the regime hierarchy. Any deeper analysis of motives and meanings must be left to historians. What we do know is that, immediately after peace was declared, Italy was peculiarly reticent about publicizing all the good things that undoubtedly had been done. Even the Ministry of Foreign Affairs was silent about what had happened in the Italian Occupation Zone in France: the document used by Poliakov as the basis for his research was stamped with a "strictly confidential" seal and to this day it has been impossible to unearth it in the Ministry archives.

Many holocaust survivors could still be found in Italy at that time: I personally heard several stories from them first-hand. They told of incredible actions performed by the Italian authorities and individual citizens to help persecuted Jews. Many of these survivors decided to remain in Italy and invest their future here.[13] The kind of work I was doing in the media at the time led me to start preparing a television documentary based on their testimonies and experiences.

Apart from some initial shooting, the documentary was never made, nor did a movie on the same subject ever get past the earliest scripting phase. Forty years were to pass before the story could be told of a train traveling across Italy just before the armistice, filled with Jews to be saved from the SS.

In order for the project to be completed, destiny had to arrange I should meet an extremely talented writer with whom I could collaborate. Our age difference (she is much younger than I am) meant she could maintain a certain objectivity which I could not, having being personally involved in the events we were relating.

That is how our book was written. Day after day, for two years, we experimented and exchanged ideas, arguing often: two generations, two naturally different ways of feeling and seeing things. Our novel, entitled "Dear Sophie," is set within a fictional framework and enriched with factual episodes. It is in circulation and defies our own judgement of it. Now and then, we can't resist rereading a chapter here and there, remembering the emotions we felt while putting these experiences and ideas on paper. By way of conclusion, at the end of this presentation, all I can say is that in writing this book I personally relived the emotions of that lengthy journey through my youth, my maturity and now — my old age. It was a journey that led me to search for and rediscover the Jewish identity I had simply ignored: a journey that confirmed my belonging to the oldest branch of a Jewish community that has lived in Italy for over twenty centuries and that forms an integral part of this country and its civilization.

And that is something which makes me very proud.

FABIO DELLA SETA

Author

The Jew Rediscovered 35

[1] The pontifical document concerning the privileges accorded the Jew, Meir di Gabriel Magino, is reproduced in "Dialoghi di M.Magino Gabrielli Hebreo Venetiano sopra l'utili sue inventioni sopra la seta," for the heirs of Giovanni Gigliotti, Rome, 1588.

[2] These immigrants left their names on some of the traditional Rome *Scola's* which survived until the turn of the century — namely, until the construction of the Rome Synagogue: among them the Castille Scola, the Catalan-Aragonese and the Sicilian Scola.

[3] For my background on this clearly compressed presentation regarding the history of the Jews in Italy in general, and in Rome in particular, I had recourse to the classical texts on the subject (Vogelstein, Rodocanachi, Roth and Berliner) but especially to the more recent research and publications of Attilio Milano. He was both a scrupulous archive proof-reader and author of two important works: "La Storia degli Ebrei d'Italia" ("The History of the Jews in Italy"), Turin, 1963; and "Il Ghetto di Roma" ("The Rome Ghetto"), Rome, 1964. Having enjoyed the privilege of both his friendship and professional collaboration, I wish to recall him here with esteem and gratitude.

[4] It is worthwhile recalling the Camondo Family: a banking family of Ottoman origin, but of Austrian citizenship, they contributed generously to financing the Italian *Risorgimento* and in exchange received both Italian citizenship and a noble title.

It is also interesting to remember that the secretary of Camillo Benso di Cavour, the political mind behind Italian unification, was a Jew by the name of Isaac Artom. His still unpublished personal archive was bought recently by the Bibliographic Center of the Union of Italian Jewish Communities.

[5] The renewed Italian civil society honored some of these personalities: thus in Rome there is a street named after Alessandro Della Seta, the archeologist who directed important digs and research in Greece; another street bearing the name of the Republican Senator, Ugo Della Seta, an eminent politician in the years immediately after the war. He wrote the lines inscribed on the plaque affixed to the wall of the Rome Synagogue, recalling the 2,000 Roman Jewish deportees and the innocent victims of the Ardeatine massacre.

[6] In this regard, see "The Rome Ghetto," by Attilio Milano, chapter 18 especially, "La parlata" ("Speech"), which includes an extensive glossary of Jewish-Roman dialect. This dialect was transcribed and documented by Crescenzo Del Monte in "Sonetti giudaico-romaneschi," Florence, 1927; "Nuovi sonetti giudaico-romaneschi," Rome, 1933; "Sonetti postumi giudaico-romaneschi e romaneschi," Rome, 1955. See also "Gli ebrei nell'opera del Belli" ("The Jews in the works of Belli"), by Fabio Della Seta, in "Rassegna mensile d'Israel" XXI (1955), and "Sulla parlata giudaico-romanesca," by Lea Scazzocchio Sestieri, in "Scritti in memoria di Enzo Sereni," Jerusalem, 1970.

[7] Article 22 of the so-called Albertine Statute, states:

"On ascending the Throne and in the presence of the gathered Chamber, the King shall swear to faithfully observe the present Statute."

[8] A particularly complete and well-documented research on this matter has been done by Eleonora Maria Smolensky and by Vera Vigevani Jarach, in "Tante voci, una storia — Italiani ebrei in Argentina 1938-1948" ("Many voices, one story — Italian Jews in Argentina 1938-1948"), Bologna, 1998.

[9] In the most recent republication of "The Tiber Afire," I included a letter I received from Massimo Mila in which he eloquently expresses his nostalgia for that period. If those friendships and meetings had continued, asserts Mila, perhaps Cesare Pavese would not have committed suicide.

[10] Among others, see Lèon Poliakov, "Breviaire de la haine — Le III Reich et les Juifs," Paris, 1951. The same study contains an account of how the French government of Vichy was about to promulgate its own race laws and requested its ambassador to the Holy See, Léon Bérard, to discover the Vatican's view on the matter. The reply they received claimed that the "Jewish Statute" raised no fundamental objections from the Roman Catholic point of view and that ecclesiastical authorities would consequently offer no opposition. The French Catholic hierarchy, on the contrary, acted with immense courage and had completely the opposite reaction.

[11] The most important element in this group in Rome was Giorgio Piperno. He survived the German occupation, although his parents were deported. Just after the liberation he published a book which manifestly expressed his attitude: "Perchè non possiamo non essere sionisti" ("Why we can't not be Zionists"), Rome, 1944.

He then emigrated to Palestine with a group of his peers and reached the religious kibbutz of Sedè Eliahu, just south of Lake Tiberius and near the River Jordan. Here, together with his young family, he pursued his battle for the civil progress of his community. An utterly convinced pacifist, he was also in the front line when it came to dealing with the successive clashes with the Arab world. He died in 1971 following an accident at work. His ideas are expressed, apart from in the aforementioned book, in a volume published after his death and entitled, "Ebraismo, Sionismo Halutzismo," Rome, 1976, as well as in letters he wrote to his dearest friend who remained in Italy. These letters are now in the possession of the Bibliographic Center of the Union of Italian Jewish Communities.

[12] There has been a marked increase recently in the amount of literature dealing with this subject. Aside from the classic study published by Léon Poliakov, "Breviaire de la haine, Le III Reich et les Juifs," there is also Klaus Voigt's, "Il rifugio precario — Gli esuli in Italia dal 1933 al 1945" ("The precarious refuge — Exiles in Italy from 1933 to 1945"), published in Italian in Florence, 1996; Jonathan Steinberg's "All or Nothing, the Axis and the Jews in the Occupied Territories, 1941-1943," published in Italian in Milan, 1997; and Carlo Spartaco Capogreco's, "Ferramonti, La vita e gli uomini del più grande campo d'internamento fascista" ("Ferramonti, the life and the men of the largest fascist concentration camp"), Florence, 1987.

[13] Some of these episodes are recounted in the book, "Dear Sophie." Here, I would like to recall the case of three former Croatian Jews who, at the end of the war, found work at the American Armed Forces Club in Palazzo Barberini, in Rome. When the Americans left, they abandoned the Club's refrigeration equipment to rust in the

garden. The three Jews, whose names were Alfred, Giga and David, asked and obtained permission to use this equipment. It was the beginning of Italy's largest ice-cream manufacturing industry which took its name from the first letters of its founders' names: ALGIDA. The company still thrives today, even if it is now part of the multinational, UNILEVER.

An Historical Perspective

First of all let me express my most sincere congratulations to the Center for Italian Studies on organizing this Symposium on The Italian Jewish experience. The very long history of Italian Jews is almost ignored in the United States where the Jewish communities came mostly from eastern Europe and belong to the "askenazi" group while Italian Jews are considered "sefardic," because they came from Spain even if, as we are going to see Jews arrived in Roma at least 200 years before Christ.

Thanks to Prof. Mignone for inviting me to address this meeting: I am an Italian Jew, I was born in Livorno and I was in Italy during the war and I survived the persecutions.

I am going to briefly recollect the long history of Italian Jews which many of you know very well but I think could be useful for some young student, and I will explain what happened to me, as a young Italian Jew between 1938 and 1945.

Guido Bedarida, in his book Ebrei D'Italia published by Belforte in Livorno in 1950 which is a broad study of Italian-Jewish participation in the Italian culture, says that maybe the name Italia comes from the Hebrew "I-Tal-Ja," the country of God's dew.

There is no need to resort to legend or hypothesis to demonstrate the antiquity of Italian Jewry. The settlement of the Jew in Europe goes back to the second or, perhaps, the third century, before the beginning of the Christian era. It may be that the Jews penetrated the southern part of the peninsula, Magna Graecia, in the early period and, if there is not in Rome an institution more ancient than the Papacy, it is the Synagogue.

According to the very ancient record preserved in the Books of Macabees, immediately after his decisive victory against Nicanor in 161, Judas Maccabaeus sent his mission to establish friendly relations in Rome.

The importance of the Roman community is attested by a well-known episode. When, in 59 B.C.E., L. Valerius Flaccus was prosecuted for gross corruption during his term of office as propraetor of Asia, one of the charges brought against him was that he had appropriated the money which the Jews of that region had brought together to send to Palestine for the upkeep of the Temple, as their coreligionists did throughout the world. He was defended by the greatest of Roman orators, Cicero.

When, with the triumph of Gaius Julius Caesar Octavianus Augustus, the Roman Republic was swept away and the Roman Empire came into being, Jewish communities were to be found solidly established in many Italian cities.

Julius Caesar's benevolent policy towards the Jews was continued, as a rule, by the early emperors. Augustus indeed extended it enjoining that they should not be summoned to courts of law on their Sabbath eve; and that, when free distribution of grain to the populace took place then, the Jews should be given their portion on the following day.

But an edict was issued in the year 19, ordering all Jews to leave Italy, unless they foreswore their fantastic religious practices, on the pain of being reduced to slavery. Moreover, on the pretext of submitting them to military service, 4000 young freedmen were seized and sent to Sardinia, to be employed in fighting the brigands.

In the year 313, Flavius Valerius Constantinus, known to history as Constantine the Great, with his co-Emperor Licinius, issued from Milan an edict establishing in the Roman Empire equal rights for all religions. This did not only stop the persecution of the Christians; it decided, in effect, their domination and sealed the fate of classical paganism.

This was the case with the Jews, and above all with those in Italy. They were brought down to the level of social outcasts and, in our own day, the attempts made to redress the balance caused the reaction which led to the phenomenon of antisemitism with all its appalling results.

The "highly distinguished religion, of indubitable legality" did not become illegal, but it began to be referred to in imperial enactments as a "sacrilegious gathering" or "nefarious sect."

The tragedy of 1096 is very well known. Pope Urbano II in November 1095 launched the first crusade in Clairemont Ferand. The crusade started by killing the infidels around them and we know, unfortunately, about the horrible massacre. Jews and Muslims were placed by Christians in the same category and this had catastrophic results for the Jews during the Crusades. In the fist three Crusades (1096-1099, 1147 and the late 12th century) organized and unorganized crusaders and mobs ravaged numerous Jewish ghettos (not yet ghettos) in the West, on the Rhine and in Bohemia, and thousands of Jews were killed. This caused the great eastern migration of the German Jews toward Poland and Russia. The forth Latin Council (1215) prescribed special dress for the Jews and excluded them from public office.

In classical times and the early Middle Ages, the Jews of Italy, as of Europe generally, had suffered from no explicit economic restrictions, as has already been made clear. They had been farmers, laborers, craftsmen, merchants, artisans, peddlers; and if any occupation were characteristic of them it was wholesale trade on the one hand and certain branches of the textile industry on the other.

The date of the re-establishment of the community of Bologna, after the expulsion of 1171, is unknown. The Jews were expelled from Milano in 1320. They were permitted to settle in Turin in 1424 and in Vercelli in 1444. By the 15th century, the Jews were solidly implanted throughout from Sicily's waters to the foothills of the Alps, and from the French frontier to the semi-Slavonic at the head of the Adriatic sea.

Only in Italy did the Jews enjoy general well-being. A few setbacks are chronicled, but they are isolated and exceptional. If, during civic disturbances, the Jews may sometimes have suffered more than their neighbors, this did not betoken a persecutory spirit among the people.

The Renaissance

The remarkable geographical and economic expansion of Italian Jewry in the course of the fourteenth century entailed danger as well as prosperity.

Pope Boniface IX, who tried to restore papal authority in the long-neglected Italian possessions of the Holy See, had been exceptionally tolerant, highly favored a succession of Jewish physicians, and in 1402 granted a charter of protection to the Roman community in which their rights as citizens were specifically recognized. But twelve years later, in 1414, an Oecumenical Council met at Constance to discuss the all-important questions of the restoration of unity to the Church, and the extirpation of the heretical movement which was spreading in central Europe. Shortly after it opened, the Spanish anti-Pope Benedict XIII, whose concern with the Jews was in the nature of a monomania, issued a series of regulations of fantastic severity.

In 1417, for example, S. Niccolo Albergati, on his appointment as bishop of Bologna, had put into execution in his diocese the friars' program, including the wearing of the Jewish badge and segregation in a separate quarter of the city.

The crowing tragedy of the Jewish Middle Ages was enacted, with the expulsion of the Jews from Spain and Sicily in 1492. Italy was the only land in Christian Europe open to the refugees, and some 9000 in all made their way thither.

Nevertheless, the fatal edict extended, not only to the Spanish mainland, but also to the insular dependencies of Aragon — above all, Sardinia and Sicily, with its great Jewish population. The edict of banishment was solemnly proclaimed on June 18, 1492, to the blare of trumpets, in every town in which Jews were to be found.

Three months only were allowed for the preparations to be made and for the settlement of their debts, whether to private individuals or to the municipalities. By September 18 — four days before the Jewish New Year — all were to have gone, any who remained on the island after that date incurring the death penalty.

The Jews in Sicily and in southern Italy had already many problems. In January 1493 they had to leave their native land and so far as we are present to tell, this date ended Sicilian Jewish history for all time.

On May 23, 1555, Cardinal Caraffa, inspirer of the Catholic Reaction and deadly enemy of the Jews, was elected to the Papacy, taking the name of Paul IV. On July 12, he issued his famous Bull, beginning with the words Cum nimis absurdum. This is one of the landmarks in the history of human persecution and of Jewish martyrdom.

From the States of the Church the reaction spread throughout Italy — in part as a result of the expansion of papal rule, in part from conventional orthodoxy, in part through political pressure. It was some while before the process was complete, but by the beginning of the seventeenth century triumph was assured.

Pius IV had insisted that his anti-Jewish legislation was incumbent on all Catholics, and it was natural for him to write to the various Italian rulers enjoining them to follow his example. The Jewish badge was obediently imposed and usury prohibited (though not for long) as early as September, 1566. In the same year isolation was enforced at Alessandria. Genoa had already expelled its Jews in 1550; now, in 1567, the central government issued orders for all the other cities of the territory to do the same within a period of three months.

By the end of the first quarter of the seventeenth century, the Ghetto and all the accompanying degradation of Italy where Jews were not allowed to live — complete segregation, the red or yellow badge, exclusion from honorable callings, the forced sermon, the censorship of literature, the House of Catechumens, and all the rest. It implied also in many areas the exclusion of the Jews from the small townships in which the establishment of a formal Ghetto would have been absurd or impossible.

The economic life of the Italian Jews was now almost intolerably restricted. General speaking, Jews were not allowed to have shops outside the Ghetto, or to engage in retail trade except among their coreligionists, or to practice any organized handicraft, or to follow any liberal profession, or to enter any branch of manufacture, or to employ Christian labor. The process of impoverishment and pauperization had caused terrible strikes all over Italy.

In 1752, intolerant Genoa readmitted the Jews, without imposing the Ghetto, in the hope to relieve the economic stagnation into which she had since fallen since the rise of Leghorn.

Napolean's Cisalpine republic abolished all Jewish disabilities, on the principle that, "Every man is born free and remains free and should fully enjoy all rights; the Jews are citizens and must be recognized as such in society."

With the fall of the Napoleon, the states of the Italian Peninsula were reconstituted much as they had existed before the Revolution, but under the aegis and domination of the house of Austria.

After a generation that had seen what freedom meant, conditions of the deepest degradation were re-established over the greater part of the Peninsula. Everywhere, the Jews lost, not only the political rights which they had enjoyed together with their neighbors under Napoleonic rule, but also the social rights they had achieved and the civil rights conferred on them, and not unworthily exercised, since the French invasion.

In the Austrian territories of the Lombardo-Venetian kingdom and the Kustenland (including Triesta) — the most efficiently administered part of the country, notwithstanding the arbitrary method of government and the hated alien control — their treatment was relatively enlightened, and their disabilities, though not trivial, could not be considered oppressive.

In the kingdom of Sardinia, by a royal edict of April 21, 1814, the whole of the former anti-Jewish code was once again enforced — more strictly tolerant inefficiency or philosophic liberalism that had characterized the eighteenth century. Piedmont now became notorious as one of the most reactionary and unenlightened areas of Europe. The Jews were now once more confined to Ghettos, from which they were not to be absent after nine o'clock at night without special reason.

But Italian Jewry had tasted liberty; and the taste of liberty, once known, is never forgotten. It is not surprising that they threw themselves heart and soul into the movement for the overthrow of the reactionary regimes, the ejection of the Austrians and the petty tyrant's whose thrones were propped up by their bayonets, and the creation of a free, united Italy. In this movement, known as the Risorgimento or Reawakening, to which modern Italy owes its being, the Jews took a part and paid a price out of all proportion to their numbers.

When the king of Italy was induced to adopt a liberal policy, it was impossible to fail to take this agitation into account. Originally, the benefits of the constitution which Carlo Alberto granted on February 8, 1848 — one of the cornerstone of the Italian revival — were confined to Catholics. Ten days later, they were extended to the Waldenses — the dissenting Christian body in the kingdom. In the following month war was declared on Austria, the symbol of foreign and reactionary control. A Jewish deputation headed by the poet David Levi, which waited on the king before he left Turin, pointed out how the victory to which all Italians looked forward so eagerly would be disastrous to the Jews of Lombardy and the Veneto, who would lose thereby those rights they possessed, being reduced to the miserable status as their coreligionists in Piedmont.

Unable to hold out any longer, Carlo Alberto signed a decree, on March 29, 1848, on the battlefield of Voghera, extending civil rights to the Jews and other non-Catholics of his dominions and abrogating all laws to the contrary.

Twenty-two years had sufficed to bring the emancipation of the Jews in Italy to fruition. In 1848, there was no European country (except Spain from which they were entirely excluded) where the restrictions placed upon them were more galling and more humiliating. After 1870, there was no land in either hemisphere where conditions were or could be better.

There was thus no part of the world where religious freedom was more real, or religious prejudice so small. It was not that the Italian Jews no longer suffered from any political disabilities, but that they no longer suffered to any serious degree even from prejudice. The profession of Judaism was regarded as an amiable eccentricity rather than a social mistake.

The most important Jew in Italian public life in the age of the Risorgimento and for some time after was Isaac Artom, a member of an ancient family of Asti, and one of the important figures in the Italian revival. He was successively private secretary to the Cavour.

An Historical Perspective

There was a symbolic importance in the appointment as mayor of Rome in 1907 of the Anglo-Italian Ernesto Nathan, a militant Freemason and son of the family which had befriended Mazzini in exile, who for six years remained responsible for the administration of the city where his kindred had so long been treated as prisoners.

Released from the Ghetto, Jewish genius became apparent in every aspect of Italian life. The long generation of intellectual training, the frequent hours of absorption in Talmudic studies, now bore a remarkable crop. It was unnecessary for the Italian Jews, as it was for some of their coreligionists beyond the Alps, to become assimilated to the ruling culture before they could contribute to it. Their Italianità was already so complete that the period of transition was reduced almost to nothing. There was thus no country of Europe where the Jewish contribution to cultural life was proportionately so great.

My personal ordeal

In 1938 I was a public school boy in Livorno. I had many friends. I used to play soccer and tennis and I was a member of the local fencing club. My problems, my projects for the future were exactly the same as any boy of my age living in Livorno. My parents used to live a normal life of a middle class Italian family: they belonged to the local social club and they had many friends. We never considered if our friends were Jewish or Catholic. Like my parents, I don't remember having any problems because of my Jewish identity. My only difference from my classmates was that every year, at the beginning of school, my father used to send a note to the principal asking him to exonerate me from attending the religion class. (I mean the only Catholic religion class where the teaching was performed by a priest). I liked this because it meant going to school one hour later or leaving school one hour earlier once a week. To be Jewish, for me, meant to go to the Synagogue about three times a year for the big holidays. I liked the atmosphere but I didn't understand anything about the Hebrew prayers. I also went to the local Jewish school once or twice a year — there was an elementary Jewish school in Livorno at that time — to participate in some performance. For instance, for Purim my class performed the history of Ester.

To be Jewish was a characteristic of mine, of my cousins and of a few of my friends. No more than that. It was more a characteristic than a difference. Some of my relatives were observant Jews: they did not work on

Saturday, they used to go to the Synagogue every week, and their children didn't go to school on Saturdays or on Jewish holidays. But they too, like myself and my family, were Italians in the full sense of the word. An uncle of mine died in World War I. His name was Gastone and my father named me Gastone in his memory. My grandmother was, of course, very sad at the loss of her son, but she was very proud of the silver medal that he was given for his heroic death in battle. My grandfather, on my mother's side, was the owner of the most important pharmacy of the town. He was proud of being Italian and, I must say, he was convinced, like many Italians were, that fascism and Italy were really the same thing. He used to keep a diary, where he recorded the events that he considered most important. These events, including the birth of one of his grandchildren, were the exploration of the North Pole, the launching of a new ship in Livorno's harbor and the visit of Mussolini or the king to our town.

In 1938 Italian Jews were Italians among Italians. In August of 1938, to show you how normal my life was, I went to Rome to participate in the Italian youth gymnastic games. I was quite good in running the 100 meter and so, I was representing the Livorno team in my age class. I am not sure that I understood the exact meaning of some news that I heard in Rome, new about the "Difesa della razza" (Defense of the Aryan Race). But I was forced to realize it soon, once back Livorno. I was not going to attend the public school anymore, my father talked of leaving Italy in order to find a job, our maid had to be dismissed and my grandfather was not allowed to own his pharmacy. And, furthermore, all my friends disappeared. My parent's friends didn't know them anymore. But most of all, the world of my Livorno, the Italian world, was crumbling around me. My beliefs, my projects, my personality, my life — even if not materially threatened — were to be reconsidered. Only then for the first time, did I hear that Jews had been persecuted often in history and not only in Italy. I learned that, for centuries in Italy, Jews were not normal citizens and not citizens at all. I used to consider myself an Italian of the Hebrew religion, but now I had to realize that my ancestors were considered and had to consider themselves Jews and only Jews. They lived in a country which did not consider them equal citizens or even citizens. My ancestors did not have the right to consider themselves citizens.

Now, we were again told that we were Jews and, therefore, different. We were not citizens anymore. We were excluded from Italian society: no longer protected by the law, forbidden to enjoy the opportunity of studying, working and living the normal life of an Italian. I can't say I felt antisemitism from the people of Livorno, but they didn't know me anymore. My father had to leave for France. My mother, my brother and I went to live with my grandparents. Money became a problem. So, not able to study, I started working at the age of 17. I was able to work because of a man's courage and generosity. This man, an engineer, was courageous because it was forbidden by antisemitic law to hire and to hide me, and he did. He was not bothered by the consequences of hiding a Jew.

Then two years later, I decided to get my high school diploma. I attended a small local Jewish school which was run by the many Jewish teachers expelled from the public school and was frequented by the young Jewish students who were also expelled. For my final exam, I sat alone in a public school classroom and took the written exam. For the oral test, I was called the last of all the students. I was different.

After this, in May 1942, the local police called about twenty Jewish boys and sent them to work on a river near Livorno. I was one of the twenty. The work was painful. It was forced labor.

In this period my relationships were limited to Jewish boys and girls. We started meeting and discussing relevant issues: why the Jews had to be persecuted, why Jews had always been persecuted and why Jews remained Jews and did not fully integrate themselves into the society. We asked ourselves, 'did we want to remain Jews' and if we did, 'would we have to emigrate to Palestine, where Jews used to live.' All of us decided we had good reasons to remain Jews. Half decided that to live a Jewish life and in order not to be persecuted every few generations, we had to go to Palestine as soon as possible. The other half, and I was among them, decided that it was impossible to put all Jews in Palestine. We considered that if Jews remained Jews for centuries in the Diaspora, even persecuted and decimated, there must be a reason. Therefore, we had to remain in the Diaspora fighting against discrimination.

The war brought for Italian Jews the same problems it brought to the Italian people. My house was destroyed by an air strike and we fled to the country. Meanwhile, my father was arrested by fascists in France. He was brought back to Livorno and put in jail because he was a Jew and an antifascist.

Our lives became endangered in September of 1943, when Germany took over Italy. It is true that many Italians did help Jews. Jews enjoyed the humanitarianism of the Italian people. But there were some rare cases of denunciation in Italy. The Catholic church aided the Jews: many convents hid Jews and many priests helped in many ways. The assistance of the church was so widespread that it is certain that some instruction to help was provided directly from top, the Vatican that is.

I may describe many meaningful and touching cases of Jews being saved by Italian gentiles and Catholic priests. These stories of heroism I know personally. I would like to take this occasion to thank the Italian people and the Catholic church. I can say that I stand here today because of the kindness and help of a gentile and, maybe, a Catholic priest as well.

And now I come to a very big BUT. But even if it is true that the antisemitic laws in Italy in 1938 had been, I believe, the first occasion in which the Italian people could not and did not approve of fascism (the first break between the Italians and fascism), it is also true that the Italian people did not react. They did nothing to express their outrage. And if the Italian people may be had the excuse that the country was under a dictator— the political parties were not allowed to exist, there was no free press and no one was free to express a non-conformist opinion— the same cannot be said about the church. Maybe Pope Pius XII had good reason for not condemning the racist law, not only in Italy but more so in Nazi Germany. But he should have said something. Even when in October 1943, more than 1000 Jews were deported from the area of the former Roman ghetto, the pope, the Vatican, did not say a word.

I am sorry for having to censure the past attitude of the roman Church toward the Jewish people but I am happy to say that things are changed and are still changing now. I am glad to mention the enormous merit of Popes Jean 23rd who once and for ever declared that it was wrong to call Jews murdered of Jesus Christ, and Pope Jean Paul the second: he did visit the Synagogue in Rome, he did call Jews "oldest brothers," he did acknowledge the Church responsibilities (he did say of some men of the Church) about anti-Semitism, he did recognize the State of Israel. He is preparing an important document which most probably will change for ever the attitude of the Church towards Jews and Judaism. Pope Jean Paul the 2nd deserves exceptional merit and not only by Jews when he removed the condemnations of Galileo and Savonarola.

Now we remember how the Italian people and the Catholic Church helped the Italian Jews. We thank the Church and the people for that.

But we must also remember that more than 9,000 Italian Jews perished in the Holocaust. 9,000 over 40,000 is of course too many but it is not comparable with the tragedies which occurred in the rest of Europe.

As I said, the Church and some Italians did help in order to save Italian Jews. But I think that the main raison which saved many Italian Jews was a different one. Many Italian cities were bombed during the war and some had to be evacuated. Many Italians had to leave their houses and cities and went to a country side. So Italian Jews had to move as well and I must say, Italian Jews were not recognizable as Jews: they look Italian like other Italians. Most of the Italian Jews arrested were in Rome and they wrongly thought that they would have been safe there. In the country side, like myself and my family, many Italian Jews did escape, it was difficult, very difficult but they did escape. There was a big difference with Jews in Poland, Germany and other European countries where Jews did look like Jews, all of them used to live in the same areas of cities, the anti-Semitism was very consistent and unfortunately they did not have any chance to avoid the arrest and the holocaust.

Today we have about 35,000 Jews in Italy: 15,000 in Roma, 9,000 in Milan and very small congregations in Turin, Venice, Ferrara, Florence, Leghorn, Padua where live less than 1000 Jews.

Italian Jews are again more Italian than Jews... they are Italian like other Italians. Hoping that they will never be persecuted again.

That is what I had to say about the history of Italian Jews and about my ordeal during the time of persecutions.

GASTONE ORTONA OREFICE

The Jews in Sicily

As I search my memory for anything associated with Jews during my years of growing up in Sicily, all I can come up with is a ditty in Sicilian which was repeated by children as they performed acts of cruelty on lizards and frogs (how painful to recall the mindlessness of it!). The ditty was "non fu io e mancu Diu, fu la spata du giudeu!" (It was not I, nor was it God, it was the sword of the Jew!) which in retrospect took a lot of gall on our part. There we were about to sever a lizard's tail or worse and we were accusing the Jews! The antisemitism contained in the ditty, however, was not of a personal nature; it had to do with the biblical guilt of the Jews as the people who had failed to recognize the divinity of Jesus and had killed him, which is what Catholics were taught through catechism (that is, before the Church had adopted a more enlightened approach). I and my comrades had no personal knowledge of Jews as persons of flesh and blood. They were a mythical people who had lived "in illo tempore." As far as I knew, (and I regard my experiences there as typical and representative) there were no Jews in Sicily, nor had they ever lived on the island. It is not that I was particularly uninformed or oblivious to my surroundings. There seemed to be no physical signs in Sicily from which you could infer that Jews once had inhabited the island in large numbers. I had never seen a synagogue, or a ghetto, or a building that could be identified as Jewish. I knew no word in Sicilian that betrayed the presence of Jews on the island. I knew no food that could be recognized as Jewish. On the other hand, I could easily spot influences of other groups that have inhabited Sicily. Physical signs of the presence of Phoenicians, Greeks, Romans, are commonplace, as are those of the Arabs, Normans, Swabians, French, Aragonese/Spaniards, and even Americans, who were the last to enter Sicily as conquerors. If you look at a map of Sicily and see cities such as Caltanissetta, Caltagirone, or Caltavuturu, you have an example of the Arabic presence on the island, (*Kalt* means *castle* in Arabic); words like *bruccetta* (fork) or *custureri* (tailor) are echoes of the French domination (*brochette, couturier*). The Normans come to mind while admiring the cathedrals of Monreale and Cefalù. But nothing of the Jews was visible to my uninitiated eye. Of course, they never conquered Sicily like the others and they never left monuments to themselves for posterity. But they were there for fourteen long centuries, sharing bad times and good times, living side by side with Christians and Arabs, in relative harmony, as teachers, as merchants, as doctors, as farmers, as textile workers, as dyers, and shoemakers, contributing not little to the economic and cultural life of Sicily. Yet today those fourteen hundred years of history seem to have been erased from the consciousness of Sicilians.

Who were these Sicilian Jews, where did they live, what did they contribute to Sicilian history and what made them disappear from our collective consciousness? Answering these questions, even as incompletely as I can on this occasion, may inspire others to study the subject more deeply and illuminate an aspect of Sicilian history that has been ignored for too long.

Fortunately things are changing and that history is beginning to be written. In November 1992, in Salemi (province of Trapani), a convention was organized by the Institute of Jewish Culture "SLM," headed by Titta Lo Jacono, to discuss the historical importance of Jewish communities in Sicily. The week-long convention, attended by important Catholic and lay personalities, represented a solid beginning and an invitation to start studying those things not destroyed by time: the documents that gather dust in town archives and in libraries.

The date of the conference was chosen, of course, to coincide with the five hundredth anniversary of a momentous event in history. No, not the 1492 discovery of America by Christopher Columbus! I am referring to another event that echoed even more loudly in the hearts of European Jews: the edict by Ferdinand and Isabella of Spain, the Catholic Monarchs, expelling the Jews from all their realms. So we will begin from the end of the sojourn of the Jews on the island they had called home for fourteen hundred years, from which they were evicted not by popular animosities of their neighbors and townsmen, but by the actions of a distant king from a distant land. Sicilian Jews were caught in the vortex of a turbulent drama that was begun elsewhere.

Having driven out the Moors from Granada, the last stronghold of the Moors, Ferdinand and Isabella, who considered themselves the champions of Christianity, wanted to eradicate from Catholic Spain any other religious groups and set about the task by ordering a massive campaign to convert or drive out the Jews. Under pressure from the Grand Inquisitor Torquemada,[1] Ferdinand and Isabella signed an edict in which they accused the Jews of proselytizing and of eating away at the well-being of Christians with their usury, and ordered them to convert to Christianity or to leave all Spanish realms within three months on pain of death and confiscation of all their wealth. Their expulsion from Spain was deemed essential to "extirpate... the apostasy and iniquitous perversion of the Jews who by their practice and conversations have induced many Christians into heresy and in some errors."[2] In Sicily, which belonged to Spain and was governed at that time by Viceroy Don Ferdinand de Acugna, remembered as one of the better Viceroys,[3] the antisemitism rampant on the Iberian Peninsula was not shared by Sicilians and they did not want to see their numerous and longstanding Jewish communities leave the island. The Viceroy, sensing the enormous impact that the edict was going to have on the island, did not make it public until June 18, 1492, two and a half months after its proclamation in Spain (March 31, 1492), perhaps hoping that its implementation would not take place. No doubt he knew that an action of that magnitude was bound to create animosities, especially among the powerful members of the Sicilian *Camera Regia* (Sicilian Parliament) which could have objected not only on legal grounds — that body had not been consulted on a matter that was of the utmost importance to them — but also for moral and economic reasons. Losing the entrepreneurial skill of the Jews would be catastrophic to the island and the elite knew it. The Viceroy also knew that public opinion was definitely against the mandate because the Jews, having lived in Sicily for so long, were already integrated into the social fabric of the country.

Once the edict was made public, Sicilians in positions of authority, which included the count of Adernò, Tommaso Moncada — Grand Justice of the *Regnum* — as well as the Judges of the Magna Curia the Masters of the R oyal P atrimony, t he T reasurer o f th *Regnum,* wrote a p etition t o Ferdinand and Isabella an attempt to stop the edict from taking effect. Other bodies protested to the Viceroy with letters and personal appearances. In essence, these petitions briefly contradicted the religious rationale given by the King for the expulsion order and focused on a number of points of economic and social importance:

1. In Sicily the Jews did not try to convince Christians to abandon their faith nor did they cause heresies;

2. The Jews spent nearly one million florins a year to feed and clothe themselves and if they were evicted the island would lose this enormous sum (Titta Lo Jacono, in his *Judaic Salem,* estimates this sum to be equivalent to three quarters of a billion dollars);[4]

3. The commerce between Jews and Christians would come to an end and cause much hardship on Christians;

4. The island would come to lose the iron works industry, which was totally in the hands of Jews. And this would have disastrous consequences on ship building;

5. The island would come to lose low-wage workers employed in the construction of city defenses against incursions by pirates;

6. The state coffers would come to lose the income from taxes levied on the Jews;

7. Some of the islands belonging to Sicily, like Malta, Gozzo and Pantelleria, which were inhabited in large numbers by Jews, would become deserted;

8. The Jews, finally, with the exception of a few individuals and families, were generally so poor that if the three months limit was not extended, many would starve to death.[5]

The tone of the petition, written in Sicilian, is one of dismay, sadness and disbelief. In a second letter written to the Viceroy by the municipal government of the City of Palermo, and similar in tone, the Jews are cleared of the accusation of proselytizing and of usury: the letter states categorically that there are no reasons for proceeding against the Jews since the accusations are not founded on fact: "And for this reason the action must not be continued against this *regnum* since there are no reasons for it, nor can the cause be that the mentioned Jews are usurers for in this kingdom it has never been known that the Jews practiced usury publicly."[6]

Sicilian Jews were in fact not engaged in money lending, even though Jews had been given permission to charge 10% on loans by the Emperor Frederick II in his Melfi Charter of 1231.[7] The Sicilian officials who signed the petition reflected the dismay, as confirmed by other sources and other testimonials, of the population as a whole who had had a long tradition of tolerance for different religious beliefs and had lived in relative tranquillity side by side with Jews, Arabs, and Christians. In the depth of the Middle Ages, while Europe was experiencing savage repressions and massacres of an ethnic and religious nature, Latins, Greeks, Muslims and Jews lived in harmony, in Sicily, practicing their individual religions and beliefs without interference from the government. It was so under the Arabs and it continued under the Normans and the Swabians, and to a lesser degree under the Aragonese.

The presence of the Jews in Sicily and in Southern Italy goes back in time to the first century before the modern era. While conquering Roman armies operating in the Mediterranean basin brought a good number of Jews into Italy as slaves, the largest number of them was brought back by Pompey after he sacked Jerusalem in 63 BC and by the Roman Proconsul Crassus who is said to have sold thirty thousand of them as slaves. To these groups a good number of merchants trading with Rome and operating out of the Eastern Mediterranean, and particularly Alexandria, may be added to make up the first nucleus of Jews to reside in Sicily. In time the small communities of Sicilian Jews grew in size and in importance through immigration from other parts of the Mediterranean. By the time they were expelled, there were fifty Jewish communities throughout the island, the largest being in Palermo with 5000 people; Trapani, Messina, Catania, Marsala, Sciacca, Agrigento, Mazara had large communities ranging from 2000 to 3600; medium s ized c ommunities r anging f rom 350 -1500 e xisted in Biv ona, Caltagirone, Caltabellotta, Mineo, Modica, Noto, and Polizzi; smaller communities existed in Salemi, with 320 Jews, in Termini, Castroreale, Randazzo, Augusta, Erice, Paternò, etc... According to some scholars the total Jewish population of Sicily was 100,000 people, which is estimated to represent 10% of the total Sicilian population. Others adopt a more conservative estimate of 50,000. But even if the lower estimate is accepted, it still constitutes a large nucleus whose weight in the life of the community, owing to the restless activism of the Jews who traveled back and forth between their communities, was certainly felt.

By far no other dominant group had as much influence on the Sicilian Jews as the Arabs did. The Jews enjoyed certain privileges, together with the general population, including the right to own real estate and to have synagogues, but they were forbidden to carry arms, to enter the army, and to build more synagogues. They had to pay, like other groups, a tax known as "ghezia" for practicing their religion freely and they had to wear a distinctive sign — a yellow belt and a special turban — which was instituted for the first time ever in Sicily in 887. These measures notwithstanding, the similarity of customs, culture and languages between Arabs and Jews worked in favor of the Jews who became the natural liaison between Arabs and Christians. The Jewish community in Palermo flourished to become the largest in Italy. Other communities existed in Agrigento, Siracusa and Catania. Sicilian Jews had even constituted a small community in Egypt.

But the golden age of Judaism in Sicily came during the twelfth and fourteenth centuries, under the Norman Swabian dynasties.

Under the Normans who came to power in 1066 and remained in Sicily until the last of their dynasty, Constance of Hauteville married Henry VI, the son of Frederick Barbarossa, the Jews enjoyed parity of civil rights with other citizens. They could hold public offices, own property, except Christian slaves. They were free to engage in any commercial activities, to travel and work. A medieval traveler, Benjamin of Tudela, who was not unlike Marco Polo in spirit of observation and in interests, has left us a detailed description of the various Sicilian Jewish communities he visited between 1170 and 1173, giving information as to their numbers and occupations. He describes Sicily as a kind of earthly paradise and the Jews who live in it as a large and flourishing community.[8] The Jews were engaged in many activities too diverse to list here, but two occupations in which they held a monopoly were the silk and dyeing industries. While the Arabs had brought the silk worm into Sicily, and built a thriving industry, it was the Jews who eventually made it grow into a monopoly. King Roger II returning from an expedition against Byzantium in 1147 stopped off in Thebes, Greece, where the silk industry was in the hands of Jews. He captured the town and took the Jewish silk workers with him to Palermo giving a great boost to the native industry, guaranteeing for Italy four centuries of domination of the market. The dyeing industry which required special skills was another favorite occupation of the Jews. Jews were also adept as fishermen, artisans and skilled workers of every kind.

But the happiest and most productive time for the Jews came when Frederick II (*Stupor mundi*, the wonder of the world) came to occupy the throne of Sicily, Southern Italy and Germany. While he was forced by political necessities to adopt policies that at times seemed inimical to Jews — he accepted the dictates of the Fourth Lateran Council that required Jews to wear a distinctive sign, an orange-colored TAU of his own design, he confirmed that they should continue to pay taxes to the bishops — he expressed his true feelings for them in his Melfi Charter, published in 1231, in which he declared that Jews were under his personal protection and that they had the same rights to justice as all other citizens. In addition, for the first time in history and against the power of the Church which had just lifted its excommunication from his head, he declared that money-lending, as noted earlier, was not illegal for the Jews as long as they did not charge more than 10% interest. While money-lending was not immediately embraced by Jews, it was to become an important activity for them. The Church, of course, had maintained all throughout that charging interest on money lent was sinful. The Jews figure prominently in Frederick's plan for economic reforms. He gave them absolute control of the silk monopoly. The Emperor at one point closed all dyeing shops in the realm except those in Capua and Naples, placing these under the direction of two Jews, as a way of monopolizing that industry as well. The two Jewish directors in turn could authorize the opening of other shops. In addition, as a way of stimulating commerce, Frederick organized fairs in various cities with Jews participating prominently in them. Under Frederick's rule, Jews prospered, being able to conduct their activities with the support of the sovereign and under his protection. Their highly specialized skills with silver, gold, (the Jews were linked to these arts so much that "orefice," a word that signifies "goldsmith" used as a family name indicates that family's Jewish ancestry), coral and iron made their contribution to the economy of their island nearly irreplaceable. One activity carried out by Sicilian Jews can be used to extrapolate the sense of safety and continuity that they felt in Sicily: many of them were farmers and cultivated the land and grew vineyards while living in small towns: Always weary of the sudden change in political climates, Jews have tended to be an urban people, as a natural defense against the unpredictability of historical events that might force them to liquidate their assets quickly and run. Such an eventuality must have appeared remote to the Sicilian Jewish farmers who invested everything they had in the land. Frederick II was only one of the last in a long line of rulers who by their action instilled such abiding faith. But he was the one who was the most appreciative of the business acumen of the Jews, and also of their spiritual and cultural patrimony. Things changed for the worse, however, after the death of Frederick and of his successors and the arrival of the French, in the person of Charles d'Anjou, in Southern Italy and in Sicily.

The destinies of the Jews in Southern Italy were parted when Sicily rebelled against the greed and abuses of the French in 1282 and threw them out, slaughtering every Frenchman in sight. Sicily became a separate kingdom under Charles of Aragon, while Southern Italy remained under the Anjou dynasty. While there is no question that Sicilian Jews fared a lot better than their counterparts under French domination, it is true that in the Kingdom of Sicily which lasted from 1302 to 1402, when it was demoted to a Viceregency, the Jews suffered a setback — although they did not suffer in the same measure as the general population — due to the deteriorating economic conditions. A crisis caused by dynastic strife and infighting among local barons engulfed the island. In addition, as the economy changed from industrial/agricultural to strictly agricultural, the Jews who had occupied key positions in the silk manufacture and dyeing industries were forced to shift their attention to trading in agricultural products. Slowly their wealth diminished. The political climate also changed. Under the Aragonese, harsher laws against Jews were enacted. Jews could not practice medicine on or give medicines to Christians, they could not hold public offices or associate openly with Christians. But as happened in the Vatican, these laws were not adhered to in daily practice. In fact, Jewish doctors were allowed to frequent the Court and were received honorably there as "familiars."

No doubt many of the problems that rose between Christians and Jews can be ascribed less to the Aragonese government than to the action of the Church which, through preachers, inflamed the population against the "murderers of Christ" and was in part responsible for some episodes of brutality against the Jews. Typically, the time of the year Jews dreaded most was the Holy Week which culminated in the reenactment of the passion of Jesus, a reenactment that still takes place in costumes and with elaborate productions worthy of Hollywood in many Sicilian towns. The fury of preachers who denounced Jews from the pulpits caused many to abandon what is truly a Sicilian way of life: "vivi e lassa viviri" (live and let live). Still, such outbreaks were sporadic, temporary and causally linked to outside agencies. They were momentary departures from the normal behavior of Sicilians. Fanaticism is totally alien to the Sicilian *modus vivendi*. Sicilians are very pragmatic people. They are extremely rationalistic and will not perform acts of brutality unless family honor is at stake. Sicilians, as Tomasi di Lampedusa observed, have a way of changing everything that comes to them from the outside and the hot wind of antisemitism in crossing the Mediterranean sea became much cooler when it reached Sicily and even then it was not easily tolerable. Racism, as Titta Lo Jacono wrote, is an imported plant, but unlike the prickly pears or orange, it has never taken roots in Sicily.[9]

By and large, in the 15th century Jews continued to enjoy autonomy as a collectivity, have their own synagogues, cemeteries, ritual baths, slaughter house; they were free to chose their work, they could own property, and they could own slaves, except Christian ones. These privileges were not cheap, however, since the authorities frequently made demands on the Jews for special purposes, to renew a license, for example, or to extend a right or to confirm a privilege already obtained. One of the most ironic "donations" the Jews ever had to make was when they paid Ferdinand 2,500 Ounces in 1481 and another 1000 Ounces again in 1489, ostensibly to obtain assurances from him that their previously established rights were not going to be altered. In actuality the money helped finance the war against Granada, the outcome of which destroyed the last stronghold of Arab power in Spain and sealed the destinies of the Jews. Unwittingly they contributed to their own expulsion!

But that was not the only irony. Once the edict was announced and the machinery set in place to extract as much wealth from the departing Jews as possible, the Spanish authorities registered and sequestered Jewish properties to make sure that any outstanding debts or obligations were paid. The most outrageous of ironies was a demand by the government to be reimbursed for all the future taxes that it was not going to collect from the Jews! They were forced to pay one hundred thousand Florins to have their properties released to them, as well as five thousand Florins to the Viceroy as a special donation. The two sums were not far from the actual value of the properties seized by the government. In other words the government expropriated these properties and left the Jews the task of transforming them into cash in the hope that something would be left over, after satisfying Christian creditors. In the end, little was left, in fact, to the Jews who out of the meager pooled resources the community had to pay for the indigent being expatriated, which for the city of Palermo alone were 1/8 the Jewish population. Those who were too poor to pay for their transportation out of the country were to be provided by the community with "una coperta di lectu...cum unu pare di linczola usati et uno mataraczo usato di pocu precio et la somma di tre tari per testa." (a blanket for the bed with a pair of used sheets and an inexpensive used mattress and the sum of three tarì per person.)

Needless to say the departure from Sicily was traumatic for both those who remained and those forced to leave. The expulsion order, however, had different effects in Sicily than it had had in Spain. Out of 200,000 Jews in Spain, 150,000 accepted banishment rather than convert to Christianity. In Sicily, there seems to be agreement among historians that a great number of Jews, and particularly those that belonged to the upper classes, preferred to convert, rather than lose their capital and their homeland to which undoubtedly they had become attached and which had been very hospitable to them.[10] The town of Salemi, where out of thirty families of Jews only four decided to accept exile, represents a special case and is certainly not typical of how Sicilian Jews reacted to the expulsion order. Nor can what happened in San Marco and Castronovo, where the scale tipped in the other direction, be considered representative. In San Marco 723 out of 728 Jews preferred to leave, in Castronovo,120 out of 130.[11] The percentage of those who left is difficult to calculate but it is generally accepted that most of the poor Jews preferred to leave, no doubt hoping to find better economic conditions elsewhere. There were also many who accepted conversion but continued to be Jews within the sanctuaries of their homes.

The Jews who had lived in Sicily since the first century BC left the island they called home on January 12, 1493, never to return again. Many of them went to Rome, where the Popes surprisingly adopted generally a protective attitude towards them. Even the Borgia Pope, Alexander VI, who was a Spaniard did not share the Spanish monarch's preoccupation with Jews and offered them his protection, even against the petition by local Jews who feared that the influx of many others would cause problems in their community. The city that received the largest number of Sicilian Jews was Reggio Calabria where the Jewish communities of Messina and Siracusa moved *en masse*. They were welcomed by King Ferrante of Naples who offered them his protection and disposed that the new arrivals should be treated as though they had been long-time subjects of the crown. But it was not long until Ferdinand took control of Naples, marking the end of their sojourn there. In 1515 most of them were forced to leave again. A small number of rich families remained in Naples for another 30 years. But in 1541, when these families were forced out, the history of the Jews in Southern Italy came to an end. Many went to the North, and especially to Rome and Ferrara, others preferred to leave for farther destinations in Albania, Greece, Siria and Palestine. The authorities made two attempts, in 1740 and in 1747, to recall the Jews in the hope of stimulating economic activity in the realm, but no Jewish communities ever returned to Sicily or Southern Italy. Yet the memory of their residence in these places lived with them for a long time, for when midway through the 16th century, they established themselves in Salonicco, Constantinople, or even the island of Corfù, many

"Aljiamas" bore the names of the places they had been forced to leave. In Salonicco a dozen synagogue-communities were called "Sicilia" "Puglia" "Calabria" "Otranto" and "Messina."

What's left of the fourteen centuries of Jewish permanence in Sicily? As I said at the beginning, not much remains to the untrained eye. But serious efforts are being made to try to recover a part of the past because respect for history is a barometer of civilization. Much work remains to be done. Each of the fifty towns in Sicily had its own "giudecca," its own cemeteries and synagogues. While a great number of the physical remnants of the Jewish presence have been destroyed or transformed, a great deal still remains; town archives contain masses of documents that need to be studied and catalogued. The most visible evidence of the Jewish presence is probably in the use of names that are very common in Sicily. Names of cities such as Messina, Catania, Palermo, Piazza, and Trapani, while not automatically Jewish in origin were adopted by them with great frequency; names of professions like Orefice, (goldsmith) Ferraro, Ferro (iron monger was a profession almost exclusively reserved to Jews) Barbera (with its many variants-Barbieri, Barberini, Barberis-identifies people who worked as barbers but who also performed small operations, pulled teeth etc.). Last names such as Angelo or D'Angelo were frequently used by Jews. It was translated directly from the Hebrew (Angelo is Malechai in Hebrew). Palumbo was a translation of the name Jonah; other common Sicilian Jewish names are: Sala, Lo Presti, (probably a variant of Pristo-Preste, priest), Forte, Leone and Moncada (this last name, belonging to one of the most renown aristocratic families of Sicily was common among the *conversos.*) Those who converted were given the chance to use the names of noble Sicilian families such as Torres, De Castro, Martines.

The integration of the Jews with the rest of the population left marks on Sicilian customs and traditions, even if we are not aware of them. The Jews continued culinary traditions imported by the Arabs and brought them north after the expulsion.[12] Until the 1600s Sicilians normally used animal fats for cooking. Gradually they began to favor olive oil which was part of the Jewish culinary tradition. A typical Sicilian dish of Jewish origin is meat fried in olive oil with garlic and sage. Another is "Artichokes a la giudea." Who knows what other Jewish customs have entered the mainstream of Sicilian life? Who knows how many people of Jewish origin walk among Sicilians without knowing anything about their ancestors?

GAETANO CIPOLLA
St. John's University

---

[1] Isidoro La Lumia (1823-1879) who wrote an excellent history of the Jews in Sicily, *Gli ebrei in Sicilia,* Palermo: Sellerio, 1984, tells the story that while an emissary of the Spanish Jewish community was asking the King and Queen to reconsider the edict, by offering them thirty thousand ducats,Torquemada entered the room and taking a crucifix from under his cape and placing it on the table, said: "Judas Iscariot sold his master for thirty pieces of silver, would you sell him for thirty thousand?" Having said this he turned around and brusquely walked out, leaving the Queen astonished a nd s tunned. As f or t he kin g, added s lyly L a L umia: " Ferdinand w as a lso stunned or at least made believe he was." La Lumia believes that Ferdinand, whose greed and ambitions are well known, was more interested in expoliating the Jews than in safeguarding Christians from the evil influences of heresies.

[2] This is part of the text in Sicilian made public by Viceroy D'Acugna, which presumably translated the original Spanish documents. See Attilio Milano, *La storia degli Ebrei in Italia,* Torino: Einaudi, 1963, p. 218.

[3] This I. La Lumia's judgment, op. cit., who viewed the Viceroy's delaying tactics in implementing the royal mandate of expulsion, which was made public on June 18, 1492, two and a half months after its proclamation in Spain, as an expression of his sympathetic attitudes toward the Jews.

[4] Lo Jacono, *Judaica Salem,* Palermo: Sellerio, 1990, p. 47.

[5] The text of these two letters is in La Lumia's volume, pp. 59-65.

[6] Ibidem.

[7] According to Attilio Milano (p. 178), in the 250 years since publication of the Melfi Charter very few availed themselves of the privilege. Jews in Sicily were accustomed to more direct means of producing wealth. In fact, in some agreements stipulated in 1363 and in 1398 between various chapters of the Jewish community of Siracusa the article that Jews were forbidden to practice usury amongst themselves and with Christians was introduced at the request of the community itself. Christians, of course, were not allowed by Christian doctrine to lend money on interest.

[8] Benjamin's writings are summarized by Milano, op. cit., and by others. They are a valuable source of information for twelfth century Italy.

[9] Lo Jacono, op. cit., p. 49.

[10] See Carmelo Trasselli, "Gli Ebrei in Sicilia" in *Nuovi Quaderni del Meridione VII,* p. 44. His views are shared by Titta Lo Jacono, *Judaica Salem,* op. cit. and by

Aliyahu Ashtor, *The Jews and the Mediterranean Economy 10th-15th Centuries,* London, Variorum Reprints 1983, p. 241.

[11] Titta Lo Jacono claims that the persecutions suffered in Spain by the Jews had given them a stronger sense of belonging to a special group and a stronger attachment to their traditions. The fanaticism of the Christians begat the fanaticism of the Jews who refused to give up Judaism. But in Sicily where only sporadic explosions of hatred against the Jews had been seen and mostly as a result of the religious propaganda, Jews felt more at home.

[12] Mary Taylor Simeti's *Pomp and Sustenance,* New York: A. Knopf, 1990. Simeti speculates that Jews were responsible for helping develop the "cucina baronale."

LA LUMIA AND THE STORY OF THE SICILIAN JEWS

> "In Sicily to do things well or badly does not matter: the sin that we Sicilians do not ever forgive is simply that of 'doing.'...It is at least twenty-five centuries that we carry on our shoulders the weight of magnificent heterogeneous civilizations, all come from the outside ready made and perfected, none germinated from within us... since two thousand five hundred years we have been a colony... Sleep is what Sicilians want, and they will always hate whoever wants to wake them up."
> From Il *Gattopardo* Tomasi diLampedusa, Opere, Mondadori, pp. 170-171

For over twenty years, I have been fascinated with the story of the Sicilian Jews. A story with an unknown beginning but with a definite ending: the edict of 1492 that expelled them from the domains of Ferdinand and Isabella, a closed chapter in Sicilian history never to be reopened. There are not too many accounts of this story; the few that exist tend to repeat the same information.[1] On a visit to the island, after careful search, it is still possible to find remnances of the Jews in Sicily in the more than fifty places where they resided. My own unsystematic search suggests that the story of the Sicilian Jews is relevant for our time, it is a sad human story that needs to be known better and more widely.

La Lumia's "Disappointment" and the Saga of the Sicilian Jews

My first encounter with this story was through a republication of Isidoro La Lumia's *Storie Siciliane*, originally published in 1881-83. La Lumia, a Sicilian historian practically ignored by Italian intellectuals, was born in Palermo on November 1, 1823, and died in the same city on August 29, 1879, almost twenty years after the unification of Italy. A brief biography of his in the newer edition of his works adds to his date of death the words "Perennemente deluso" (forever disappointed). The story of the Jews of Sicily in my mind is intertwined with La Lumia's "disappointment." The systematic elimination of one people or ethnic group by another is a historical reality. It has repeated itself; in fact it keeps on repeating itself, in this century and in our own days, from the Holocaust to genocide in some African countries, to the more recent ethnic cleansing in the former

Yugoslavia.Nationalism, the hallmark of modern world history, carries in its blood the virus that leads some to the desire to eliminate others. The exaltation of group or nation can lead to the demand that "the other" be eliminated.[2] As Italy emerged as a new nation, La Lumia apparently wanted the new nation to be as much as possible the sum total of the parts that were put together by the Risorgimento. History, unfortunately, did not go according to his wishes. In fact, the new Italy ostracized him, as it ostracized all those who resisted joining the bandwagon that, in the name of the new nation, obscured and obliterated the diversity of the many parts that had been brought together. The regions were forced to shed their identity and were fused in the homogeneous, artificial construct of the new nation, the new culture, and the new beliefs. Eventually, Fascism emerged as the extreme logical conclusion of the new construct and an exaltation of nationalistic myths. The democratic reality that ensued after World War II, in part as a rejection of the extreme nationalistic manifestations of Fascism, tried hard to revive the diversity of the many parts of the nation. The regions were recognized as sources of cultural identity and revival. Ethnic, religious and linguistic identities were recognized. However, after half a century it is safe to conclude that such efforts were too late and perhaps not too sincere; to many they meant very little.[3] This is not unlike what happened in Sicily after the Jews were eliminated from the island. As La Lumia tells the story, the city of Messina, once a thriving port, after suffering from a serious slump in trade and in its economic vitality, invited the Jews to return. The attempt, however, failed miserably. A natural reality that has been destroyed cannot be recreated artificially.

The Story of the Sicilian Jews

Prince Fabrizio, in the *Gattopardo*, described Sicily to the Piedmontese envoy Chevalley as a melange of "magnificent heterogeneous civilizations, ready made and perfected, none made by ourselves, none germinated from within us... " (Lampedusa 170). The Jews brought to Sicily their civilization, their value system, their way of living and of doing. The Jews did not come to Sicily all at once. Where did they come from? When did they start coming to the island? These are unanswerable questions. No date exists marking their arrival. Unquestionably, however, their presence dates back to very early times. La Lumia and others believe that the first influx may have occurred during the First Century A.D. After the fall of Jerusalem, the Jews were dispersed into various parts of the Mediterranean and a number of them may have found their way into Sicily. But this, in our estimation, need not be their first appearance on the island. There is a Christian bias to make the Jews date to the death of Christ, but the Jews existed long before that.[4]

There are definite records attesting to the presence of a Jewish community in Siracusa in the VI Century A.D. during the pontificate of Gregorius Magnus. There is no doubt of the presence of the Jews in Sicily during the Moslem domination. They, like the Christians, were required to pay a tax on religion, the *gesia*. There are records indicating that they were allowed to own their own "meschita" (In Sicily the term for Mosque (Meschita) is used also for synagogue.) However, they were forbidden to build new ones or to proselytize. Under Pope Sergius VI, 1009 to 1019, the Jews in Europe suffered from persecution; the Sicilian Jews, however, like the Spanish Jews, under the Moslems, were spared such experience. Economic class and not religion was the most relevant distinction that existed at the time among inhabitants of the island. There were basically two classes, free men and slaves. Free men could own real estate and enjoyed some civil rights.

Under the Normans, the golden age of Sicily, the Jews like all other ethnic and religious groups enjoyed extensive freedom and rights. In this era, in Sicily, the concept of "states within the state" is perfected. Some rights were taxed. Jews, but not Christians, continued paying the *gesia* and a tax on winemaking. The Jewish community in Palermo under the Normans had 1500 members, in Messina 200. After the Sicilian Vespers, under the Aragonese monarchy, the Jews gained more rights. Frederick II, in 1321, ordered that in civil proceedings the Jews be subject to secular magistrates. Frederick III, his nephew, required that the Inquisition proceed against Jews only in the presence of ministers of the King. La Lumia reminds us, though, that under the same monarch, the Jews of Palermo were ordered to move to a community built outside the walls of the city. In the rest of the island, by the same order, the Jews were ordered to live apart from the Christians. But, La Lumia hastens to conclude, nothing came from this order; a century later its enforcement was still under discussion.

With each succeeding king, the Jews managed to improve their status. Alfonso the Wise brought into his court a number of distinguished Sicilians, among them Rabbi Moses Bonavoglia from Messina, a renowned physician. The story is told that when Alfonso needed cash he would feign a threatening attitude against the Jews of the island. The rabbi would intervene on behalf of his people; and for a price, the King would relent.

For La Lumia, the Sicilian Jews fared better than the Jews in the rest of Italy. It should not be surprising therefore that over the years there may have been a continuous influx into Sicily from the northern coast of Africa, especially from Morocco. A last large contingent of Jews came to Sicily in 1491 from Provence after Louis XI occupied that region. His predecessor, Charles VI, had expelled them from the rest of France. As La Lumia notes, it would have been a lot easier for these Jews to reach Spain instead of going to Palermo.

By the middle of the XV century, the island counted Jewish communities in fifty-seven different cities and towns. The largest community, in Palermo, had supreme jurisdiction over all the others. Each community had its own form of self-governance. A group of elders administered the business of the community, resolved disputes among its members and made sure that the laws were enforced. King Martin I attempted to superimpose a representative of the Crown over the entire structure of self-governance, the Dienchelele.[5] Two rabbis served in this position, first Rabbi Giuseppe Abbanascia and then Rabbi Moses Bonavoglia. King Alfonso, however, through the intercession of Rabbi Bonavoglia, eliminated the office upon receipt of six hundred ounces from the Jewish community.

Each community owned one or more "meschitas" (synagogue), a cemetery and a place for the purification of women. New synagogues could be built only with the approval of the crown. In 1450 with 10.000 florins, the Jews bought the right to live wherever they wished. However, Christian and Jew could not share the same roof, the same table or the same bed. In essence such an arrangement was not inconvenient for the Jews. Even the ghetto became a matter of convenience and not a strict legal mandate.

The ancient obligation that all Jews, male and female, wear distinctive clothing was eventually changed to the wearing of the "rotella rossa" (the red wheel), a round patch. The same "rotella" was used to distinguish shops and stores owned by Jews. The Jews in addition to the taxes levied on all subjects of the crown continued paying the *gesia*. Here and there special tax obligations remained in some communities. In Mazzara, for instance, at Easter, Christmas and on the day of San Salvatore, the Jews had to supply the local bishop with a certain quantity of pepper. In Palermo, a nominal fee had to be paid for weddings, and for the birth of a child, much lower if the newborn was female. Also in Mazzara, at some point, the local bishop issued an order that all Jews attend Christian services. However, in 1399 King Martin rescinded the order. Through the intervention of Rabbi Bonavoglia, the order that Jews listen to the sermons of an itinerant preacher, Fra Matteo da Girgenti, was also rescinded. The Jews were required to abstain from manual work during mass on Christian holidays. In court, Christians could testify against Jews, but the reverse was not permitted. Money lending with interest, traditionally forbidden to Christians, was permitted to Jews; interest, however, was fixed at no more than ten percent.

The Number of Sicilian Jews and Their Occupations

There are but speculations about the total number of Jews on the island at any time from their earliest arrival to their expulsion. Giovanni di Giovanni claimed that, in 1492, the Jews were ten per cent of the total population, one million people. Hence, the order of expulsion must have affected about one hundred thousand individuals.[6] That by the time of the exodus, the number of Jews in Sicily was not insignificant is confirmed by other historical records. More important, however, than the absolute number of Jews, is their presence throughout the island, in large cities such as Palermo, Siracusa or Messina and in small towns such as Castroreale, Cammarata or Nasi. There were Jewish communities along the coast and in the interior. Giovanni di Giovanni chronicles the presence of Jews in fifty-eight places, including the islands of Malta, Gozzo, and Pantelleria. Di Giovanni's chronicles of the 58 communities are supported by accounts of the crown concerning events in most of the same communities around the time of the expulsion.[7]

The economic activities of the Sicilian Jews spanned the entire gamut of known economic activities. The Jews were involved in financial and commercial activities and were also prominent in the professions and in the crafts. They were physicians, weavers, goldsmiths, and metal workers. Some small towns had no other traders but Jews. Denis Mack Smith reports that "they were especially celebrated as doctors" (107), a profession also opened to women. This is so in spite of the standing edict that Jewish physicians could not practice medicine on Christians. As it emerges from La Lumia's account, the story of the Sicilian Jews is the story of a distinct religious group with a strong attachment to its own religion, cultural values and way of life. From today's point of view, they also had much charity and patience in putting up with an attitude, fanned by religious fanatics, that called for symbols to differentiate them from the rest of the inhabitants of the island. They fought to expand their sphere of freedom from inconvenience and interference, but fought harder to protect the integrity of their faith and their independence in the face of the fierce determination of the Catholic church to make Christianity the sole religion of the island.

While all groups in Sicily fared best under the Normans who made an example of their ability to govern ethnic and religious groups with respect for diversity, the Jews in particular, managed to protect their cultural and religious independence as long as they were dealing with temporal powers. If necessary, money would buy freedom and rights. Their worse enemy, through their many centuries on the island, was the Catholic Church. Prelates and lay people, many of whom, probably uncertain of their own faith, fought hard to eliminate all other faiths and homogenize the entire island into their alleged superior spirituality. The struggle of the Catholic Church to conquer the minds of the Sicilians through the centuries must have been both fierce and difficult. It had to conquer the poverty of spirit of a large permanent underclass more concerned with the needs of the body than of the soul. The Church took on all the civilizations that had been present on the island, Sikelians, Moors, Greeks, Romans, and Jews. Faced with stubborn resistance to evangelization, the Catholics complained that the Jews wanted to seduce people away from Christianity; thus, the insistence on separateness and distinctive symbols to mark all people and things Jewish. Preachers out either to convert non-Christians or to reconnect to their church nominal Catholics resorted to scare tactics portraying the Jews as the instrument of the devil. With each wave of evangelization, anti-Semitic stories and fantasies were revived such as the one, that reportedly happened in Messina, that the Jews used the blood of Christian children for their rituals.

As the state, the embodiment of temporal power, fell under the influence of the church the Jews suffered and their ability to maneuver and buy rights failed. Most telling on this account is the story eagerly repeated by Giovanni di Giovanni that after the issuing of the edict of expulsion, Ferdinand and Isabella were approached by leaders of the Jewish community in Spain with an offer of thirty thousand ducats to lift the order. Torquemada, however, stopped the deal. He broke into the meeting, crucifix in hand, and cried "Judas sold his master for thirty pieces of silver: you (the kings) want to sell him for thirty thousand." (Giovanni di Giovanni 195). Under Ferdinand and Isabella, the power of the state and the power of the church became one and the same. The Inquisition, originally an ecclesiastical institution, was taken over as a power of the crown. "Ferdinand took it (the Inquisition) as his own power, and made it an attribute and concern of the Crown." As of this event the days of the Jews in Sicily or in Spain are counted. Each individual has a simple decision to make: to convert or to leave. The number of conversions was much larger in Spain than in Sicily. Why this is so should be the subject of an interesting study.

The very wealthy of Sicily, the Barons, most comfortable in their large estates, had little or no incentive to come to the rescue of the Jews. The Jews were part of the active classes; many worked with their hands, some traded or lent money. Their elimination was no cause of concern for the aristocracy. On the other hand, the political leaders of the island, those active in the economic life realized that the Crown had doomed the economic system. As the Jews left, the island lost a substantial segment of what in later economic development becomes identified as the core of the modern economy: the middle class and the upper lower class. In the words of La Lumia, "the population that was especially productive and useful."

The Spanish Edict of 1492 and Its Enforcement in Sicily

The edict to expel the Jews from all the Spanish domains was issued in Granada on March 31, 1492. The edict with instructions prepared especially for Sicily was sent to Ferrando de Acuña, Viceroy of the Crown for "Sicily and adjacent islands." The intent and logic of the edict are simple. The Inquisition has concluded that the Jews constitute an irremediable threat to Christianity in the Kingdom of Spain, therefore the Kingdom must be rid (cleansed, in today's language) of them. All must be eliminated, so that,

> "alcuno Judeo masculo ne femina, grande ne picciolo di qualunque stati sia non possa stare, ne stara in parte delli nostri regni & dominationi, ne pozzano tornare a quelli per stare ne passari per quelli o per alcuna parte di quelli sub pena della morte...." (Giovanni di Giovanni 222).

> "No Jew, male or female, grown up or child of any age can reside, and shall not reside in any part of our Kingdom and domains. Nor can they come back to our Kingdom and domains or parts of them to live permanently or temporarily under the penalty of death..."

As the edict continues, every attempt had been made to resolve the problem of coexistence between Christians and Jews short of the final solution of expulsion; death is prescribed for those who dare return. The Jews in various places and at various times had been ordered to live in quarters of their own, the *juderias*, but they continue "to subvert and draw away faithful Christians from our holy Catholic faith." (David Raphael 190). The Jews insist on teaching Christians their laws, their ways, their ceremonials a nd r ituals. C hristians ha ve s ubjected t hemselves t o " the abominable circumcision" and have been made to "blaspheme the holy name of Jesus Christ our Lord and Redemptor." (Giovanni di Giovanni 217). Hence the King as defender of the Catholic faith must "withdraw his grace" from the Jews and expel them from his kingdom. By the end of July 1492 all Jews must be gone from Spain and its territories. So that they "may better dispose of themselves, their belongings and their estates, all Jews are placed immediately under the protection and guardianship" (David Raphael 192) of the Crown. No one is to cause them any offense. Finally, the Jews are reminded that in settling their affairs before departing, they are forbidden to take with them "gold, silver, minted money, or other items prohibited by laws of [the] kingdom, except for nonprohibited merchandise or exchange bills." (David Raphael 192). The edict is issued by the Crown, but the true moving force is the Inquisition, which, as the edict states, continues finding the Jews in violation of the relations between the two faiths. The Crown takes literally the word of the Inquisition.

The edict of Ferdinand and Isabella must have stunned the Sicilian leadership and most likely Acuña himself, if not for humane reasons, for two practical considerations. First, because of the major task involved in the execution of the order. Second, because it violated the existing practice of consultation with, if not consent of, the island leadership. Acuña took his time in making the order known. It is possible, according to La Lumia, that he asked for further clarifications from Spain, maybe even for an exemption for Sicily. The requirement written in the very edict that it be "proclaimed in the plazas ... in the principal cities and villages ... by a public crier" (David Raphael 193) was not observed by the viceroy for some time. It is not known when the edict arrived or how long it took to arrive in Sicily. Acuña must have kept it secret for a considerable time. On May 24 and 28, 1492, he issued two orders without ever mentioning the edict. The first, placing all the Jews, their property and all their belongings under the protection of the Crown. The second, prohibiting all citizens from carrying weapons unless they were charged with the protection of the Jews and their possessions. The rationale for such orders is worth considering:

> "...*havemo havuto informacioni* (emphasis mine) ... chi la maiesta del Rey nostro signuri per certi causi moventi lo animo di sua altecza voli & intendi distachari & expelliri fora di soy regni et dominio li Iudey..." (Codice Diplomatico DCCCLXXII).

> "... *we have received word*... that his majesty the King our lord for certain reasons moving the spirit of his highness wishes and intends to detach and expel the Jews out of his kingdom and domain..."

With the edict safely put away in his office, such maneuvers can be interpreted in a number of ways. To prepare the island by degrees for the shock of the proclamation. Working behind the scene to gain a possible reprieve from the Crown. Or, just fear of an insurrection, given the number of individuals affected, and the implications for the economy of the island. In the meantime the Jews were under the "protection" of the Crown and their possessions were being identified for subsequent inventory. The insignia of the King was placed on the "meschitas" and on the door of all Jewish homes. A copy of the orders issued by Acuña in Messina, where he was in temporary residence, was sent to all major "cities and villages." At least forty of them are mentioned.

On May 31, 1492, a summary of the Monarch's edict is transmitted secretly by Acuña to the officials of Palermo ordering them to collect the weapons from all private citizens and to place all Jews under royal protection. (Codice Diplomatico DCCCLXXIV). They were also ordered to requisition all the possessions of the Jews and to start inventorying them. In a very different tone, on June 3, 1492, Acuña sends a letter to the bishops of Sicily exhorting them to instruct "in the Catholic faith any Jews who, recognizing the error of their way, are willing to convert to the said Catholic faith." (Codice Diplomatico MLXI). This letter is indicative of the desire to also remind the public of the very nature of the edict, to expand and to protect the Catholic faith. Much of Acuña's concern during the process leading to the departure of the Jews from Sicily deals with: first, economic realities, satisfaction of debts towards the Crown on the part of Jews; second, making sure that all the Jews are gone, including those who are in jail. The approach Acuña takes towards these chores is the purely Weberian approach, *sine ira ac studio*, of the emerging modern bureaucratic mind. If one considers instead the immense relevance of the morality of what is involved in carrying out the edict, Acuña's actions and meticulous concern, as we shall see below, are the quintessence of Hannah Arendt's *Banality of Evil*.

Only on the 18th of June, 1492, Acuña makes the royal edict public, "so that everyone learns the news, especially the Jews." On that day the edict is promulgated "*voce preconia de verbo ad verbum*, (to be proclaimed out l oud f rom b eginning t o e nd) s o t hat t here c annot b e a ny do ubt." (Giovanni di Giovanni 229).[8] As of this date, also, the tempo of the execution picks up, as do the communications out of Acuña's office. Legality is to be observed scrupulously. The Jews must pay the taxes to the Crown and the Christians must pay their debts to the Jews. Those who convert to Christianity will stay, but they must pay the equivalent of forty percent of the value of what they own for this privilege. This is not totally consistent with Acuña's letter to the bishops of Sicily of July 6, 1492 in which he wants to put to rest the "vulgar rumors" (vulgari dictu) of some who claim that even if they convert, the Jews will be "mistreated both with regard to person and wealth." To advance further the Christian faith, Acuña writes, the Jews that convert will receive no mistreatment, either to their person or the their property. ("Non sarra facto danno alcuno in persona ni in beni tanto mobili como stabili.") (Codice Diplomatico DCCCXV). What each person, poor or rich, can take out of Sicily is spelled out. How the Jews of the inland towns must reach the port cities for embarkation is mapped out.

The deadline for expulsion originally set for September 18, 1492 soon appears too unrealistic for an orderly execution. The Jews make an appeal to the Crown and, reminiscent of the old way of doing things, their appeal is granted, in exchange for five thousand florins. The September deadline is moved to December 18, 1492 and eventually to January 12, 1493. The many orders issued from Acuña's office are the quintessence of modern "bureaucracy." The edict must be enforced efficiently, legally, and with no questions asked about its morality. On July 3, 1492 an order goes out to remind all that the Jews must be treated properly because they are under the protection of the Crown, they must not receive offense or mistreatment of any kind. (Codice Diplomatico DCCCXIV). The order was prompted by the complaint of some Jews who had been harassed by Christians in economic transactions. On July 6, 1492 Acuña sends one of his officers to Girgenti to investigate the complaint of some Jews who claimed to have been robbed and defrauded. (Codice Diplomatico DCCCXVI) On August 29, 1492 emissaries are sent to all cities that have Jewish communities to find out if local officials in executing royal orders extracted bribes from the Jews and if there was any corruption in the execution of the edict. (Codice Diplomatico DCCCCLXXI).

Neither Jew nor Christian must enrich himself at the expense of the Crown. The elders of the Jewish communities are ordered to extract an oath from their members that there has been no fraud and that they have not bribed any public officials. Those who have, must be excommunicated on the Sabbath in the "meschita" according to the practice of the Jews (more Iudeorum). Because of a complaint from the Jewish community in Randazzo, on July 8, 1492 Acuña issues an order that all goods and property requisitioned for over fifteen days, if no creditors have come forward, be returned to their owners so that they can be disposed of properly, in preparation for the departure. If any creditors have made a claim, they should be paid forthwith what is owed them and the rest be given back to the owners.

On July 17, 1492 assurance is given to the Jews, this time directly, not through the Catholic bishops, that if they convert, contrary, once again, to "vulgar rumors", they will suffer no mistreatment and will be treated like Christians. (Codice Diplomatico DCCCCXXVII). At the end of July as the September deadline for departure approaches, an order is sent to the officials of Palermo to let out of prison thirty days before departure all the Jews incarcerated for debts, who have no means to repay their creditors. (Codice Diplomatico DCCCCXXXI). Having heard that in Castroreale the Jews could not get their inventoried goods transported to Messina, Acuña orders the officials of that city to see that the royal edict is followed. The goods must be transported to Messina and turned in to the Royal Treasurer. "We are not little surprised," writes Acuña, "that our orders which are those of the Crown are not being followed." He threatens a fine of one thousand florins against the public officials if they don't see to it that his instructions are properly followed. (Codice Diplomatico DCCCCXIII).

In another case, also in Castroreale, Ferrando Acuña intervenes in a private matter to ensure that the spirit as well as the letter of the law prevails. A Joseph Settuna pleaded that a house that his father-in-law had given to the "meschita" and had been inventoried with the possessions of the congregation, be returned to him, so that he can sell it and get the money necessary for his departure. Acuña orders that the house be excluded from the general inventory and returned to Settuna for a private sale. Further, the same Settuna and his brother Bonavoglia have a home and a certain quantity of incense on lease from a nobleman named Filippo, for which the two brothers pay Filippo six florins per year. Acuña orders that the house be sold, that Filippo receive a sum of money equivalent to the value of the house, and that the two brothers get the rest. Once again, the officials are reminded that if the order is not executed properly a fine of one hundred ounces will be imposed on them. (Codice Diplomatico MX).

The Reaction of the Officials of Sicily to the Edict

The official reaction and response of the island to the edict of the Spanish Monarchs is best contained in two documents prepared shortly after the official proclamation of the edict against the Jews. Both documents are written with the proper respect and deference that vassals owe a King or the Viceroy but do not hesitate to analyze and portray how the island will suffer if the edict is executed. Both documents seem to beg the fundamental question: why did the Crown in this most critical edict fail to consult with the very people that are faithful and loyal to it? The first document sent from Messina is the result of the deliberation of the members of the Royal Council meeting as individuals, not officially as the Council, and is dated June 20, 1492, two days after the issuance of the edict in Sicily. The second document was prepared by the leaders of the city of Palermo and was sent to the Viceroy Ferrando Acuña, hopefully to strengthen his will and his hand in negotiations with the Monarchs, and is dated July 11, 1492.[9]

Together both documents challenge and rebut the royal edict in economic, social, and military as well as religious terms. According to La Lumia, had the barons of Sicily joined in with these complaints of the island leadership, the Sicilian Jews might have fared differently. However, given the universality of the Royal edict, the emergence of a modem national state with an efficient bureaucracy, the merging in Spain of temporal power with religious power, and the fact that the order caused a number of conversions, La Lumia's assumption seems less than realistic. As later historical developments in the Spanish empire show, the Crown was quite determined with the purpose of the edict. As the Sicilians generally found out the Crown of Spain under Ferdinand and Isabella is quite different in its relationship with its subjects from the Crown under the previous kings. The title of Catholic Monarchs, the defenders of the faith, which may have not pleased Rome completely, is taken by Ferdinand and Isabella quite seriously, after all, it is a useful means to consolidate the empire.

For the Sicilians it is quite clear that the royal edict will be the cause of a major disaster for the island and especially for a number of cities, large and small. What may be compelling reasons for the Spanish Monarchs are not so for Sicily. At least, the Crown must allow more time in the execution of the edict so that a proper case can be made both for its reconsideration and for a delay in its execution. The island officials clearly want to show to the Crown that they can better speak for the interest of the island and ultimately for that of the Crown when it comes to local issues. For sure, they argue, the Monarchs and the Viceroy should not damage the island to inflict pain on the Jews and thus end inflicting worse punishment on the Christians.

As far as the religious issue is concerned, the island officials and those from Palermo suggest that whatever the Jews may be doing in and to Spain, which the Crown finds offensive to the Catholic religion, is not at all true in Sicily. Whatever the tension may be between Jews and Christians, it is not the Jewish faith that is expanding. In actuality, in Sicily, the Catholic faith is expanding to the detriment of the Jewish faith. The Jews do not undermine the existence and mission of Christianity; to the contrary, a number of Jews are becoming Christians and once they convert they behave like good Christians, (perfecti Christiani.) To prove that the Jews do not "behave in a manner that is contrary to, or insults the Catholic Christian faith," there is the testimony of a father Antonio de la Pegna who has conducted a recent inquisition on the state and practice of religion on the island, searching for practices contrary to the tenets of the faith. Father Antonio has uncovered "no error or scandal" in the practice of religion. The document from Messina, the more important of the two, because it is addressed personally to the Monarchs, concludes on this issue that had they, the leaders of the island, been aware of any way in which the Jews undermined the Catholic faith, they themselves would have petitioned the Crown not to expel the Jews, but to burn them. "...videndo nui di tali horribili crimini dicti Iudey essiri mundi per la practica hanno cum christiani..." ["...we see *these* (emphasis mine) Jews (the Sicilian Jews) to be free of such terrible crimes (those reported in the edict) in the interaction with Christians."]

As to military defense issues, the Messina document reminds the King that the island would be quite weakened, if so many people, so integral to the economy, are forced to leave. The Turks, whose navy is ever present in the Mediterranean, may very well take advantage of this opportunity to launch incursions into the island. Coast cities and towns will be left in no position to defend themselves for lack of human power. The Jews, they maintain, may not make great soldiers, but they can provide support to the military; they are useful because they are dependable. Some of the islands surrounding Sicily such as Malta, Gozzo and Pantelleria, with large numbers of Jewish inhabitants, will become easy prey to invaders.

The economic issue is the one most emphasized in both documents. The Messina document, in fact, is divided into two parts: the first deals with the Jews, the second with the surplus production of grain in the island and the need to find some way to sell some of it to the "barbaria," (the Moslem lands.) Spain had prohibited trade with the Moslems. The document concludes by rejoining the issue of the Jews with that of the trade embargo. The prohibition to sell excess grain to the Moslems and "the great harm ... that will befall this kingdom with the departure of the Jews ... will result in so much damage to the revenue, taxes from exchange, entry taxes, and tolls that accrue to the interest of your Royal Majesty." With regard to usury, historically the economic activity most associated with the Jews, the island "has nothing to complain about."

If the Jews are expelled from Sicily, the leaders calculate that the economy will lose over one million florins worth of activity per year. This is what the Jews spend for their existence. Crown, churches, cities, barons, and private citizens will all suffer from such loss. The Christian, in the final analysis, will suffer because of the absence of the Jew. To throw out of the island so many people will cause a collapse in the value of real estate. Finally, the Jews are involved in so many occupations, crafts and trade that the economy of entire towns and of the island will collapse. To conclude with the words of the document from Palermo, if the royal edict would have "caused harm to the Jews only, we (Christians) would be quiet nor would we be making such a plea. However, we do all we are doing because we can see the destruction and ruin of the entire island, of cities in particular and generally. It would be a thing too incredible to explain." (La Lumia 351).

Isidoro La Lumia died, *perennemente deluso*, because the new Italy, instead of building itself from the ground up on the foundations of its diverse regions, highlighting the best traditions of each, chose a top down mode of development which imposed a new reality on the rich diversity of its base. In fact, it may have even contributed to the destruction of that richness. Essentially, it was no different from other powers that had taken over Sicily not to make it part of a whole but as a "colony." While there may have been historical justification for the previous experiences of "colonization," the last experience, the one of the united Italy, called more for integration than submission of the island. This raises the issue, which has reappeared in one form or the other over the past century and a half, of Why Italy? What is Italy? Who are the Italians? Where does Italy begin? Where does it end? "Campanilismo," as social scientists keep on pointing out, has remained the hallmark of Italian culture. It is the most relevant reality of Italy today and of Italy (however one may want to define it) through the centuries. Maybe, all of this points out to the major weakness of modern nationalism: it can create constructs out of crises but finds it hard to hold on to them, because they are too artificial. La Lumia was led through his research to the conclusion that evil to the island has usually come from the outside.[10] One should not interpret this as meaning that what is inside, as against what comes from the outside, is all necessarily good. The issue is more one of the fit between what comes from the outside and what is inside. Had the Monarchs of Spain paid attention to the views of the Sicilian leaders and spared the island the loss of an important part of its population, Sicily would have not suffered from a major economic disaster. Had the new Italy of Savoy taken into consideration the true state of the island and integrated it into the union as a part with its identity, the "unitá" would have been a better reality for Italy and for Sicily.

And perhaps the same reasoning can be applied to events after the union such as the attempts by the fascist regime to improve the socioeconomic condition of the island or the Cassa del Mezzogiorno under the first Republic. One fact seems to be sure, even today in the relation between Sicily and the outside world, especially Italy, what is most known are the negative features of the island's life: the Mafia, the corruption, the unfinished roads, the non-existing railroads, funding used up three or four times with the original project yet to be started, hosting international sport competitions with no facilities ready and with construction still going on two years after the competition is completed. One wonders if the same kind of tragedy or comedy will continue in the context of the united Europe. For all the writing and concern about Sicily, one thing is sure, the island is still a mystery to the outside world and perhaps to the Sicilians themselves. La Lumia's *Storie Siciliane* (which should be read more widely) may be an important first step in gaining an understanding and appreciation of this island loved by some and yet a mystery to many.

SALVATORE G. ROTELLA, PRESIDENT
Riverside Community College

---

[1] Most of the information about the account of the Jews in Sicily comes from *Isidoro LaLumia Storie Siciliane*, in which can be found the section entitled, "The Sicilian Jews," pp. 311-345.

[2] The concern with nationalism had its heyday especially among American scholars during Fascism and Nazism and World War II.

[3] The Italian Constitution after World War II provides for the safeguard of linguistic minorities and liberty of religious worship. It provides for decentralization of the state and the establishment of twenty regions, five of which, (Valle D'Aosta, Trentino-Alto-Adige, Friuli-Venezia Giulia, Sardegna and Sicilia) with special autonomy for ethnic, historical and peripheral reasons.

[4] See in addition to LaLumia, Giovanni di Giovanni *L'Ebraismo della Sicilia* pp. 1-7 On pp. 2 and 3, DiGiovanni writes "The number of Jews in the Roman Provinces increased after Jerusalem was won and demolished by Titus..."

[5] The institution of the Dienchelele had its origins in Spain, where the occupant of that office had the title of Judge and Highest Rabbi.

[6] See Giovanni di Giovanni, pp. 19-28. The subtitle under the title of Chapter II "Of the Number of Jews in Sicily reads," "The Jews Abhor Continence."

[7] DiGiovanni, part II, pp. 246-405. This part chronicles communities. In an addition ("Aggiunta per gli Ebrei di Sicilia"), he includes the story of the Jews of Scicli which apparently he had not considered in the main body of the work. Scicli "is situated in the Valle di Noto and in the diocesi di Siracusa." p. 421.

[8] Apparently the order issued by the Crown differed from possession to possession. The version for Sicily is reprinted in its entirety in Giovanni di Giovanni, pp. 216-229.

[9] These two documents are *Codice Diplomatico* DCCCXCV, the one from Messina which is dated June 20, 1492; the second, *Codice Diplomatico* DCCCCXXII, from the city of Palermo, dated July 11, 1492. La Lumia in his *Storie* reprints both documents; however, the one from Messina leaves out completely the section of the document dealing with the issue of grain surplus.

[10] La Lumia, pp. 311-313. "...la persecuzione arbitraria e violenta arrivava da fuori....il male è stato quasi sempre alieno ed esotico innesto." (The arbitrary and violent persecution came from the outside.... evil has almost always been a grafting both alien [from the outside] and exotic.)

Devils Without Horns:
The Festa dei Giudei*

The Festa dei Giudei (Feast of the Jews) is part of the rites that occur during holy week in San Fratello, Sicily. This ancient festa mixes carnival motifs with the Church's Easter liturgical feast, a combination not typically found in Italy or other parts of the Mediterranean. Little is known about how the festa originated. Whether the festa existed in its own right or was inserted into the Catholic Easter liturgy remains a mystery. The identity of the Giudeo, a character central to the festa, has stimulated a great deal of debate but little agreement. Is the Giudeo meant to portray the tormentor/executioner of Christ? Is this Giudeo, with mask and tail, similar to the "diavolate" of other Sicilian feste or do the trappings of the costume disguise a more ancient character? Is the costume a disguise within a disguise? These questions along with a score of others have been debated since Giuseppe Pitre first wrote about the festa in the early 1900s.[1]

One can see in the preparations for the festa the complex intertwining of tradition and ritual. The women of the town prepare lavuri, wheat sprouted in darkness, invoking a pre-Christian rite absorbed by the Easter liturgy. At a certain point in the festa, the women will bring the lavuri in plates and place them in front of the alter. Women also bake the bread which is placed in baskets on the massive platform that will later carry the heavy crucifix. Although the women of the town play a central role, their work is very much behind the scene.

It is the women who make the costume of the Giudeo. The costume consists of a hood-like mask, a helmet, and a red and yellow jacket that is richly embroidered with floral patterns on the front and other designs on the back. The embroidery, I was told, follows an Arabic style and in fact many of the Giudei wear Muslim symbols on their helmets. Red pants, leggings and shoes of unshorn goat skin and a tail(s) complete the costume. A tail is sometimes worn at the base of the hooded mask. Fox, rabbit or wolf are typical of the types of animal selected for these tails. The fox and the wolf are considered to be the most effective mediums of magic. Along with these tails the Giudeo sometimes also wear a horse tail attached either to the bottom backside of the coat or else to the rear of the pants.[2]

In San Fratello, liturgical observations begin nine days before Easter with a high mass in the parish church. Mass is followed by other rites and services internal to the parish. This, however, changes with the public representation of the passions of Christ in theatrical form. The passion play begins in the late afternoon on Wednesday of holy week. On the following day, the Giudei make their appearance. At first they are a fleeting kind of presence. In late morning you begin to see them darting out of doorways only to disappear into the maze of alley ways that wind through the town.

Cosa state aspettando? (What are you waiting for?)

Eventually, hundreds of Giudei dressed in gaudy bright red and yellow costumes, will turn the town upside down, doing things that the most permissive carnival would not allow. Making noises with their trumpets, singing vulgar songs and making erotic gestures, they travel the streets, piazzas and alley ways in small groups, noisily assaulting anyone in their path. They enter any and all public and private places, except for the church. They drink wine or grappa and remain in an inebriated state, many for the duration of their festa. Many drink from flasks they carry on the tops of their helmets. Others sit in bars and drink with their friends. Writing at the turn of the century, Giuseppe Pitre described their presence in the following way: the Giudei "...run here and there staying close to the churches, agitating with chains consisting of flat links, playing the trumpet disparately. Now they gather together, now they divide, defusing themselves among the pious congregation. They slip through the crowd kicking and jumping in crazy ways."[3]

The Giudei carry on in this fashion for two days. Their part in the Festa officially culminates on Holy Friday with the last procession. In this procession a group of men carry the massive 15th century Spanish wooden crucifix on a huge platform. They are followed mainly by women, many in mourning clothes, sometimes shoeless, singing laments and songs for the dead. From another direction the statue of the Madonna is carried up the hill to a place where she will encounter her crucified son. The Giudei assault the procession as it winds through the narrow streets transforming, what in the Christian vision is the most mournful and penitent moment, into an explosion of pirouette dances. As they dance they position themselves closer and closer to the people in the procession, intimidating them as they dance, singing and blowing meaningless or silly songs on their trumpets. The trumpets and laughter of the Giudei can be heard late into the night, but by morning, they are nowhere to be found. The festa continues through Easter Sunday with a mass and a procession in which Mary is united with her son. This is followed by a large Easter lunch and the lighting of fires in the house, as part of a kind of purification ritual intended to drive away any lingering evil spirits.[4]

Crocifisso Spagnolo con Giudei e la nonna.
(Spanish crucifix with Giudei and Grandmother.)

Before the unification of Italy, the Giudei played a ritualized role of actually personifying the crowd of tormentors that attended the crucifixion of Christ. However, problems began when persons selected to play the role of Christ were too severely beaten.[5] With the ending of this practice, Sabina Cuneo observed that: "...the function of the Giudei was transformed to concentrate more on the carnavalesque aspect of ritualized violence and disorder ... the Giudei are not the tormentors of Christ anymore but they are

Madonna della Pieta

those that disturb public peace."[6] In spite of this transformation, the costume still positions the Giudei as the "killers of Christ." The Roman style helmet and epaulets, for example, retained from the original costume, ironically identify the Giudeo with the Roman soldiers that carried out the orders of Pontius Pilate.

Most scholars believe that the Festa dei Giudei was inserted into the Easter festa sometime during the Middle Ages.[7] No one knows at what point or what role the church might have played. Salvatore Mangione, the mayor of San Fratello and an authority on the festa, told me that to "understand the Festa dei Giudei one needs to know the history of San Fratello."[8] That history dates back millennia, to the time of the Siculi, the people believed to be the island's original inhabitants. How far back in history one must travel in order to unravel the festa's meaning is a difficult question to answer. Why the festa came to be known as the Festa dei Giudei and what form the festa might have had before it was incorporated into Christian liturgy, remain mysteries.

The festa is not widely publicized. In San Fratello people are reluctant to talk about it with outsiders. Few of the Sicilians I met in the towns around San Fratello knew from direct experience about the Festa dei Giudei. They passed along stories — that Mussolini outlawed the holiday in the 30's and that clerics didn't like it. They warned me that it could be dangerous. My cousin's friend remembered hearing that someone had been killed in San Fratello, many years ago, when a masked Giudeo exacted his revenge. In Sicily there are rumors that some of the masked festivals are considered illegal and therefore not publicized.

I trombettieri. (The trumpeteers.)

In *Religious Festivals in Sicily*, Leonardo Sciascia addresses part of the festa's mystery. In his brief commentary he discusses aspects of the festa that are, for the most part, ignored by other writers. He begins by noting the biblical interpretation imposed by Catholic liturgy that positions the Jews as the killers of Christ. Sciascia, however, feels that to understand the festa, we must go beyond the symbolism imposed by the church. He reminds us that Sicily was one of the places where the Jews were defended against Spain's edict of expulsion (1492).[9] Towns like San Fratello, in Sicily's interior, not only provided refuge for Jews and other heretics, but were also sites of resistance, since these mountain towns were not only difficult to reach, but also dangerous. There is the story of a town's people who piled wood alongside the house of the visiting inquisitor, his servants and officials. They would have burnt them all had not the Baroness de la Florida with her kinsmen and retainers affected a siege that enabled them to escape. In other places the Inquisitors were ambushed between towns. These dangers finally forced the Inquisition to confine their labors to the cities. Even there, the Inquisition ran into trouble. For example, on March 7, 1516, an immense crowd in Palermo besieged the vice regal palace with artillery taken from its arsenal. After sacking the palace the crowd turned its attention to the Inquisition. They freed the prisoners, burned the records and pillaged the property of the Inquisition's headquarters. The Inquisitor, who had recently arrived from Spain, barely escaped with his life.[10]

Though far from a celebration of the defeat of the Inquisition, researchers have connected the Festa dei Giudei to other types of festivals that involve a struggle or quest for freedom. Italo Sordi found that in Cuneo, a town in the Piedmont area of Northern Italy, carnival is utilized in a similar way that involves the chasing of the Saracens from the town. This finding is significant since much of San Fratello's population is believed to have migrated from towns in this province. Utilizing Sordi's work, Nuccio Lo Castro has connected the respective feste in Cuneo and San Fratello with others in Belgium, Mexico and South America. He argues that these festivals all demonstrate syncretic connections to the Festa dei Giudei. Lo Castro offers what he calls a "synthesis" of existing literature on the festivals and places it within the category of those that involve a quest for freedom.[11] While syncretic connections are important they unfortunately offer little in resolving the basic questions fundamental to developing an understanding of the festa. Who the Giudei represent, how this representation has been used/modified, what might be said about the role of cultural selection and memory, and what part of tradition is kept or discarded, continue to be questions central to an understanding of the festa. Finally, the crucial question of whether the Giudei are fighting a battle or acting out an old rite, is not addressed.

We can gain some insight into the complexity of the Giudeo's identity through the work of Franco Ingrille and Lucia Birnbaum. Ingrille argues that all the ingredients of the Dionysian feast are present in the Festa dei Giudei. To support his thesis he focuses on both the carnivalesque behavior of the Giudei and specific elements of the costume. He draws our attention to the tail and the shoes made of unshorn goat skin and argues that they are evident reference to satyrs, creatures devoted to Dionysus. In his reading of the festa, pagan or pre-Christian elements combine at some unspecified moment with the Christian celebration of the passion of Christ. The festa, Ingrille theorizes, is evidence of a confluence between Christian and pagan communities, experienced at some point in the region's history.[12]

Birnbaum also sees ancient symbolism in the festa. However, she reads the symbolism of the costume very differently. Commenting on the tail of the Giudeo she writes, "Witches, heretics and Jews are recalled in the tail of the devil, with whom the inquisition identifies all three."[13] The Inquisition used the imagery of the devil to inspire hatred of the condemned and the family of the condemned. This was done through the sanbenito or saco benito ("sacred sack"). Cecil Roth describes the garment in the following way:

> It consisted of a long yellow robe, traversed by a black St. Anthony cross (in the case of those convicted only of formal heresy, only one of the diagonal arms was necessary). Where the heretic had escaped the stake by confession, flames pointing downwards (fuego revuetto) were painted on the garment, which in these instances was sometimes black. Those condemned to burning bore in addition a representation of the devil thrusting heretics into the fires of hell. All wore, moreover, a tall mitre (coraza), similarly adorned.

The sanbenito had to be worn in certain cases in public, particularly on Sundays and festivals. This was true even after the prisoner was released by the inquisitional authorities. Released prisoners were sometimes made to wear these costumes for months or years, exposing themselves to scorn and derision. After its immediate utility had passed, the sanbenito was hung in the parish church of the delinquent. Hanging in the church, the sanbenito included an inscription identifying the family of the wearer so that they would be marked as objects of lasting shame, humiliation and suspicion.[14]

In Sicily there were strong objections to the use of the sanbenito, particularly the practice of hanging the sanbenito in the church after the heretic was burned at the stake. Following a large protest in 1543 the practice of hanging the sanbenito in the church was stopped in Sicily. This protest in Sicily was part of other actions against the Inquisition. These actions objected to the manner in which the Inquisition used public imagery and religious ritual to obscure the horrific form of torture used by the Inquisition to exact confessions.[15] The costume of the Giudeo as a whole, makes reference to the Inquisition and its Sicilian tenure. This is accomplished in several ways. The Giudeo wears the mask of the torturer while making light of instruments used either to extract confessions or as means of self flagellation. The Giudei use these instruments as noise makers, for jokes and to intimidate and frighten the pious.

Traditionally, it was the peasants and sheepherders who wore the disguise of the Giudeo. With the disguise came certain privileges and liberties, inherited from the carnival tradition. These traditions involve the reversals of the social order and roles. Anyone wearing the costume of the Giudeo, for example, could mock and insult those of higher status and wealth. They could even insult the priest and his congregation in the most blasphemous way imaginable, including deriding the sacrifice of the cross. In these ways, the festa can be seen as a symbol of the revolt of the disenfranchised against the powers based on Christianity. The fact that the church continues to carry out periodic campaigns aimed at ending the tradition, suggests that the festa continues as a form of protest against the powers of the Catholic church.

The costume of the Giudeo embodies a multiplicity of characters in addition to the satyr. Cuneo writes, "The carnavalesque aspect of the costume of the Giudeo is without a doubt characterized in a demonic manner by the tail of a beast making it similar to the "diavolate" of other Sicilian Festivals."[16] Lo Castro also describes the festa as a "diabolical event":

> For many of the inhabitants of this little city, it (Festa dei Giudei) represents also a moment of necessary and collective exorcism. It looks like the devil has unleashed devils — obsessed and possessed by an ecstatic state of rebellion and exaltation. The procession of Friday, infected by their being, is an authentic diabolic event.[17]

The mask of the Giudeo is a hood that fits over the head. It is red with holes outlined in black for the eyes, has a yellow nose and a mustache over a mouth with a leather tongue that has a studded cross. The mask can also resemble the colorful masks worn in carnival, the Roman soldier/flagellator of Christ, and the mask of the inquisitor who tortured the supposed heretic. What is particularly unusual is how both the devil and satyr are represented without horns. I will return to the peculiar absence in a moment.

The bulk of scholarship on the festa has avoided making comparisons with other spiritual traditions, save paganism. Additionally, comparisons have not been made with other feste that continue to use Giudei in their Easter celebrations. Easter festivals, for example, in parts of Calabria continue to use Giudei in their dramatic representations of the passions of Christ.[18] Though Purim does not coincide with Easter, it nevertheless contains important parallels to the Festa dei Giudei. Purim is the first festival to celebrate the victory of the Jews over anti-Semitism. It is a three day carnival festival of masquerade, abandonment and wine drinking that turns religion on its head. Participants were allowed to drink until they "do not know the difference between 'Cursed be Haman' and 'Praise be Mordecai'."

In his comprehensive history of festival, Doniach draws out attention to the importance of Italian carnival in the development of Purim:

"The golden age of the troubadour saw the birth of this Purim child who, as a babe in arms, was rescued from the fierce French rioting and carried to Italy. There, the carnivals, despite the rough treatment they meted out to the child's parents, fostered and encouraged his playful habits and endowed him with that adolescent energy which maintained him till ... his features were well formed."[19]

"The fierce French rioting," refers to a millenialist panic that seized southern France in the first quarter of the fourteenth century. Jews were accused, along with lepers, of poisoning wells and acting as a 'fifth column' who aimed to destroy Christian society. Jews fleeing France eventually settled in Asti, Fossano and Moncalvo, and Purim entered the Piedmont phase of its diasporic odyssey. The Jews of Province contribute the Masseket Purim, a humorous parody, which involves a custom embodied in the Hymn for the Night of Purim. This hymn lauds the indiscriminate virtues of red, white and green wines. A month before Purim, towns would elect Purim kings to rule over "the vineyard of the community."[20] These connections suggest that Purim and the Festa dei Giudei share syncretic connection to carnival, particularly the form of carnival that developed in the Piedmont area of Italy.

The idea of the Jew and the devil as allied in their opposition to Christ, and thereby to contemporary Christian civilization, became a popular belief by the Middle Ages. "The Jew was thought to have physical characteristics setting him apart from human beings, and identifying him with the devil — and horns were an integral part of this image."[21] If horns are both an integral and popular part of the iconography of the devil and were the symbol that equated the Jew with the devil, their absence in the costume of the Giudeo is important. How might this absence be interpreted? As we have seen, the absence of horns does not prevent an association with the devil, but prevents the identification of the Giudeo with the devil, per se. In the Festa dei Giudei, the Giudeo is, therefore, associated with a character under the devil's influence. Why the Giudeo does not directly represent the devil is difficult to answer. In fact, the symbols of the costume connect the Giudeo to forces of evil, at the same time that other symbols connect the Giudeo to positive forces, symbolized by the festival's association to the bacchanalian feast. While this question cannot be answered in a definitive way, we may continue to look to the festa as a whole for other clues that might help us understand the festa's complexity.

This association of the Jew with the devil made Easter a particularly dangerous time for Jews. On Christian feast days Jews had to keep within their houses, with their doors and windows closed, and were forbidden from doing any work that could be seen from the street. Many places maintained the ancient abuse that started in southern Europe, of stoning the houses of the Jewish quarter on Good Friday. Popular belief held that the Jews made an annual practice of reviling Christ. As part of this yearly ritual, Jews were believed to crucify and burn a wax image in mockery of Christ. The reference to the wax image makes it clear that the myth was based on the Purim tradition of burning a wax image of Haman. Other stories circulated that Jews mocked the name of Christ in the streets and went so far as to erect a cross on, which they fastened a Christian boy, whom they whipped with out mercy. To this rumor may be traced the legend, which states that Haman met his death on the second day of passover.[22]

The spectacle of the Giudei in the festa reinvokes this myth of Jews who revile Christ and torment his devoted followers during Easter. In fact, these myths and legends describe the activities of the penitents, who in many towns had a highly ritualized reenactment of the crucifixion. There is no accounting of what outsiders who witnessed these practices thought about them or, whether feste such as this, became the stuff out of which subversive myths were woven. What is clear, however, is that the costume and role act like a palimpsest — a parchment whose original meaning has been lost or erased and written over. Sometimes part of the original manuscript remains — barely visible at the margins — giving a sense of what has disappeared. It is through such an entanglement of fields and confused parchments, that the tradition of the Festa dei Giudei continues to be reborn.[23] In spite of the retraditionalizations and new meanings that the festa has acquired, it continues in its demonization of the Jew even though the Giudeo is no longer cast as the tormentor and executioner of Christ. In fact, the festa uses pre-Christian carnival motifs in this context to also demonize pagan and Islamic spiritual forms. At its most oppressive moment, nevertheless, the festa stands as a symbol of freedom and for the people of San Fratello "... an irrenouncuible moment of their own identity."[24]

It was several months before I was able to interview the mayor of San Fratello. Our interview was very brief and I was only able to ask a handful of questions. My questions were an attempt to confirm what I had learned through the stories people told me. "Has the festa ever been outlawed?," I asked. "Yes," he answered. "During Fascism Mussolini put a decree prohibiting anyone in San Fratello from wearing the costume of the Giudei, no one is sure exactly why Mussolini outlawed the festa. Perhaps Mussolini thought that an enemy could be hidden under the mask. The Fascists really persecuted the young people," he said. "They would arrest them and put them in jail or send them to confinement for just dressing as Giudei. The youths accepted their fate and sometimes got five to six months on the Aeolian Islands. Since the Fascist authorities and Catholic church have both been unable to stop people from performing the role of the Giudeo, the festa has become a symbol of freedom."

I cavalli. (The horses.)

Finally I asked if he knew why the festa was called the Festa dei Giudei? Isn't it in fact anti-Semitic? Turning his attention to the first part of my question, he said, "We can think about the famous edict of Ferdanando the Catholic or the other edicts made in Spain that expelled all the Jews from Sicily — from cities such as Palermo, Messina and Catania. The Jews took refuge in the small mountain towns. In San Fratello they probably asked to be converted to Catholicism and asked to adorn themselves with this mask during the passions of Easter week. ...Historically, the reason they are called Giudei could also involve the symbolism in the Bible of the cheering Jews in front of the dying Christ. When the Christian Church is internationally mourning the death of Christ, in San Fratello it is celebrated." He then explained that it was mainly people from Rome who thought that the festa was anti-Semitic. They thought that way, he said, because they had never actually seen the festa.[25]

Mangione then glanced at his watch and abruptly ended the interview. The official beginning of the festa was drawing near. The mayor led us back down the long hallway that returned to the front of his house. Once outside, we walked in the direction of the church. On our way to the church I noticed another building with one of Mussolini's slogans stenciled high on the wall just below the roof line. Just below the slogan was the floor where a small club of Fascists continued to meet. Later, they appeared on the balcony dressed in dark suits to leer or stare sternly at all the commotion beneath them. We entered the piazza and passed the priest who moved about frantically, first in the direction of the area where the last supper was soon to be staged and then toward via del Calvario to the path where the villager who once played Jesus would have been beaten and tied to a cross.

A group of Giudei motioned and then yelled out to me. I pretended not to hear or see them. They walked in my direction. I turned away. They altered their direction. Again they approached. Some lifted their masks and lit cigarettes. The one in the center of the group extended his gloved hand. They asked me to join them in the bar across the street. At the bar one of the men explained that we were related and ordered grappa. He then gave me a new name and invited me and my companion to a feast which was to take place at his house on the morning of Venerdi Santo. When we left, the group recited my new name in unison.

We arrived at the house mid morning. Again the men have their masks pulled back. They were sitting in front of a table of meat and cheese, bread and wine and pastry. When we were finally seated parody took the place of prayer. Jokes were made about how in the past they would perform the miracle that changed the meat into fish. They had all been drinking since early morning. Outside the pious were preparing to carry the heavy fifteenth century cross through the streets. Inside the party was warming up for carnival. The Giudei would taunt the processioners, interrupt their prayers and songs with shrill and meaningless noise from their trumpets, turn pirouettes, hang upside down from balconies and do everything possible to erase the boundaries between the sacred and profane, right and wrong, good and evil.

SALVATORE SALERNO

Macalester College

I would like to thank the following people for their help and support — Professor Bernie Bachrach, Franco Ingrille, Lucia Chiavola Birnbaum, Linda Schloff and

Toto Serio. A special thanks to Piercarlo Grimaldi for sharing his research on the Festa and for the many conversations in San Fratello during the festa, to Professor Bernie Bachrach and Rabbi Bernard Raskas for their insights, questions and suggestions, Denise Mayotte, Jennifer Guglielmo, and Janet Contursi for their critical reading of earlier drafts of the paper and to Monica Barbieri for her help with translation. Lastly I would like to thank the Jerome Foundation for their support of my work on the Sicilian festa.

* The photographs that appear in this essay are from "Easter in My Grandfather's Sicilian Village" an exhibit of photographs and text based on my experiences in San Fratello during Easter.

[1] Giuseppe Pitre, *La Famiglia, La Casa, La Vita Del Popolo Siciliano* (Palermo: Il Vespro, 1978), pp. 300-302; *Cartelli. pasquinate, canti, leggende, usi popolo siciliano* (Palermo: Il Vespro, 1978), pp. 226-228; Benedetto Rubino, *Folklore a San Fratello,* (Palermo, 1914); Antonio Buttitta, "I giudei de San Fratello," in "Atlante", n. 35,-ll, 1962; Leonardo Sciascia, *Feste Religiose in Sicilia* (Bari, Italy: Leonardo Da Vinci, 1965); C. Naselli, "Note sui Giudei di San Fratello," in Demologia e folklore, Palermo, 1974; I. Soldi, "La Sicilia pagana dei Nebrodi," in Que Touring, VI, 1979; Nuccio Lo Castro, "La Festa dei Giudei a S. Fratello, kermesse diabolica della settimana santa, Feste, Provenca Regionale di Messina, 1980; Salvatore Mangione, et al.. *I riti della settimana santa nella vita e nel folklore di san fratello*. San Fratello: Villaggio Cristo Redentore, n.d.; Franco Ingrille, Unpublished Manuscript on the Feste of Sicily e Sabina Cuneo "Festa dei Giudei," Schede di catalogazione," Museo Nationale delle Arti e Tradizioni Popolari, Rome, n.d. .

[2] Naselli, Note sui Guidei, p.297.

[3] Pitre, *La Famiglia*, p.300.

[4] Lo Castro, "kermesse diabolica," p. 461.

[5] Rubino, *Folklore a San Fratello*, pp. 58-59. See also C. Naselli, Note sui Guidei, p. 301.

[6] Cuneo "Festa dei Giudei."

[7] Pitre, *La Famiglia*, pp. 300-302; Rubino, *Folklore a San Fratello*, p. 56-57 e Mangione, et al.. I riti della settimana

[8] Salvatore Mangione, Interview, April 12, 1995, San Fratello, Sicily.

[9] Sciascia, *Feste Religiose in Sicilia*, pp. 30-32.

[10] Henry Charles Lea, *The Inquisition in the Spanish Dependencies* (New York: The Macmillan Company, 1922), pp. 1-25; Edward Peters, *Inquisition* (New York: The Free Press, 1988), pp. 113-114 & A.S.Turberville, *The Spanish Inquisition* (New York: Henry Holt and Company, 1932), pp. 199-200.

[11] Mangione, et al.. *I riti della settimana santa*.

[12] Ingrille, Unpublished Manuscript.

[13] Lucia Chivola Birnbaum, "Godmothers and Others of Color: Le Comari," Chapter 7, Unpublished Manuscript. See also: Benedetto Rubino, *Folklore a San Fratello*, pp.56-72 and Lo Castro, "kermesse diabolica."

[14] Cecil Roth, *The Spanish Inquisition*, (New York: W.W. Norton & Company, 1964), pp. 109-110 & Peters, Inquisition, pp. 94-95.
[15] Peters, *Inquisition*, pp. 226-227.
[16] Cuneo "Festa dei Giudei."
[17] Lo Castro, "kermesse diabolica."
[18] I would like to thank Sabina Cuneo for pointing this out. See also her brief but insightful essay on the Festa dei Giudei cited above.
[19] N.S. Doniach, *Purim or The Feast of Esther*, (Philadelphia: The Jewish Publication Society of America, 1933), pp. 125-126, Goodman, Philip, *The Purim Anthology*, (Philadelphia: The Jewish Publication Society of America, 1949), pp. 3-13, Peters, Inquisition,pp. 76-80, Schauss, Hayyim. *The Jewish Festivals* (Cincinnati: Union of American Hebrew Congregations, 1938), pp. 237-250.
[20] Doniach, Purim, pp. 128-130.
[21] Ruth Mellinkoff, *The Horned Moses in Medieval Art and Thought*, (Berkeley: University of California Press, 1970), pp. 135, Professor Bernie Bachrach, Interview, October, 1998,.
[22] Rabbi Bernard Raskas, Interview, October, 1998. See also Doniach, Purim, pp. 171-196, Roth, Cecil. *The History of the Jews in Italy*, (Philadelphia: The Jewish Publication Society of America, 1946), pp. 228-261.
[23] I would like Giorgio Bertellini for suggesting the concept of the palimpset. See his insightful paper, "Restoration, genealogy and palimpset. On some historiographical questions," Film History, Vol. 7, 1995, pp. 227-290. See also Michel Foucault, " Nietzsche, Ge nealogy, H istory," in D onald F . Bo uchard, (ed.), *L anguage, Counter-Memory, PracticeT*, Ithaca, N.Y.: Cornell UP, 1992; Carlo Ginzburg, Myths, Emblems, Clues, London: Hutchinson Dadius, 1990.
[24] Cuneo "Festa dei Giudei."
[25] Salvatore Mangione, Interview, April 12, 1995, San Fratello, Sicily.

IDENTITY OF A JEWISH COMMUNITY IN A PROVINCIAL TOWN: ANCONA

Those who leave Ancona to go abroad soon become aware that their city is not very well known outside of the Italian borders. They have often to provide further coordinates (south of Venice, east of Rome, etc.) in order to make sure that people know where they approximately come from. Yet, in spite of its marginality in the imaginary geography of Italy, Ancona occupies a rather central place in the historic memory of Italian Jewry, as it hosted for centuries one of the largest Jewish communities in the country. Precisely because of its geographical position and its commercial and strategic relevance as the main harbor on the Adriatic shore of the State of the Church, Ancona consistently attracted a large Jewish community and hosted, along with Rome, the only other ghetto in the State after the expulsion of the Jews, decreed by Pope Pius V in 1569. As I am not an historian nor a sociologist, I will chiefly look at this community through the magnifying glass of literature. In particular, I will focus on the opening pages of Madame de Staël's novel *Corinne, or Italy*, which present in a dramatic fashion the conditions of the Ancona ghetto at the end of the eighteenth century, and on a much less known novel, — entirely devoted to this milieu — which has not received yet the attention it deserves. Mario Puccini's novel, *Ebrei* (1931), takes place in Ancona around the years of World War I and presents in a very subtly nuanced way the attitude and reaction of a Jewish community in the rearguard, so to speak, vis-a-vis the conflict.

George Ticknor, who visited Ancona in 1817, noticed the presence of "the Jews," along with "the grave Turks, and Persians, and lively Greeks that throng its narrow, inconvenient streets."[1] The description of the city that we find in Madame de Staël's *Corinne* is consistent with the American traveler's, though the historic moment she evokes predates the Napoleonic era. The male protagonist of the novel, Lord Oswald Nelvil, who is traveling to Italy in the winter of 1794, is forced to spend a few days in the city on his way to Rome:

> Ensconced between the mountains and the sea, the city is beautiful by its very location. The throng of Greeks seated oriental style at work in

the shop fronts and the variegated Middle Eastern clothing of the Levantines in the streets give the city an original and interesting look. [...] The Greek, Catholic, and Jewish religion exist peacefully side by side in Ancona. They are strikingly dissimilar in their ceremonies, but the same feelings rise up to heaven through their different rituals, the same cry of pain, the same need for sustaining strength.[2]

De Staël goes on to describe the most immediately visible landmark in the city, San Ciriaco's cathedral, which "on the mountaintop looks precipitously down on the sea;" but her description soon turns into a reverie on human destiny that the place seems bent to inspire, as it also inspired the final page of Carlo Levi's *Christ stopped at Eboli*, a text I will address later. DeStaël writes:

> The sound of the waves often intermingles with the chanting of the priests. Inside, the church is overloaded with a host of rather tasteless ornamentation, but stopping a moment under the portico of this sanctuary, one takes pleasure in associating religion — the purest of the soul's feelings — with the spectacle of this splendid ocean upon which man may never fix his mark. He may work the land, cut his roads through the mountains, lock rivers into canals to carry his wares. Yet though his ships furrow the waters, the billows come swiftly to erase this slight trace of servitude, leaving the sea once more as she was on the first day of creation.[3]

The gentleman traveler is witness to a fire the people of the city are unable to control because of the absence of properly functioning pumps, but even more so because of their lack of resolve. As he decisively intervenes and manages to sedate the flames with the help of an English crew at anchor in the bay, Lord Nelvil is appalled to realize that the inhabitants of the Jewish Quarter have been left trapped in their houses, as "the police officer made a practice of closing the gates of the quarter at night," — a practice that, briefly interrupted after the arrival of Napoleon's army, was discontinued in Ancona only in 1831.[4] When the English traveler asks that the gates be opened at once, he is confronted by several women, who entreat "him to let the Jews burn," as they are deemed responsible of bringing bad luck to the city. "The rioters were in no way evil," de Staël charitably comments, "rather their superstitious imaginations had been sharply struck by a great misfortune."[5] Nelvil proceeds to free the Jews, and eventually also rescues the inmates of a madhouse, who had been left to their destiny, too, by their fellow citizens. The story dramatizes the tensions between the Jewish community and its Gentile counterpart that have led to a variety of episodes of bigotry and hatred throughout the history of the city, — a backdrop against which it appears justified the statement of one of Puccini's characters that "Ancona is not a philosemitic city."[6]

The first extant document of a Jewish presence in Ancona goes back to 1279, an elegy composed on the occasion of a catastrophic earthquake,[7] but it is noteworthy that Christian hagiography identifies the first bishop of Ancona and saint patron of the city, Ciriaco, as a native of Jerusalem and a rabbi, who assumed the Greek name as he converted and revealed to the empress Helen the whereabouts of Christ's cross.[8] The obviously apologetic nature of the narrative does not render the genealogy less intriguing, as it indirectly confirms the memory of a community that dates its presence in Ancona from immemorial times.[9]

The most memorable event in the history of the community is certainly the execution of twenty-five Marranos, who had found refuge in the city out of their native Portugal, decreed by Pope Paul IV and carried out in Campo della Mostra in 1556, which provoked a boycott of the Ancona harbor by the Jewish communities in the Eastern Mediterranean.[10] The ghetto was then established in 1569 by Pope Pius V, who banished all Jews from the State of the Church, except those of Rome and Ancona.

Here are some statistical data that may be useful in order to properly situate Ancona among the other major Jewish communities in the country.[11] In 1763 the community counted 1,290 members, in 1877 1,906, in 1938 1,177, in 1967 400, now about half that number.[12] Within the State of the Church, around the midst of the nineteenth century, Ancona hosts by far the largest Jewish community in relative numbers, as it makes up 4.6% of the total population. In the country as a whole,

> between the beginning of the sixteenth and the end of the eighteenth century, Ancona hosts one of the eight ghettoes (along with Ferrara, Mantova, Modena, Roma, Torino, Venezia, Livorno) that gather a population of at least 1,000 inhabitants. In 1871 Ancona has the seventh largest Jewish community in absolute numbers; the sixth in relative weight as far as the total number of inhabitants is concerned (3.6%). However, if one excludes some small, though concentrated communities (Pitigliano, Acqui, Moncalvo), Ancona can well figure among the large

ones, being only outnumbered by Mantova (6.2%) and Livorno (5%), as Trieste was still Austrian.[13]

The community was particularly proud of its educational institutions, there were more than 10 *Yeshibot*, and "at a time when in the Marche the rate of analphabetism was higher than 80%," the Hungarian Rabbi Haym Rosenberg could later boast, "in the ghetto of Ancona there was nobody who could not read the Bible in the original."[14] Ancona was also the site of the first Zionist organization in Italy, funded in 1898.[15] However, signs of a decline of the community were clearly perceivable by the turn of the century. Rabbi Rosenberg looks with nostalgia (in 1929) at the once intense religious life of the community, whose fading already embittered the last years of the life of his predecessor, Rabbi Isaac Raffaele Tedeschi,[16] a scholar of the Kabbalah whose last writing, dated *Ancona 1 novembre 1900*, is devoted to a defense of "The Authenticity of the 'Zohar.'"[17] By a remarkable coincidence, this classic text of Jewish mysticism had been first printed in Italy in 1558 by Immanuel Benevento, a student of Moses Bassola, who was rabbi in Ancona at the time of the boycott and was hailed by the French Christian kabbalist Guillaume Postel as "pope and chief of all the Jews of this century."[18]

We can measure the rapidity of the decay from a revealing passage in the moving "Memories of a crepuscular community: Ancona," by Gina Del Vecchio, a delicate essayist and novelist. She writes:

> My mother prayed with fervor, even if she did not know the meaning of most of the words she was reading; and once that I dared to ask her how that would be possible, she gave me an answer that was less imperative than my father's "Worship and be silent," but no less meaningful and deep: "I know that I am praying."[19]

The quote may help us to understand the climate of Mario Puccini's novel, full of characters who remind us of this maternal figure. Mario Puccini was born in Senigallia, the site of another ancient Jewish community along the Adriatic shore, (whose name he lends to one of the characters in the novel, the orthodox merchant Davide Sinigaglia) but spent most of his early years in Ancona working for the publishing house funded by his father, which deserves credit for having published writers such as Saba and Lucini at a time when they certainly did not enjoy the critical acclaim they were granted in later years. One of the few critical appreciations of the novel rightly defines it "one of the most important books to be published between the wars" and "maybe the only novel of ideas of our recent literature."[20] *Ebrei* is, simply stated, the story of an averted conversion: Susanna, the example of a modern Jewish woman, is temporarily seduced by Christian sensuality, but is finally able to withstand temptation and continue to uphold the values of Jewish spirituality. Massimo Mila, in an insightful review of the third edition of the novel in 1954, remarks that such a "sentimental crisis" is treated by Puccini "with a delicate hand," until it "dissolves itself in a serene rainbow, like an ephemerous spring storm."[21]

Carlo Moscato, the protagonist, has moved out of Ancona to the town of Lorina (i.e. Loreto), where he has initiated a textile factory, abandoning thus the paternal trade. However, he has kept intact the memories of his Jewish upbringing and his aspiration to represent the type of "the true Jew, the pure Jew, even the absolute Jew,"[22] whose model appeared to him Manasse, a translator of the Psalms and a Zionist, who ends up a suicide. Carlo is married to Susanna Sacerdoti, a young sensitive woman, also raised in the religious atmosphere of the ghetto, but exposed to the seduction of Christian religion, as it manifests itself in music, the leitmotiv of the novel being the sound of the bells: "Susanna had always liked the sound of the Christian bells."[23] Whereas to Carlo is the sound of Manasse's voice that resounds like "a gentle music coming from afar [...] it was as if through his voice I were listening to our prophets of ancient times."[24] Carlo, too, is not insensitive to the power of music, but expresses scepticism over the ambivalence of music in Christian lithurgy: "Curious religion, that of the Christians: it is a holiday, and the bells toll; one dies, and once again the bells announce the pain and anguish of the people."[25]

Susanna enters for the first time in a church attracted by the music,[26] and is aware of the disruptive effect her musical upbringing had on her religious feelings: "I was, as a child, so attached to prayer. [...] But, when I started to study music, what happened? I go to bed, start to think and pray; but then, all of the sudden, I start to think about the master's classes."[27] But the centrality of the theme is nowhere more evident than in the different attitude the two protagonists display in front of what Susanna regards as "one of Liszt's most beautiful scores, St. Francis praying to the birds;"[28] in listening to the music, however, Carlo thinks of the "arrival of the Messiah (*arrivo del Messia*,)" and this even becomes the title he chooses for and by which he then refers to the piece, in spite of Susanna's protestation that the sound of the *shofar* is nowhere to be heard. To which Carlo replies that

> the *shofar* is the instrument that expresses our pain, not our joy; that day the Jews will express their happiness without the horn, softly, chastely, just with treble, gentle voices [...] how many times, as a boy, I thought of that day that will have to come, even if we will not be there: and it will have to be quite a feast... Noisy, and yet muffled; full of hurrahs, and yet also of silences, of wonder...[29]

The scene shifts from Ancona to Udine with the beginning of the war. Carlo is ordered to the front, where he works as a translator, due to his knowledge of Serbo-Croatian. His absence triggers a crisis in Susanna, who considers conversion to Christianity, as she is involved in the activities of an orphanage organized by the local priest; until the priest betrays his prejudice by handing her a pamphlet on an alleged case of ritual infanticide that provokes Susanna's return to the faith of her forefathers.

The novel ends with a flash-forward, when the family is recomposed and back in Ancona, breathing again "our air, the air of the Loggia" (*via della Loggia*, the street in which Jewish merchants had traditionally their stores.)[30] Such a nostalgic evocation of the atmosphere of the ghetto may sound naive if we compare it to Saba's much more problematic "tormentosa aria natia,"[31] but it becomes illuminating, along with it, of the "several attitudes about breathing" (to use the title of a poem by Anthony Hecht)[32] that made up Italian Jewry at a crucial juncture in its history. Aldo Camerino was right in observing that nobody handled the situation of the Italian Jews before the Fascist racial laws with so much clarity of ideas and no less knowledge of the argument than Puccini did in *Ebrei*.[33] In the epilogue to the novel, one of the two sons of the couple, Davidino, asks a question whose naiveté is maybe the best measure of the pride of the Ancona Jewish community: "is it really true, dad, that Jerusalem is a more beautiful city than Ancona? (*è proprio vero, papà, che Gerusalemme sarebbe una città più bella di Ancona?*)"[34] A pride once justifiable, if we consider that, in order to describe the holy city, an Italian-Jewish traveller of the end of the fifteenth century, Rabbi Isaac ben Meir Latif, could write to his friends in Italy that "Jerusalem is twice as big as Ancona."[35]

Carlo Levi's final meditation in *Christ stopped at Eboli*, as he anticipates the new, indeed unprecedented catastrophe to come, takes place in

Ancona, in front of San Ciriaco's cathedral, whose outline also ironically adorns the frontespice of Puccini's novel, the cathedral supposedly named after a Jewish convert:

> I went up to the cathedral of Ancona and looked out at long last upon the sea. It was a quiet day and from this height there was a wide view over the water. A fresh breeze was blowing from Dalmatia, making tiny whitecaps on the smooth surface of the waves. Vague notions floated through my head: the life of this sea was like man's fate, cast for all eternity in a series of equal waves, moving through time without change. I thought with affectionate sorrow of the motionless time and the dark civilization which I had left behind me. But already the train was carrying me far away, through the mathematical fields of Romagna, toward the vineyards of Piedmont and the mysterious future of exile, of war and death, which I could then but barely perceive, like an uncertain cloud in the boundless sky (*come una nuvola incerta nel cielo sterminato.*)[36]

Sterminato: the Italian word that ends the book paradoxically gathers both meanings, unlimited, and exterminated. Twenty-five Jews from Ancona, as their Marrano ancestors in the sixteenth century, fell victims of hatred, as they were deported to the Nazi concentration camps.[37] That the sky can never be exterminated, however, lends us unlimited hope.

DAVIDE STIMILLI

Northwestern University

---

[1] *Life, Letters, and Journals of George Ticknor*, 2 vols. (Boston: Houghton Mifflin 1909) 1:167. The most recent impressions of an American traveler I am aware of, those reported by William Weaver in *The New York Times* under the title "Plucky City on the Adriatic," are quite flattering, and confirm an image of the city as surviving all adversities (both natural and human-provoked) that is dear to the local imagination, both of the Jewish and Gentile population. I quote his final period: "Before heading for my train, I stopped for coffee at one of the cafes within the port area. The other tables were crowded with sailors and tourists; I heard half a dozen languages being spoken, and the man at the next table was reading a newspaper that I finally figured out was Maltese. Ancona may not be a city for tourists, but it is certainly a city for travelers." *The New York Times*, June 25, 1995, xx: 9.

[2] Madame de Staël, *Corinne ou l'Italie* (1807), trans. Avriel H. Goldberger, *Corinne, or Italy* (New Brunswick: Rutgers UP 1987) 12.

[3] da Staël, *Corinne*, 12.
[4] *La comunità ebraica ad Ancona*, ed. Ercole Sori (Ancona: Comune di Ancona 1995) 18, 21.
[5] da Staël, *Corinne*, 14.
[6] "Ancona non é una citta filosemita." Mario Puccini, *Ebrei* (Milano: Ceschina 1931) 94.
[7] Cf. Cecil Roth, *The History of the Jews of Italy* (Philadelphia: The Jewish Publication Society of America 1946) 118; Maria Luisa Moscati Benigni, *Marche: Itinerari ebraici* (Venezia: Marsilio 1996) 24-25.
[8] Cf. Giuliano Saracini, *Notitie historiche della città d'Ancona* (Roma 1675) 52-70.
[9] Cf. Attilio Milano's statement, in his *Storia degli Ebrei in Italia* (Torino: Einaudi 1963) 73, that "la colonia ebraica si dà vanto di una antichissima residenza nella città," in spite of the scant documentary evidence. Only *en passant* I mention the apocryphal narrative of Jacob d'Ancona, who supposedly visited China four years before Marco Polo, a figure whose historical existence is highly questionable, but not beyond *all* conjecture, if one may apply Sir Thomas Browne's generous criterium (cf. Dinitia Smith, "China, Pre-Marco Polo? Publisher Puts Off Book," *The New York Times*, September 30, 1997, A6.)
[10] Cf. Haym Rosenberg, "Alcuni documenti riguardanti i Marrani portoghesi in Ancona," *La Rassegna Mensile di Israel* 10 (1935) 3-20; Roth, *The History of the Jews of Italy*, 298-302; Id., *Doña Gracia of the House of Nasi* (1948; Philadelphia: The Jewish Publication Society of America 1977) 134-175; Milano, *Storia degli Ebrei in Italia*, 250-252; Ariel Toaff, "Nuova luce sui Marrani di Ancona (1556)," in *Studi sull'ebraismo italiano*, ed. Elio Toaff (Roma: Barulli 1974) 263-280.
[11] I rely for the following infomations on Ercole Sori, "Una 'comunità crepuscolare': Ancona tra Otto e Novecento," in *La presenza ebraica nelle Marche. Secoli XIII-XX*, ed. Sergio Anselmi and Viviana Bonazzoli, Quaderni monografici di "Proposte e ricerche", 14 (1993) 189-278: 192-194.
[12] Moscati Benigni, *Marche: Itinerari ebraici*, 33, 41.
[13] Sori, "Una 'comunità crepuscolare'," 194.
[14] "In un tempo nel quale nelle Marche si contavano più dell'80 per cento di analfabeti, nel ghetto di Ancona non vi era una persona che non sapesse leggere la Bibbia nel suo testo originale." Dr. H. Rosenberg, "Prefazione e cenni biografici," *Saggio degli scritti degli eccellentissimi rabbini David Abraham Vivanti di v.m. ed Isacco Raffaele Tedeschi di v.m.*, Pubblicato a cura della Università Israelitica d'Ancona (Casale Monferrato: Lavagno 1929) v-xli: xxii.
[15] Roth, *The History of the Jews of Italy*, 519.
[16] Rosenberg, "Prefazione e cenni biografici," xxiii.
[17] I. R. Tedeschi, "L'autenticità dello 'Zoar,'" *Vessillo israelitico* 48 (1900) 370-373, in *Saggio degli scritti*, 196-199.
[18] Cf. Cecil Roth's entry *Basola, Moses ben Mordecai*, in the *Encyclopedia Judaica*.

[19] "Pregava fervorosamente mia madre, pur non conoscendo il significato della maggior parte delle parole che leggeva; e una volta che osai chiederle come ciò fosse possibile, mi diede una risposta meno imperativa dell'"adora e taci' di mio Padre, ma non meno significativa e profonda: 'so di pregare.'" "Ricordanze di una comunità crepuscolare: Ancona," *La nostra rivista: Rassegna dell'ADEI-WIZO* 2 (1955) 4.

[20] Salvatore Battaglia, "La narrativa di Mario Puccini (storia di una vocazione)," in *Omaggio a Mario Puccini*, ed. Sergio Anselmi (Urbino: Argalia 1967) 56. Battaglia remarks that the novel "meriterebbe un'analisi minuta, che eccederebbe i limiti di questo scritto." I can only in part fulfil such a *desideratum*. On Puccini (Senigallia 1887-Roma 1957) cf. also the more recent collection of essays *Mario Puccini: due giornate di studio e di testimonianze* (Senigallia: Comune di Senigallia 1987).

[21] "si scioglie poi in un sereno arcobaleno, come un effimero temporale di primavera." Massimo Mila, [*Ebrei*], *Omaggio a Mario Puccini*, 161.

[22] "il vero ebreo, l'ebreo puro, l'ebreo, vorrei dire, assoluto," Puccini, *Ebrei*, 7.

[23] "Sempre era piaciuto a Susanna il suono delle campane cristiane." Puccini, *Ebrei*, 28.

[24] "una musica gentile che giunge di lontano [...] ed era come se per la sua voce io udissi parlare i nostri profeti dei tempi antichi." Puccini, *Ebrei*, 13.

[25] "Curiosa religione quella dei cristiani: che si fa festa, e suonano le campane; che si muore e ancora sono le campane che annunciano il dolore e l'angoscia degli uomini." Puccini, *Ebrei*, 40. Cf. also the description of the first meeting of the two lovers, underscored by the sound of the bells from the Chiesa del Sacramento, which Carlo interprets as meaningful: "the bell [...] tells me: "Run, run, don't lose her. She is your woman" (*la campana* [...] *mi dice: "Corri, corri, non la perdere. È la tua donna"*.)" Puccini, *Ebrei*, 31.

[26] Puccini, *Ebrei*, 44.

[27] "Io, da piccola, ero così attaccata alla preghiera.[...] Ma, quando cominciai a studiare musica, cosa succede? Vado a letto, comincio a pensare e a pregare; ma poi, ecco, mi vengono in mente le lezioni del maestro." Puccini, *Ebrei*, 71.

[28] Puccini, *Ebrei*, 498.

[29] "lo chofar è lo strumento che esprime il nostro dolore, non la nostra gioia; quel giorno gli ebrei la loro felicità la esprimeranno senza corno, pian piano, castamente, appena con voci bianche, gentili... [...] quante volte, da ragazzo, pensavo a quel giorno che ben verrà, anche se noi non ci saremo: e dovrà essere proprio una festa così... Chiassosa, e pure in sordina; piena di evviva, e pure anche di silenzi, di stupore..." Puccini, *Ebrei*, 498-499.

[30] "l'aria nostra, l'aria della Loggia." Puccini, *Ebrei*, 368.

[31] Cf. *Trieste* vv. 19-22: "Intorno/circola ad ogni cosa/un'aria strana, un'aria tormentosa,/l'aria natia."

[32] Cf. "Songs for the Air or Several Attitudes About Breathing," in his *A Summoning of Stones* (New York: Mac Millan 1954) 27.

[33] Aldo Camerino, 1962, *Omaggio a Mario Puccini*, 176.

[34] Puccini, *Ebrei*, 671.

[35] Attilio Milano, Storia degli ebrei italiani nel Levante. (Firenze: Casa editrice Israel 1949) 30-31.

[36] "Salii alla cattedrale di Ancona, e mi affacciai, per la prima volta dopo tanto tempo, sul mare. Era una giornata serena, e, da quella altezza, le acque si stendevano amplissime. Una brezza fresca veniva dalla Dalmazia, e increspava di onde minute il calmo dorso del mare. Pensavo a cose vaghe: la vita di quel mare era come le sorti infinite degli uomini, eternamente ferme in onde uguali, mosse in un tempo senza mutamento. E pensai con affettuosa angoscia a quel tempo immobile, e a quella nera civiltà che avevo abbandonato. Ma già il treno mi portava lontano, attraverso le campagne matematiche di Romagna, verso i vigneti del Piemonte, e quel futuro misterioso di esili, di guerre e di morti, che allora mi appariva appena, come una nuvola incerta nel cielo sterminato." Levi. *Cristo si è fermato a Eboli*. Torino: Einaudi, 1947. 239-240; *Christ stopped at Eboli*, trans. Francess Frenaye. New York: Farrar, Straus, and Co., 1947. 267-268.

[37] Sori, "Una 'comunità crepuscolare'," 226.

The Jewish Risorgimento and the Questione Romana

Thinking involves not only the flow of thoughts, but their arrest as well. Where thinking suddenly stops in a configuration pregnant with tension, it gives that configuration a shock, by which it crystallizes into a monad. A historical materialist approaches a historical subject only where he encounters it as a monad. In this structure he recognizes the sign of a Messianic cessation of happening, or, put differently, a revolutionary chance in the fight for the oppressed past.
   Walter Benjamin, "Theses on the Philosophy of History," XVII

...all'uscita del giorno di Simchat Thorà, dell'anno 5628, verso le due di notte, [...] tutti noi ebrei eravamo chiusi nelle nostre case con catenacci e chiavistelli di ferro, perché tutti sapevamo che di sera ci sarebbe stata una grande confusione tra i servitori del papa e gli uomini del regno d'Italia, per scontrarsi gli uni con gli altri.... Cominciò ad uscire gente da ogni angolo della città al grido: "Viva Garibaldi", "Viva il Regno dei Savoia", "Non abbiamo niente in comune con il figlio di Pietro", "Tornatevene alle vostre tende, o cristiani"....[1]

For the Gregorian calendar, it is October 25, 1867. Angelo Citone, Rabbi *ad interim* of the congregation of Rome, has locked himself in his little room in the ghetto, and is anxiously writing these notes down in his family book of memoirs — the *Croniche*. On the very same day, only a few miles from the ghetto, Giuseppe Garibaldi has been fighting the Pope's army in Monterotondo, while his Roman followers are leading a popular insurrection within the Eternal City itself. For the *garibaldini*, Rome is the last tile to be annexed to the mosaic of unified Italy. For the Roman Jews, who have heard of the wonders that the Italian *Statuto Albertino* grants to the Jews of Turin, Genoa, and Livorno, Garibaldi renews Messianic images of freedom. He is the new Moses, as Citone's biblical simile puts it, who will free the Jews from their new oppressor.

Alas, Citone's hopes are soon to be crushed. Garibaldi's mission fails, and the repression begins promptly and fiercely. Giuseppe Leti, among others, witnesses the fury of priests, monks, and Jesuits, who, "con una gran croce in mano, gustava[no] il feroce delitto di percuotere con quel sacro strumento di redenzione"[2] whoever had participated in the insurrection. The situation worsens especially for the Jews, accused of being sympathetic with the red shirts.[3] The consequence, recorded by Citone, is that "La casa di studio del Talmud Thorà, le scuole, le Yeshivoth e gli asili rimasero chiusi a causa della paura e del timore per ogni istante. Chi ci potrà dire quando finiranno queste disgrazie e questi malanni?"[4]

No one can answer the question, yet. For three more years, Angelo Citone has to wait locked in his room, cleansing his *Croniche* from any reference to history and politics, and reducing the journal to the mere inventory of family births, marriages, bar mitzvahs, and deaths. But on the 20th day of September of the year 1870, finally, jubilantly, history comes back in the *Croniche*: "In questo giorno ventiquattro del mese di Elul dell'anno 5630...Vittorio Emanuele re d'Italia... che regna sulla casa d'Israele come regnò Ciro... ispirato dal Signore [è entrato in Roma]."[5] Transfigured by myth, the king of Italy has entered Rome through the no less mythical *breccia di Porta Pia*, opened on the city's walls by the artillery of Captain Segre, a Jew. The news quickly spread in the ghetto that it was another Jew, Captain Mortara, who led the first combat unit of the Italian army into the city. Rumors even have it that none less than General Cadorna himself had been seen embracing the seven-year-old son of the Roman Jew Abramo Giuseppe Mondolfo, while the latter, waiving the Italian flag, was crying "Italia! Italia!" And while the legends of this new Massada multiply and prosper, the Jewish press salutes with greatest joy the epochal event: "Il potere temporale è caduto," writes the *Educatore israelitico*: "È questo, senza dubbio, uno dei più grandi avvenimenti del secolo."[6]

It is such a great event, in fact, that we should leave, for the moment, the intimate and familial atmosphere of Citone's *Croniche*, and lend our ear to what the wider world of the Italian Jewry has to say about it. With the *presa di Roma*, a symbolic victory of the Jews is celebrated. What has been conquered, writes the *Educatore israelitico* a few days after, is not a city like any other, but Rome:

> quella Roma che un tempo otteneva la conquista della Palestina dopo lungo assedio e tremende vittorie, che menava prigionieri migliaia e migliaia de' nostri correligionari; Roma, quella Roma in cui si macchinarono tanti infami attentati contro la famiglia d'Israele, quella Roma ch'era il focolare dell'intolleranza religiosa, il sacello del fanatismo...[7]

As remarked by the only other Jewish paper of the time, *Il Corriere israelitico*, the conquest of Rome thus means the very end "di quel governo che a guisa degli antichi Faraoni teneva avvinti a giogo codardo i nostri fratelli." The Jews are now free, "sulle sponde del Tevere, come un giorno su quello dell'Eritreo."[8]

From words like this, it sounds as if the longed for solution of the *questione romana* represented for the Jewish population nothing less than a theological — rather than merely historical — resolution. Differently from the gentile chroniclers of the time, the Italian Jews demonstrate in fact a rather consistent tendency to refuse, in a way, the "historical" interpretation of the event. What they seem to have in mind, on the contrary, is to *isolate* the event from the continuity of history and transfigure it on the plane of symbol and myth. This refusal of the historical approach has, to be sure, nothing whatsoever to do with naïveté. It is, rather an *appropriation* of what would otherwise be "Italian history," and the transformation of this timemonad into a Jewish story — the story of Moses, in fact, which repeats itself again and again throughout time. In an allegorical way, to put it differently, the liberation of the Jews finds its first and more immediate accomplishment in their *appropriation* of history, and in the transformation of teleology into a theology of Messianic redemption. The *presa di Roma* is a Messianic moment, a "cessation of happening, or, put differently, a revolutionary chance"[9] for the return of a repressed and oppressed Jewish tradition which returns now to the fore as repetition of the Moses' myth.

As a moment of Messianic redemption, the *presa di Roma*, bringing back the memories of the Red Sea, bypasses the linear succession of continuous, historical time, and opens up a space for a return, in fact, of Jewish narrative — that which had been repressed, pushed out of history, by the prevailing religion. The abundance of metaphors engaging the *presa di Roma* in the terms of the Old Testament brackets away, along with the New one, the whole of history, and goes back to the theological moment of redemption. It is as if, for the Italian Jews, the time between the flight from Egypt and the arrival of Vittorio Emanuele II had been an empty, unredeemed time, and history the very accounting of this emptiness.

In the Jewish literature of the Risorgimento, the very symbol of such emptiness had been, not surprisingly, Rome itself — the city which the popes wanted "holy," and which the Jewish poet Giuseppe Revere, writing in 1862, saw Godless and empty:

> Non è Dio dove ha carcere la vampa
> del pensier; non è dio dov'è delitto
> amor di libertà, dov'è proscritto
> Quel che primo nel core egli ci stampa.
>
> Dio non è, dove il giusto è derelitto,
> ed il triregno i nostri voti inciampa;
> Dio non è dove, al ver tolta la lampa,
> furor di prete è sol legge e diritto.
>
> Perciò deserto il Vaticano resta[10]

If history is not, as Walter Benjamin once said, "a document of barbarism,"[11] it is at least — and the difference might not be great — a document of Catholicism: priestly furies, public executions, and forced conversions are the material of the history that Revere recapitulates, and which hinges upon the fate of Rome.

David Levi, other illustrious Jewish poet of the Italian Risorgimento, also devoted to "Roma" a poem of his own. Here, the Eternal City is, again, a desert filled only by the debris of history. The poet's gaze concocts the image of the numerous civilizations that succeeded in Rome, one after another, and of their eventual, fatal fall. Presiding to this locus which remains symbolic of linear history, and giving continuity to the flow of historical time, is the everlasting presence, from the Vatican, of the black raven of Catholicism:

> Noi, noi, parevan dir le strida acute,
> noi fummo ognor presenti
> a le lotte, a le glorie, a le cadute,
> e agli sfracellamenti...
> Sol io, cra, cra, cra, crò,
> qui regno — gracchio e sto.[12]

In this sense, if Rome is the very symbol of history, and the Catholic raven is what presides to it, the resolution of the *questione romana* becomes the Messianic moment of discontinuity, of rupture, at which the continuity of (Catholic) history is suspended, and the original myth — the Jewish Testament — returns.

Yet, if myth suspends history in the ex-static moment of redemption, it does so only for one moment. The reign of the Holy — we know — is not destined to rule the secular, for which history advances inexorably — even in the holy city itself. With Vittorio Emanuele II, Moses of the Nineteenth century, the doors of the last Italian ghetto are sprung open — and with it, the whole of the Jewish culture is opened now to the winds of transformation. Not extraneous to some opportunism, only five days after Porta Pia a committee of middle-class Roman Jews addressed Vittorio Emanuele with the following words:

> Noi pronunciamo per l'ultima volta il nome di Israelita. Nell'istante in cui dallo status di riconoscimento legale passiamo al benedetto regime di uguaglianza civile, questo è un dovere di riconoscenza. Sotto lo scettro di Vostra Maestà noi d'ora innanzi fuori dal nostro tempio ci rammenteremo che dobbiamo essere e che null'altro saremo che Italiani e Romani.[13]

In all fairness, if the Pope were to accept to be "re di tutti i Cristiani *solo* per quanto concerne la religione di Gesù,"[14] also the Italian Jews had to yield to the same rule, and be Jews only within the temple. This secularization of religious life, especially for a community hardly accustomed to having to make such distinction, was certainly problematic. It will not take long before Angelo Citone, in a later entry of his family journal, would lament, for instance, that "si è ora diffusa la cattiva consuetudine di non ricordare nomi biblici."[15] The ghetto, whose post-Risorgimento life Citone sadly records, is crowded now with little Giulios, Guidos, and Alfredos. The *Mizvot* are scarcely observed. Circumcision, as Rabbi David Panzieri notes, is performed only for medical reasons. And even the synagogue, the only space within whose walls Jews could still call themselves "Jews," is scarcely attended.[16]

The history that unfolds from the *presa di Roma*, in other words, seems to run inexorably towards what Gramsci, following Attilio Momigliano's suggestion, had called "disebreizzazione":

> il superamento del cosmopolitismo cattolico e in realtà quindi la nascita di uno spirito laico non solo distinto ma in lotta col cattolicismo, [dovette] negli Ebrei avere come manifestazione una loro nazionalizzazione, un loro disebreizzarsi....[17]

And the Jewish historian Eugenio Artom, grandson of that Isacco Artom who worked Cavour at the resolution of the *questione romana*, also maintains:

> La storia del Risorgimento diventa così la storia degli italiani nel loro superare il gruppo in cui ciascuno viveva, per la creazione di una nuova, più vasta e completa collettività: nel loro passaggio spirituale dagli stati patrimoniali o cittadini, dalla Regione, dalla classe, dalla confessione religiosa alla idea di Nazione...[18]

Jewish identity remains, to use Artom's own metaphor, a "regional" one — transcended in fact in what David Levi called "the religion of Nation." In the nation, "[t]utte le credenze si univano, si mischiavano in una fede, la religione della patria — l'Italia."[19]

This *disebreizzazione* of the Italian Jews, and the transformation of their identity into a secular Italian one, represents undoubtedly a central problem for the current studies on the Jewish Risorgimento. Dan Segre, Stefano Caviglia, and, in the United States, Andrew Canepa,[20] have all commented on the problematic notion of "integration." If the Italian Jews were "integrated" by the process of nationalization, in what way were they "emancipated"? Were they not, in fact, disappearing *as* Jews? And in what is "integration" different from the old plague of "conversion"? "E se gli ebrei — asks Caviglia — non fossero stati solleciti nel lasciarsi nazionalizzare?"[21]

The problem, needless to say, was deeply felt by the Jewish intellectuals of post-unification Italy themselves — and it is to one of them that I would like to turn our attention. Giuseppe Revere devoted to the very problem of integration his long Preface to the collection of poems *Osiride*, published in 1879. With a move between irony and humility, he decides that the question is such a complex one that a higher mind needs to be confronted with it. Who else but Moses, the "prophet," "[il] condottiero degli Ebrei,"[22] could clarify this entire business of emancipation and integration? Who, better than the Jewish prophet, could see what had really changed for the Italian Jews after 1870, and how? Yet, where could Revere ever find Moses now, in unified, *disebreizzata* Italy?

> Io voleva il mio Mosé autentico e non contraffatto, co' suoi raggi in fronte, con le tavole della legge nell'una mano e con l'altra libera per

> percuotere, un Mosé che non si fosse impacciato di Statuti, dispotico, assoluto come il suo Jehova, de' propri dogmi tenace, ne' riti inflessibile, delle opinioni degli infedeli noncurante...[23]

Where, indeed, could this original Moses be found? Well, we should not be *that* surprised by now to find that the quest will end in Rome — the symbolic center, indeed, of a Jewish identity liberated only to be now torn between secular and religious allegiance — between, in Revere's words, dogma and Statute. And, within Rome, the quest cannot end anywhere else than in a church — symbolic figure, again, of the Italian Jew's relation with a State still largely catholic. It is in San Pietro in Vincoli, sculpted by Michelangelo, that Giuseppe Revere finds, finally, his "true," unadulterated Moses, "con la sua faccia divinamente diabolica al suo solito posto, tenendo sotto il braccio destro le sue brave tavole della legge."[24]

Engaging Moses in a dialogue that sounds already a bit like catechism, Revere does not linger long before asking the fatidic question:

> Dacché qualche volta parlo del vostro povero popolo eletto, il quale è ora anche elettore ed eleggibile, vorrei pure un po' sapere come la intendete intorno alle sue nuove condizioni.[25]

Moses, as expected, starts his rather elaborate answer from the times of the Pharaoh. Yet, quite more unexpectedly, he starts talking of the New Testament as much as of the Old, and even begins pondering about the merits of Jesus Christ. Moses, alas!, is himself *disebreizzato*?! "C'entra forse Michelangelo — advances Revere — in questa, che, se non temessi di offendere la vostra grandezza, direi conversione?"[26]

The "condottiero," known to us all for his proverbial anger, does not betray at least this expectation: Can Revere — *bestemmiatore!* — really believe that, after living in a church for three centuries, one could talk as if there was no such a thing as Christianity? At any rate, did Revere ever see Moses doubt the unity of God, or proclaim, with Catholic zest for metaphysical technicalities, His "unity in trinity"? "[Io] tengo duro a ciò che mi appartiene di vecchio" — roars Moses. But — he adds soon, with a touch of *realpolitik* — "[p]er mandare innanzi la barca qui, gli è un altro paio di maniche."[27]

Religious faith is one thing, and this, says Moses, is one and unbending. But life, "here," is a different matter. An abyss still lies between history and the prophesied Empire of Freedom. Regarding the latter, Revere may have been right: the unification of Italy has not realized the reign of the Messiah, and nothing has changed for the Italian Jews. But, in the face of history, Moses does not seem to have any doubt: what is at stake is not to realize a lost paradise in Rome, but the possibility of opening, there, a space for what Revere's Moses calls a "Gerusalemme politica." To open, in other words, a political space distinguished from the religious one — a space that will also be one of negotiation between Jews and Catholics. Freedom and emancipation, for the Italian Jews, are concrete possibilities only within the limits of the nation — within the discourse, that is, of politics, which is the art of compromise and negotiation. That this emancipation cannot coincide with the Messianic promise is for Moses a truism: *that* freedom has little to do with politics.

Is not this declaration of the abyss that lies between God and a yet unredeemed history the very affirmation of Judaism *vis à vis* Christianity? Is not the *presa di Roma*, this end of the confusion between religion and secular power, the vindication, indeed, of Judaism? It is on this more positive note that the little dialogue between Revere and the old prophet ends. And here I would like to stop myself, taking my leave from you like Revere took his from Moses: "laonde, mi tolsi senza batter becco dalla sua presenza, chiedendogli soltanto la permissione di baciargli la mano poderosa. Credo anzi m'abbia anche benedetto; segnato non direi, per non mescolar l'una fede nell'altra..."[28]

ROBERTO MARIA DAINOTTO
Duke University

---

[1] Angelo Citone, *Le "Croniche" della famiglia Citone*, trans. Alberto Piattelli (Roma: Edizioni di storia e letteratura, 1988) 380-1.

[2] Quoted in Riccardo Rinaldi, *Roma papale: dalla Repubblica alla monarchia* (Roma: Nuova Editrice Spada, 1992) 236.

[3] Bruno Di Porto, "Gli ebrei di Roma dai Papi all'Italia," *1870. La breccia del ghetto. Evoluzione degli ebrei di Roma*, ed. Salvatore Foà (Roma: Barulli, 1971) 41-42.

[4] Citone 380-1.

[5] Citone 92.

[6] In Yoseph Colombo, "Il XX settembre 1870 nella stampa ebraica dell'epoca," *1870. La breccia del ghetto. Evoluzione degli ebrei di Roma*, ed. Salvatore Foà (Roma: Barulli, 1971) 100.

THE JEWISH RISORGIMENTO AND THE QUESTIONE ROMANA 115

[7] Flaminio Servi, *Educatore israelitico*, ottobre 1870, in Yoseph Colombo, "Il XX settembre 1870 nella stampa ebraica dell'epoca," *1870. La breccia del ghetto. Evoluzione degli ebrei di Roma*, ed. Salvatore Foà (Roma: Barulli, 1971) 104.

[8] In Colombo, "Il XX settembre 1870 nella stampa ebraica dell'epoca," 106.

[9] Walter Benjamin, "Theses on the Philosophy of History," trans. Zohn, Harry, *Illuminations*, ed. Hannah Arendt, 1968 ed. (New York: Schocken, 1966) 262-3.

[10] Giuseppe Revere, *Versi*, Opere complete di Giuseppe Revere in parte inedite o rare, ed. A Ròndani, vol. 3, 4 vols. (Roma: Forzani e C. Tipografi del Senato, 1898).

[11] Benjamin 256.

[12] David Levi, *Ausonia.Vita d'azione (dal1848 al 1870)* (Roma: Loescher, 1882) 129-30.

[13] Citone 200.

[14] Citone 200; my emphasis.

[15] Citone 210.

[16] Stefano Caviglia, *L'identità salvata. Gli ebrei di Roma tra fede e nazioni, 1870-1938* (Roma: Laterza, 1996) 39-48.

[17] Antonio Gramsci, *Il Risorgimento* (1977; Roma: Editori Riuniti, 1996) 209.

[18] Eugenio Artom, "Per una storia degli ebrei nel Risorgimento," *Rassegna storica toscana* (gennaio-giugno 1978): 138.

[19] Levi 81.

[20] Andrew M. Canepa, "Considerazioni sulla II emancipazione," *Rassegna mensile di Israel* XLVII.1-2-3 (1981): 56-71; Andrew M. Canepa, "Emancipazione, integrazione e antisemitismo liberale in Italia. Il caso Pasqualigo," *Comunità* (giugno 1975): 165-203; Stefano Caviglia, *L'identità salvata. Gli ebrei di Roma tra fede e nazioni, 1870-1938* (Roma: Laterza, 1996); V. Dan Segre, *L'emancipazione degli ebrei in Italia*, trans. Toscano, Mario, Integrazione e identità. L'esperienza ebraica in Germania e Italia dall'illuminismo al fascismo (Milano: Franco Angeli, 1998).

[21] Stefano Caviglia, *L'identità salvata. Gli ebrei di Roma tra fede e nazioni, 1870-1938* (Roma: Laterza, 1996) 6.

[22] Revere 258.

[23] Revere 259.

[24] Revere 261.

[25] Revere 264.

[26] Revere 268.

[27] Revere 268.

[28] Revere 281.

REFLECTIONS ON THE PRIEBKE AFFAIR
ON MASSACRES, TRIALS, HISTORY AND MEMORY

In the late afternoon and early evening of 24 March 1944, the Nazis carried out a massacre just outside the walls of Rome. For Italians, the event has become synonymous with its locus, *Le Fosse Ardeatine*, the Ardeatine Caves, a labyrinth of catacombs used by the early Christians. While this episode p ales in c omparison w ith w hat c onspired in t he e xtermination camps, its details and subsequent repercussions shed light on the horror of the Fascist-Nazi alliance and the convoluted, often-contested terrain of history.[1]

A day before, Communist partisans had completed a successful attack against the heavily-armed Bolzen Battalion of SS police in Via Rasella, killing thirty-three soldiers. The partisans no doubt were offering their own bitter and ironic response to the festivities taking place that very day marking the 22nd anniversary of Mussolini's "March on Rome." In savage reprisal, Hitler ordered ten Italians executed for each of the thirty-three dead soldiers. The task of compiling a list of prospective victims fell to Herbert Kappler, a lieutenant-colonel in the SS and his immediate subordinate, Erich Priebke. Kappler had already distinguished himself in the mass arrest and deportation of the Jews of the Roman ghetto to Auschwitz in October of the previous year (1943).[2] He was assisted by Pietro Caruso, police chief of the Eternal City. Pope Pius XII, when informed of the impending massacre, decided neither to intervene nor protest an outrageous act planned and committed within his temporal and spiritual domain.

Kappler, Priebke and Caruso spent the night of 23-24 March typing up a list of men to be executed. When 330 victims could not be located within Rome's notorious prisons, men were added to the list indiscriminately, including seventy-five Jews who had managed to avoid the 1943 deportation. The list of death — a perverse and obscene counterpart to the "list of life" made famous in Spielberg's film — contained a cross-section of men and boys from Roman society aged 14 to 74: soldiers, business-men, professionals, farmers, artisans, workers, students and even a Roman Catholic priest. Not one of the victims was involved in the partisan attack of the previous day. The victims were taken to the caves, just off the ancient Roman Appian way, and forced to kneel while a bullet was fired into the base of their skulls. Priebke admitted to executing two men; he then returned to his duty at the mouth of the caves, checking names off his list. In order to conceal their crime, the Germans dynamited the entrance to the caves. But there were witnesses and rumors in the city. When the Allies entered Rome ten weeks later on 4 June, they were directed to the site, uncovered the bodies and assisted in the gruesome task of identification.[3]

Even before the war ended, a furious debate began over the meaning and significance of the massacre. The official Vatican newspaper blamed the partisans ("irresponsible elements") for provoking the Nazis who were entrusted with the solemn responsibility of upholding "history and civilization." In the context of the Cold War, rightwing newspapers and commentators (Italian, not German) decried the partisan attack as "barbaric" while defending the Nazi massacre as a legitimate act of war.[4] Meanwhile, an attempt was made to bring those responsible to justice: Pietro Caruso was tried, found guilty, and executed. Kappler and five German accomplices were turned over to Italian authorities and tried in 1948; Kappler was found guilty; fortunately for him, the new Italian republic had outlawed the death penalty and he was sentenced to life imprisonment; the other five were acquitted. Priebke was not among them — he had fled to Argentina after escaping from a British POW camp in Italy. In an interview, he implied that he was assisted by the notorious "Rat Line" established by the Vatican and under the direction of Bishop Alois Hudal. The military court in 1948, though, by ruling that the partisan attack was not a legitimate act of war, paved the way for one of the more bizarre aspects of the story: some relatives of the victims filed suit against the partisans responsible for the attack. The suit was rejected. The site of the massacre was consecrated as a national memorial and the partisans of via Rasella were recognized for their military valor even as they began receiving death threats from anonymous sources.

The Ardeatine Caves massacre was neither the first nor the last of Nazi reprisals against partisan acts. It was, in a way, unprecedented, for it unfolded within the shadow of the Vatican which conflated the partisan attack with the massacre onto the same moral plane and with the full knowledge of the Pope. The struggle concerning the contested meaning of the event is far from over. More broadly, the history of what happened in Rome on March 23-24, 1944 must be seen in the context of an on-going fifty year campaign by well-organized forces to defame and discredit the ideals and actions of the Italian partisan Resistance.

Just how divisive the massacre continues to be was forcefully brought home in the last few years. In the spring of 1994, the American telejournalist Sam Donaldson approached a distinguished looking older gentleman on the streets of San Carlos Bariloche, a pristine town reminiscent of an Alpine village in Argentina. The gentleman acknowledged that he was indeed Erich Priebke, a former SS and Gestapo officer. Within days, the slow-moving machinery of international law was at work. Italy demanded his extradition to stand trial for his role in the Ardeatine Caves massacre. The Italian government contended that the massacre was an unhealable tear in the fabric of Roman life and that Priebke was guilty of "crimes against humanity." The massacre had torn through entire families, affecting different social and economic classes.[5] One of the worst offended was the Jewish community. Today the Jewish community flourishes in Rome, approaching its third millennium of existence, despite the persecutions of Imperial Rome, the Catholic Church, Fascism and Nazism. Ironically, the community was divided over a contemporary reminder of the recent past when Priebke was extradited from Argentina to Rome in 1995 for his role in the Ardeatine Caves massacre. In May of 1996, his trial began before a Military Tribunal of three judges and lasted until August 1. Priebke never spoke in his own defense at the trial, another affront to the many relatives of the victims present. His legal defense claimed he was merely a lowly soldier following orders. Yet as an officer, Priebke was undoubtedly familiar with paragraph 47 of the German military code then in force which clearly stated that a German soldier could not be punished for refusing to carry out illegal orders or war crimes. One official at the Caves, Gunther Amon, fainted and did not take part in the executions; he was not punished. Captain Gerhard Schreiber of the German Navy and a respected military historian, presented documentation of eighty-five cases in which army or SS officials refused to carry out war crimes, with little or no punishment.[6] Daniel Goldhagen's recent work, *Hitler's Willing Executioners*[7] shows that German soldiers routinely requested other duties when it came to civilian massacres and that they were never punished. The trial generated another controversy when the dean of Italian journalist, Indro Montanelli, wrote that Priebke should be acquitted. The Chief Rabbi of Rome, Elio Toaff, suggested that even if convicted, Priebke should not be sent to prison.[8] In a decision that stunned the world, the three military judges ruled on 1 August 1996 that Priebke was guilty, but not subject to punishment for his role in the massacre.[9] That evening, the mayor of Rome, Francesco Rutelli, ordered all the lights on the public monuments in Rome turned off in protest except those at the Fosse Ardeatine. Thousands marched through the streets of the city in outrage. Priebke was re-arrested several hours later, based on an extradition request from Germany, but this action raised new legal questions.[10]

Besides the moral and legal issues raised by the Priebke trial are questions concerning the use and abuse of history. Several years ago, a proposal by the mayor, Rutelli, to rename a street in Rome after Giuseppe Bottai, a key figure of the Fascist regime under Benito Mussolini, was a striking example of how history is continually manipulated for political ends. It also broaches the more intriguing question of the intricate relationship between history, memory and writing. Who has power over the past? Who are the guardians of our collective memory?

Bottai was one of the more subtle and sophisticated figures of the Fascist regime: influenced by the avant-garde Futurist movement, he edited the important cultural journal *Critica fascista*, which supported the idea of a technocratic "left" Fascism. As Minister of Corporations, he attempted to implement the vision of the "corporate State:" Fascism's method of defusing the revolutionary potential of labor by absorbing the workers and peasants into the framework of capitalism and the modern nation-state. As Minister of Education (1936-1943), Bottai was instrumental in the persecution of Jewish teachers and professors, before and after the passage of the "Racial Laws" in 1938.

In an ironic twist of history, the mayor of Rome was a Green Party member and former Communist, Francesco Rutelli, who defeated the leader of the neo-Fascist (or "post-Fascist") National Alliance, Gianfranco Fini, in a close election. Rutelli argued that the proposal to name a street after Bottai would work toward reconciling Italians still divided by the bitter legacy of twenty years of Fascist rule. The proposal was, instead, another step on the treacherous road of making Fascism "respectable." During the Priebke trial, graffiti and posters regularly appeared overnight on Rome and other Italian cities demanding Priebke's release. For Italian Fascists, neo-Fascists, post-Fascists, and "naziskins", Priebke was the victim.

For fifty years, post-World War II Italy has maintained a "cult" of anti-Fascism and a "myth" of the Resistance. In reality, the intellectual and armed resistance against Fascism was more often employed for rhetorical purposes than as a guide to implement real political change. Anti-Fascism was a "sacred patrimony" as long as it did not contest the hegemony of the conservative Christian Democratic governments of the post-war period. Anti-Fascists who were assassinated by Mussolini's regime such as Giovanni Amendola, Piero Gobetti, Giacomo Matteotti, the Rosselli brothers and Antonio Gr amsci w ho s uffered a s low de ath in p rison, w ere s olemnly placed in the pantheon of martyrs while their political ideas were conveniently ignored. Every large city in Italy has a street or piazza named after these figures, but their real legacy was maintained only by a few maverick intellectuals and politicians like former prime minister Giovanni Spadolini and the former president of the Republic, Sandro Pertini.

In the context of the Cold War, conservatives managed to maintain political power in Italy as a murky radical right-wing continued to operate behind the scenes. The media potentate Silvio Berlusconi skillfully manipulated the country's fanaticism with soccer to his advantage and cynically resurrected the phantom of "Red Communism" to reach the office of prime minister in 1994. From that office, he nearly managed to create a "media dictatorship" by controlling the state-owned television stations along with his own private networks.

April 25, celebrated as the liberation of Italy from the forces of Fascism and Nazism, has recently been appropriated by the Right as a "day of reconciliation." Alessandra Mussolini, the granddaughter of the dictator and member of Parliament, claimed that the holiday should honor all who fought, from whatever side. Berlusconi, for his part, insists that the divisions between Fascists and anti-Fascists are merely a "piece of history."

These events of the last few years are only the most obvious in the attempt to normalize Fascism and present it in a favorable light. Berlusconi, Fini and Alessandra Mussolini are intelligent, attractive and, most importantly, media-savvy. Fascism is no longer recognized by the "Black Shirt" but by the double-breasted suits of Berlusconi, the professorial spectacles of Fini and the designer wear of Ms. Mussolini. Surely such well-groomed and articulate persons cannot be in any way related to those murderous thugs of an earlier age.

The reasons behind the proposal to rename a street after Bottai bring to mind Ronald Reagan's trip in 1985 to the cemetery at Bitburg, Germany, where former Nazi officers were buried: it was claimed that they too had been "victims" of Adolf Hitler's madness. Nazis and victims of the

Holocaust; Fascists and partisans: all are reduced, in the memory of the Right, to the same moral plane. In the process, "history" becomes an obscenity.

The historical legacy of anti-Fascism in Europe is today under attack on several fronts. Politicians openly question the most basic tenets of democracy and seek to redeem past regimes while some intellectuals consciously foster a "culture of nostalgia" which later manifests itself in various guises within the realm of popular culture. Although the nature of the anti-Fascist resistance has been closely examined and criticized from within, now we are witnessing a concerted effort to rewrite history and denigrate the struggle against totalitarian and authoritarian regimes. "Revisionists" grasp for academic legitimacy while their political counterparts mask strategies of domination with the rhetoric of national pride. A favored technique among neo-Fascists (or as they prefer to call themselves, "post-Fascists") is to place themselves on the same moral plane as their victims and anti-Fascists. Fascists were "victims" as much as Jews, anti-Fascists, and partisans. 25 April, celebrated after the war as a national holiday of liberation from Fascism and Nazism, should now be, according to the leader of the post-Fascist National Alliance, Gianfranco Fini, conceived as a "day of national reconciliation." In the winter of 1933, the leader of the largest non-Marxist leftist anti-Fascist movement, Justice and Liberty, Carlo Rosselli, presented a talk on Fascist foreign policy at the Royal Institute of Foreign Affairs in London. He warned that Fascist nationalism led inevitably to imperialism, racism, and war. Sixty-two years later, Gianfranco Fini was invited to the Royal Institute where he declared that F ascism a nd a nti-Fascism ha ve p assed int o his tory a nd s hould b e treated accordingly.[11]

Historians find themselves central to this debate concerning writing, memory and the preservation of a particular vision of the past. The fiftieth anniversary of the end of the Second World War generated a debate in Italy similar to the German *Historikerstreit*, in this case over the nature of Fascism and the anti-Fascist Resistance.[12] In addition, the fiftieth anniversary of the end of the war was an occasion for historians to convene and reassess the Resistance legacy.[13]

What, though, became of Erich Priebke?

Outrage at the original verdict placed the Italian Minister of Justice, Giovanni Maria Flick, in an embarrassing situation. With some lightning-fast legal maneuvering, he managed to have Priebke re-arrested, based on an appeal for extradition from Germany. Another trial was scheduled, raising legal and philosophical quandaries.[14] In April of 1997, Priebke — now 84 years old and another associate, the 85 year old Karl Hass were convicted, sentenced to 15 years — reduced to five — and placed under house arrest in the residence of his legal adviser, Paolo Giachini.[15] In a moment of supreme irony and no self-consciousness, Priebke announced that he would appeal the verdict to the European Court of Human Rights in Strasbourg, France. Another appeal was heard and finally, in March of 1998, a court upheld the conviction, and in a rare moment, imposed a harsher sentence of life imprisonment. When Giulia Spizzichino, a Roman woman who had lost seven relatives in the Ardeatine massacre and another eleven in the gas chambers at Auschwitz, stated in a television interview that she was happy with the verdict, she received death threats. Tullia Zevi, president of the Union of Jewish Communities in Italy, applauded the sentence but indicated that she favored an act of clemency that would allow Priebke to go free.

There were further repercussions: in June of 1998, Theodor Saewecke, 87, was tried *in absentia* for his having 15 Italian partisans shot in 1944 in an attempt to discourage others from supporting the Resistance. Saewecke worked for the CIA from 1949 until 1951 and then for the German Federal police. Also in June of 1998, Italian military prosecutors indicted two other SS officers, Lieutenant Colonel Siegfried Engel (age 89) and Lieutenant Otto Kaess (age 90) for the executions of prisoners. In October 1998, a 90 year old former officer of the SS, Siegfried Engel, was ordered to go on trial before a military tribunal in Turin for his role in the deaths of 200 Italian civilians and partisans during the war. The trial is scheduled to open May 25, 1999. In November 1998, Italy's highest court, the Corte Cassaz-zione, reaffirmed the life sentence imposed on Priebke. For his part, the former SS official continued to insist that moral responsibility for the massacre lay with the partisans. Most recently (February 1999) Priebke was released from prison and placed under house arrest.

Questions, though, still surround the Ardeatine Caves massacre and Priebke's trial. Major Karl Hass, described as one of the most wanted of Nazi war criminals for his actions in Italy, revealed in an interview that he had lived for the past fifty years in Rome.[16] The presiding judge, Agostino Quistelli, was not removed from the bench nor did he recuse himself after it became public that he had already come to a decision to free Priebke *before the trial had begun*. Witnesses for the prosecution were reduced to the bare minimum and the trial took place in the physically cramped quarters of a small military courtroom with barely enough room for the principal players. More seriously, the decision to proceed with a military trial was of the utmost significance. Priebke could be assured of receiving a sympathetic hearing of his defense that he was merely following orders. But Priebke was not, strictly speaking, a member of the German military. Both the Gestapo and the SS were police organizations; hence Priebke should have been tried in a civilian court. In fact, Priebke never performed any *military* service for Germany. The Nuremberg trials had already established a legal precedent that certain organizations such as the SS were criminal enterprises.[17] Documents of the U.S. government from the Second World War reveal that Priebke was well-known as a torturer of partisans in Rome.[18]

Some may argue that placing a ninety-year-old man in jail for actions that occurred a half century ago do not constitute an act of justice; rather, they argue, some mercy should be shown to a man who clearly will come to some final reckoning in the not-too-distant future. Yet don't the victims and their families deserve some final reckoning as well?

STANISLAO G. PUGLIESE

Hofstra University

---

[1] The only account of the massacre in English is by Robert Katz, *Death in Rome*. New York: Macmillan, 1967. The work has been continuously in print in an Italian translation a s *M orte a Roma. Il massacro delle Fosse Ardeatine*. 5 th e d. R ome: Riuniti, 1996.

[2] See Robert Katz, *Black Sabbath: A Crime Against Humanity*. New York: Macmillan, 1969.

[3] For the story of the exhumation and examination of the remains, see the study by the doctor in charge of the work, Attilio Ascarelli, *Le Fosse Ardeatine*, Rome: Palumbi, 1945; reprint Bologna: Canesi, 1965 with new material and full text of the sentence in the Kappler trial.

[4] An example of this literature questioning the motives of the Resistance and laying responsibility for the massacre with the partisans is Aurelio Lepre, *Via Rasella. Leggenda e realtà della Resistenza a Roma*. Rome-Bari: Laterza, 1996; for a defense of the via Rasella attack by one of its members, see Rosario Bentivenga, *Operazione via Rasella. Verità e menzogna: i protagonisti raccontano*. Rome: Riuniti, 1996.

[5] Of the 335 victims, only 322 were ultimately identified by Ascarelli and his forensic team. Following is a statistical analysis of the victims:
Age: 14 years: 1; 15 years: 1; 17 years: 2; 18 years: 5; 18-60: 31; 60-70: 10; 74 years: 1
Profession: Soldiers/Officers: 39; Shopkeepers: 54; Clerk/Employee: 28; Professionals: 24; Students: 9; Farmers: 10; Artisans: 31; Traveling salesmen: 16; Workers: 39; Industrial workers: 2; Priests: 1; Other: 82
See Katz, *Death in Rome*, pp. 259-270.

[6] Robert Katz, *Dossier Priebke. Anatomia di un processo*. Milan: Rizzoli, 1996, p. 126.

[7] Daniel J. Goldhagen, *Hitler's Willing Executioners: Ordinary Germans and the Holocaust*. New York: Knopf, 1996.

[8] "Rome Rabbi Asks Leniency for ex-Nazi Accused of '44 Atrocity." *The New York Times*, April 18, 1996, p. A7.

[9] *New York Times*, August 2, 1996, p. A3.

[10] On the Priebke trial, see *Processo Priebke*. Cinzia Dal Maso and Simona Micheli, eds. Rome: Il Mondo 3 Instant, 1996; Robert Katz, *Dossier Priebke. Anatomia di un processo*. Milan: Rizzoli, 1996; Mary Pace, *Dietro Priebke*. Casale Monferrato: Piemme, 1997; Walter Leszl, *Il processo Priebke e il nazismo*. Rome: Riuniti, 1997. Sam Donaldson's "interview" with Priebke was broadcast on ABC, *Prime Time Live*, 5 May 1994.

[11] Carlo Rosselli, "La politica estera fascista" translated and edited by Costanzo Casucci, *Il Mulino* XXXIII, 1984: 241-261.

[12] See especially Giovanni De Luna and Marco Revelli, *Fascismo/Antifascismo. Le idee e le identità*. Florence: La Nuova Italia, 1995; Gian Enrico Rusconi, *Resistenza e postfascismo*. Bologna: Il Mulino, 1995; Pietro Scoppola, *25 aprile. La Liberazione*. Turin: Einaudi, 1995. Much debate was stimulated by Claudio Pavone's, *Una guerra civile: saggio storico sulla moralità nella Resistenza*. Turin: Bollati Boringhieri, 1991; Romolo Gobbi, *Il mito della Resistenza*. Milan: Rizzoli, 1992; Renzo De Felice, *Rosso e Nero*. ed. Pasquale Chessa, Milan: Baldini & Cartoldi, 1995 and De Felice's *Fascismo, antifascismo, nazione*. Rome: Bonacci, 1996. For an excellent study of the historiographical problems of antifascism and the Resistance, see Alberto Aquarone, *Fascismo e antifascismo nella storiografia italiana*. Rome: Edizione della Voce, 1986. For a spirited defense of both Rosselli and the Resistance, see Nicola Tranfaglia, *Labirinto italiano: il fascismo, l'antifascismo, gli storici*. Florence: La Nuova Italia, 1989; and Paolo Bagnoli, *Rosselli, Gobetti e la rivoluzione democratica*. Florence: La Nuova Italia, 1996. More debate was generated with Ernesto Galli della Loggia, *La morte della patria: La crisi dell'idea di nazione tra Resistenza, antifascismo e Repubblica*. Rome-Bari: Laterza, 1996; Enzo Collotti and Lutz Klinkhammer, *Il fascismo e l'Italia in guerra*. Rome: Ediesse, 1996; Nicola Tranfaglia, *Un passato scomodo: Fascismo e postfascismo*. Rome-Bari: Laterza, 1996; Furio Colombo and Vittorio Feltri, *Fascismo/Antifascismo*. Milan: Rizzoli, 1994.

[13] Two conferences in particular were fruitful: "Passato e presente della Resistenza. 50 anniversario della Resistenza e della Guerra di liberazione," 1-3 October 1993 in Rome; "Antifascismi e Resistenze" organized by the Gramsci Institute in Rome, 5-6

October 1995. The proceedings of the latter conference have been published as *Fascismo, antifascismo, democrazia. A cinquant'anni dal 25 aprile* in *Studi Storici* 36, n. 3 luglio-settembre 1995.

[14] For an extensive study of the philosophical and legal issues revolving around the trial, see Walter Leszl, *Priebke. Anatomia di un processo*. Rome: Riuniti, 1997.

[15] A friend offered her home after the sentence of house arrest; see her account of how Priebke took advantage of their friendship in Mary Pace, *Dietro Priebke*.

[16] Katz, *Dossier Priebke*, p. 123.

[17] This point is made by Leszl, *Priebke*, p. xxii.

[18] As reported in the June 4, 1996 issue of the Italian-American daily, *America Oggi*, p. 4.

Risking All for Brotherhood*

For all its horror and tragedy, the story of the Holocaust contains some chapters of great human solidarity, many of them written by the caring Italians who put their own safety at risk in order to lend support and assistance to their endangered neighbors, members (if Europe's oldest Jewish community, established in Rome 2,000 years ago).

With the fiftieth anniversary of the end of World War II, the timely topic of the Holocaust is being examined in a perspective centered in southern Europe. Due in part to the recent tremendous success of Spielberg's *Schindler's List* and other media coverage, much of the world has been informed of efforts to rescue Jews in northern Europe from the horrors of the death camps. Oscar Schindler, for instance, was an individual working within the bureaucracy to save Jews. The entire Danish population was involved in a massive rescue effort, while Swedish diplomat Raoul Wallenberg worked virtually alone, achieving noteworthy results on his own.

Not many are aware, however, of the rescues effected in southern Europe. There, in contrast, we see not only civilians helping both neighbors and strangers, but also bureaucrats working within the bureaucratic framework to save Jews. Italian efforts of this kind were carried on in Italy as well as in Italian-occupied territories in southern France, Albania, Croatia and Greece. The Italian experience also is unique both because Italy was officially allied with Nazi Germany until 1943 and because the Italians were concerned not only about the fate of Italian Jews but also about that of foreign Jews as well.

Italian bureaucrats and diplomats defied orders to save Jews. The Italian army saved Jews in Croatia by taking them into Italy and in southern France by hiding them in hotels. Many Jewish survivors, including Imre Rochlitz, whose son produced *Righteous Enemy,* a documentary film on the subject, and historians and survivors Menachem Shelah of Israel and Ivo Herzer of America have attested to the fact that when the Ustachi in Croatia were rounding up Jews and sending them to death camps, Italian Army officers and soldiers organized an efficient effort to save the Jews by getting them to safe haven in Italy.

Giorgio Perlasca, an Italian businessman posing as a Spanish diplomat (see Italy Italy, No. 1,1992), falsified exit papers for more than 10,000 Jews in Budapest. Guelfo Zamboni, the Italian consul in German-occupied Salonika, in Greece, in 1943, saved more than 280 Jews from being deported by doggedly exerting his waning official diplomatic powers.

But there were many heroic, ordinary Italian citizens, including priests and nuns, who helped rescue 25 percent of Italy's Jews. In her book *The Italians and the Holocaust,* Susan Zuccotti points out that in 1942 there were about 37,100 Italian Jews and about 8,100 foreign Jews in Italy, making a total of 45,200. Only after 1943, when Italy was occupied by the Nazis, 6,801, or about 15 percent, were deported to the Nazi death camps.

During the period from World War I to 1938 the Jews had little reason to feel at risk in Italy. Many Jews had served with honor and attained high rank in the Italian army in World War I, and they were thoroughly assimilated in Italian society. In fact, while Jews in other European countries were concerned about Hitler's official antisemitism, the Jews in Italy seemed to have been little affected. It was during this period that many foreign Jews were further assured by Mussolini's repeated public statements that there was no Jewish "problem" in Italy. One can only imagine the shock that ran through the community when Mussolini took two measures against the Jews to prove to Hitler that he was his comrade and ally.

The first measure was the Racial Laws of 1938, which stated that the Jews of Italy no longer enjoyed the rights and privileges of ordinary citizens. Consequently, Jews had to leave their professions and Jewish children were forced to leave school.

The second measure was the establishment of internment camps throughout Italy for the confinement of the foreign Jews who had arrived in Italy. One such camp was built in 1940 by the Fascist regime in Calabria, near Ferramonti Tarsia, in an area infested by malaria-carrying mosquitoes. But unlike similar camps in northern Europe, in this camp the interned were allowed to set up a cooperative kitchen, library, schools, medical care unit, recreation center and even a synagogue.

Carlo Spartaco Capogreco, who has documented the camp extensively, notes that the camp's official policy was based on tolerance and respect so long as the Jews maintained discipline and order. Eventually the inmates of the camp were freed by the Allies. Other Italian internment camps, such as Fossoli in northern Italy, were not so fortunate. When the German death machine swept through to occupy Italy in 1943, the Jews there were sent to Auschwitz.

There are many theories as to the Italians' motivation in rescuing Jews. Some have concluded that they may have acted for reasons other than altruism: that is, because of their hatred of the Germans or a desire to assert their sovereignty, or as a political maneuver to win favor with the Allies should they lose the war.

Another possible motivation may be that the Jews were an important component of Italian society. The history of the Jews in Italy dates back to ancient Roman times. The Popes never expelled the Jews from Rome, which was the home of the oldest Jewish community in Europe, dating back two thousand years. Although Jews were forced to live in ghettos in Italy for centuries, in 1870 they were "emancipated" and could aspire to positions of high rank. Jews had served in the Italian army as generals, and Italy had had a Jewish prime minister. This may in part explain the widespread benevolence and sympathy toward Jews on the part of the Italian army. Another reason may lie in the fact that many Jews worked as doctors, teachers and government officials, and the non-Jewish Italian public related to them as neighbors and friends.

The Jews in Italy referred to themselves simply as "Italians," and they felt instinctively that their Italian neighbors would not just stand by in case of persecution but would reach out a hand to help. And so they found the fortitude to resist or, at least, to hide. And the Italians helped not only their Italian Jewish neighbors but foreign Jews as well. Many Jewish survivors in America come from families who immigrated to Italy from other countries as Hitler was gaining power in Europe or, later, to Italian occupied territories in southern Europe. Their stories are somewhat different from those of native Italian Jews, but the theme remains the same.

Ivo Herzer of Washington, D.C., tells of having seen his relatives, then living in Zagreb, Croatia, rounded up by the Ustachi for the Nazis, who sent most of them to Auschwitz. His immediate family was saved because an Italian soldier took pity on them. He took them to his commanding officer, who hid them in an army truck and took them overland into Italy, saving their lives.

Helen Deutsch of Chicago relates that, as a young German woman living just outside of Rome, she was left behind, pregnant, when her husband was sent away to an internment camp. The Giustini family took her in and helped her with her baby. She recalls that the Giustini grandfather slept on the floor so that she could rest with her child on his bed. The family watched over her for two years.

There are many such stories, of Jewish children hidden in convent schools, where they learned all the Latin prayers, and of entire families being taken into Italian households. Villa Emma served as the home of Jewish children in Nonantola, Italy where Mayor Stefano Vaccari honored Father Don Arrigo Beccari, an unsung hero of the Holocaust. Beccari was responsible for the rescue of 109 Jewish orphans from Berlin. He was arrested four times by the Nazis but continued his mission to save the children by insuring false identification papers were issued. The children were sent to Switzerland and rescued.

These survivors are living testimony that the people of Italy reached out to help save their lives. They all declare that they had no money or jewels to give in exchange. The Italians saved them out of love for their fellow human beings, and for no other reason.

These stories have remained untold until now, partly because most of the Italian rescuers themselves do not feel that what they did was remarkable. As many put it, "It was just the right thing to do."

MARIA LOMBARDO**
NIAF Education Director

---

* Part of this article was published in *Italy Italy* magazine. With financial support from the National Endowment for the Humanities and the National Italian American Foundation as well as other Italian and Jewish organizations, Dr. Maria Lombardo conducted 23 conferences in 23 U.S. cities titled, "The Holocaust in Southern Europe." The conferences described Italy's role during W. W. II through historians, survivors, films and exhibits. The conferences were conducted at the U.S. Holocaust Memorial Museum, and in conjunction with 18 U. S. Federal agencies in Washington, D.C.

** Dr. Maria Lombardo is the daughter of a Nazi slave labor camp survivor. She is documenting Italy's role during W. W. II and her family's personal experience in a book titled, *A Camp without Walls* to be published by *Italy Italy* magazine.

Notes From an Interview With Rabbi Aldo Piattelli

The Jewish community in Italy is the oldest in Europe and one of the oldest in the world. It can be traced back to the 2nd century B.C. and it was mentioned by ancient authors Horace, Cicero and Julius Caesar. By the 1st century A.D., when Roman emperor Titus (A.D. 79 -A.D. 81) was in power, the Jewish Community in Rome had become a very large one. Many of the Jewish prisoners brought to Rome from Palestine as slaves were redeemed by the members of Rome's Jewish community. Jews also settled in southern Italy, especially in Puglia, Calabria and Sicily. About the year 1000 the Jews began to, migrate northward, mainly into what are now the regions of Tuscany and the Veneto. In these areas the Jews were very active as pawnbrokers.

At present there are about fifty thousand Italian Jews residing in many cities. The most sizable communities are in Rome and Milan. In each city, the local community organizes the religious and cultural activities for its members. A central body, the Union of the Italian Jewish Communities, coordinates their activities and speaks for the entire national community. Every four years representatives of all the communities meet at a national congress, electing a Council that is charged with representing the Community for the next four years.

In April 1986 Pope John Paul II made an historic visit to the Rome synagogue — the first time that the head of the Roman Catholic Church had crossed the threshold of a synagogue. What effect did the pope's important initiative have on relations between the Jewish community and the Catholic Church?

"The pope's visit to the synagogue," explains Rabbi Aldo Piattelli, assistant to Chief Rabbi Elio Toaff, "was not decided on the spur of the moment but came in the wake of contacts initiated many years ago which strengthened the bond between Jews and Catholics, especially in the fields of scholarship and social action. In particular, however, the visit signaled that antisemitism based on religious prejudice is no longer admissible."

On March 14, 1944, at the Fosse Ardeatine, a quarry near Rome, the Nazis killed more than three hundred Italians, most of them Jews, in reprisal for an attack on Nazi troops in the city. To commemorate this tragic episode a ceremony is held every year on the site, where Jews and Christians pray together. "For the Fosse Ardeatine," explains Rabbi Piattelli, "a kind of ecumenical prayer has been devised, partly in Italian and partly in Hebrew, in which biblical evocations common to both religions are evident, as opposed to a prayer based on dogmas or beliefs peculiar to one religion or the other."

In the Campidoglio, Rome's city hall, the Jewish community of Rome recently awarded medals to several persons who helped the Jews during the dark years of the Nazi persecution. "It should be remembered," says Rabbi Piattelli, "that in Italy, unlike other countries in Western Europe, a majority of people did much for the Jews, often at great risk to themselves." Between the two world wars, many Jews emigrated from Italy, mainly to the United States. What is the nature of relations today between those emigrants and the Jewish community in Italy? "There is, of course, an affectionate relationship," says the Rabbi, "but above all there is a link with Jewish-Italian history and culture."

Mussolini and Fascist Anti-Semitism:
Turning Point of a Regime

On July 14, 1938, Benito Mussolini approved the publication of a "Manifesto on Race" in which ten "scholars" asserted the following: (1) race is a biological concept, and Italy belongs to the Aryan race, (2) the a pure "Italian race" exists, (3) Jews do not belong to the Italian race, and intermarriage between Jews and Aryans is not to be permitted.

Some two months later, on September 1, the Council of Ministers approved a decree law announcing that foreign Jews residing in Italy would have to leave the country, and defining a Jew as "any person... born of parents both of whom are of the Jewish race." On September 2, the Council of Ministers passed another decree law stating that all persons of the Jewish race were excluded from teaching and from all schools and universities. His Imperial Majesty Victor Emmanuel III, king and emperor, signed both measures.

On October 6, the Fascist Grand Council — the highest political body in the regime — adopted a series of resolutions to the effect that measures against the Jewish race formed part of a broader process in which the Jewish problem was simply the domestic aspect of a more general racial situation made necessary by the creation of the Italian empire. The resolutions spelled out in detail prohibitions against mixed marriages, set guidelines for the expulsion for foreign Jews and for the further definition of the Jewish race (adding, for example, persons born of Jewish fathers and Aryan mothers), and laying out areas of Italian life for which legislation would exclude Jews. A series of exemptions were listed for people who fought for Italy as volunteers in World War I, were Fascists of the first hour, and others for whom a special commission would make allowance.

How does one explain these measures in a country in which Jews constituted less than one tenth of one percent of the population, and in which in modern times Jews had experienced extraordinary degrees of freedom, assimilation, and success? Can we simply identify racism as a fundamental component of all "fascisms" and leave it at that? Certainly the anti-Semitic policies of 1938 came as a shock to most Italians, including Fascist Italians, for the Fascist movement itself had counted Jews among its earliest adherents and leaders, the Fascist regime had included a number of Jews in high-ranking ministerial positions, and Mussolini had exhibited little personal anti-Semitism in his early career — indeed, it was an open secret in Italy that for more than a decade and a half he had maintained as his most intimate lover and one of his closest advisers a Jewish woman, Margherita Sarfatti.

Over the last three decades a growing body of scholarly literature, both Italian and foreign, has examined the question of Fascist anti-Semitic policies. By far the broadest consensus on the question is that first offered by the eminent Italian historian, the late Renzo De Felice, whose multi-volumed biography of Mussolini has long set the basic terms of the debate over the meaning and nature of Italian Fascism. In 1961, De Felice's exhaustive study, *Storia degli ebrei italiani sotto il fascismo* (4th revised edition 1988) staked out the main argument that Fascist anti-Semitic measures were adopted by a Mussolini who, while himself never rigidly pro- or anti-Semitic, did so because of "his basic conviction that, to make the Italian-German alliance hard as iron, it was necessary to eliminate every major difference between the two regimes." In other words, Mussolini made the decision because of political calculation designed to demonstrate the ideological solidarity of the Rome-Berlin Axis.

In a more recent commentary in the Italian press, De Felice went so far as to argue that "I know that Italian Fascism is free from the accusation of genocide, and entirely beyond the shadow of guilt for the Holocaust."

Subsequent writers have elaborated variations of this theme — that, for example the Italian people as well as the Catholic Church rejected the racism of the Fascist measures, and did whatever they could to ignore or get around the real persecution of the Nazis after the German occupation of northern Italy in 1943-45. These are the arguments made, for example, by scholars Meir Michaelis in his *Mussolini and the Jews* (1978) and Susan Zuccotti in her *The Italians and the Holocaust* (1987). Others followed with examinations of how Fascist civilians and military officials in occupied zones outside Italy worked to undercut the impact of German persecutions, citing the case of regions such as Croatia, France, Tunisia (I think here of the research by Daniele Carpi and Jonathan Steinberg).

These and other works have given rise to the notion which underpins the very conference in which we are participating this weekend, that of *"italiani brava gente"* — that is, a warm, fuzzy view of Italians as humanitarians, in stark contrast to the bestial Germans who are the center of the controversy swirling around Daniel Goldhagen's recent book, *Hitler's Willing Executioners*. George Mosse, himself a Jewish refugee from Nazism and one of the leading scholars of Fascism, remarked many years ago that for him the difference between Nazism and Fascism was "a difference of national character."

Such views have given rise in recent years to a flurry of conferences and public programs that constitute a virtual "Italy and the Jews" industry that at once contributes to cross-ethnic discourse, generates easy funding for academic programs, and provides a message that Italian American audiences find comforting.

Against the interpretive grain of this wave of positive scholarship, a few authors — including this presenter and Italian writer Alessandro Stille — have challenged the simplicity of the "brava gente" argument, complicating the discussions, for example, by raising questions about the existence and meaning of Jewish Fascism.

Today I would like to take the issue a step further, suggesting ways in which we might want to place Fascist anti-Semitic policies in a wider context that challenges the notion of an almost anecdotal emergence of measures produced at the political whim of Mussolini. True, Italian Fascist measures did not go to the extremes that they did in Nazi Germany, and there was no Italian "Holocaust" equivalent to that perpetrated by the Nazis. And Jews did fare better under Italian jurisdiction. My argument is, however, that Fascist anti-Semitism was not just a late manifestation derived from a set of special circumstances in 1938; that its roots go back much further, and began to manifest themselves quite soon after the establishment of the Fascist regime, that Italian Fascist anti-Semitic policy was intimately tied to aspects of Fascist ideology as well as to Mussolini's personal metamorphosis; and that together these factors constitute a "turning point" in the historical evolution of Fascism after coming to power.

This is, of course, not the venue for an exhaustive narrative of the record of anti-Semitic or racist ideology in modern Italian history, nor can we recount here the details of the Fascist movement toward anti-Semitism. A brief, if selective and inadequate, overview will have to suffice.

Mussolini was appointed prime minister of Italy in October 1922, after three years of political manipulation and Blackshirt violence. Over the next four years he laid foundations for his personal dictatorship and by 1927 had consolidated the essential bases of the Fascist regime. It was in this context that on May 26, 1927 he delivered to the Italian parliament his important

"Speech of the Ascension," a detailed examination of long range programs and policies for the future. This speech for all intents and purposes represented Mussolini's first, if perhaps only partially articulated, foray into racial thinking. Mussolini, who had read Oswald Spengler's *Decline of the West* and the population theories of Richard Korherr, was preoccupied with demographic issues in a broad sense, raising concerns about Italian "decline" and "decadence" — he spoke at length about the physical and mental strength of the people, about fertility, "vitality," motherhood, biological vigor, and the overall "health of the *razza italiana*." The connections that took him from these ideas to more theoretical notions of race were not very difficult to make.

This was also the same period in which Mussolini began thinking deliberately and openly about Fascist totalitarianism, for any concern with the future was inextricably linked to Fascism's ability to reshape and mold ordinary Italians into what the regime's ideologues called the "new man." Fascist totalitarianism demanded not only biological and physical vitality, but a new "morality," and to this end all the institutional agencies of the new regime were to be employed. All established social values and systems were to be jettisoned and replaced by Fascist sensibilities and myths, and the regime would, in the words of Italian scholar Emilio Gentile, seek to "sacralize" the political and social order to accomplish this goal.

While preoccupied with these long-range matters, Mussolini himself underwent a serious internal evolution during the years from 1928 to 1932, with results that would move Fascism and the regime in a direction that I would argue would end logically with the racial measures of 1938. Put simply, Mussolini became increasingly isolated from those associates and advisors with whom he had worked closely since the founding of the Fascist movement in 1919, pushing many of them to the margins of power or purging them from his inner circle altogether. His governing style was more and more that of a micro-manager through whose hands all decisions had to pass. Moreover, as the cult of the all powerful *duce* became one of the central motifs of Fascist propaganda, he himself was captured by his very own myth. In December 1931, with the sudden death of his brother Arnaldo, Mussolini lost the one man on whom he relied heavily and whom he trusted without reservation. His isolation became more complete as he grew estranged from Margehrita Sarfatti, to whom he had been attached since 1913, and by 1932 she no longer had open access to him. As their relationship dissipated, her position within the regime grew precarious.

Indeed, the case of Sarfatti was most suggestive in regard to the racial question. In 1928, Mussolini had suddenly unleashed a tirade against the Italian Zionists and had used Sarfatti, who had been born into a prominent Jewish family, to warn the Jewish community about their loyalties. That same year, in anticipation of the signing of the Lateran Accords with the Vatican, Sarfatti had quietly converted to Catholicism. Nevertheless, her powerful influence in the cultural and intellectual life of the country had sparked resentment among many extremist Fascists, and now they began to criticize her advocacy of artistic modernism as a foreign, decadent, "Bolshevik," and finally as a "Jewish" internationalism that ran counter to Fascism's values. Her principal enemy in this regard was Roberto Farinacci, a leading Fascist intransigent and one of the major Jew-baiters of the Fascist movement. As the 1930s opened, Farinacci and his minions intensified their attacks and increasingly raised the "Jewish question" in her regard.

Mussolini's personal trajectory and Sarfatti's fate were signs of a broader transformation. In 1932, Mussolini appointed as secretary of the Fascist Party Achille Starace, a particularly simple-minded man whose personal worship of the *duce* knew no bounds. Under Starace's leadership, which lasted until 1939, the Fascist Party became a major instrument of totalitarian policy, attempting to force Italians to change their outward manner and customs as well as their values — Starace sought to discipline and harden the Italian people, to impose a cult of physical fitness on the country, to dress Italians in uniforms and substitute the Fascist salute for the bourgeois handshake, to militarize society and forge Italians into a nation of warriors.

It was during the so-called "Starace era" that Fascist racial policies began to unfold, both as a logical collorary of the new totalitarian programs and in the context of Mussolini's increasingly aggressive foreign policy. Hitler's coming to power in Germany in 1933 was a pivotal factor in this regard. Without delving into a detailed examination of Mussolini's attitudes toward Hitler and the Germans, suffice it to say that his views were at best ambivalent, for while he loathed and feared Hitler, he was also fascinated by German power and overwhelmed by Hitler's seeming mastery over the German people. Starting with 1933, and with increasing intensity, Mussolini began to articulate publicly conflicting thoughts about race and the Jews, ridiculing Hitler's anti-Semitic obsession while simultaneously unleashing an anti-Jewish press campaign in Italy through his own anti-Semitic mouthpiece, Telesio Interlandi, editor of *Il Tevere*; he gave encouragement to the Fascist racists centered around Farinacci and the defrocked priest Giovanni Preziosi, the most ideologically committed anti-Semite in the Fascist movement.

Around Mussolini a pro-German faction began to exercise growing influence, including his son-in-law Galeazzo Ciano. Ominously, in March 1934, Mussolini's mounting anti-Jewish statements reached a new level when Fascist police agents arrested sixteen anti-Fascists in Piedmont for conspiracy against the regime, and it turned out that fourteen of those arrested were Jews, among them distant cousins of Sarfatti. In his own mind, Mussolini now linked Italian Jews with anti-Fascism.

Some scholars have suggested that in view of the fact that Mussolini's record of public comments on the Jews was so inconsistent, that his final determination in 1938 to enact anti-Semitic measures must have been influenced by his ever-closer relationship with Hitler. I would argue, however, that no matter how conflicting his public utterances, the very fact of inconsistency on the part of the man who had become the all-powerful dictator of the nation created a moral climate in which Fascist anti-Semites could operate with ever-greater certainty and opened up possibilities for the unfolding of official racist policy. When Mussolini said, for example, that "Every regime has not only the right but the duty to eliminate untrustworthy elements from positions of authority," or that "Jewish blood is always Jewish blood and does not change," the signals received by his audiences were unmistakable.

One further aspect of Fascist policy in the mid-1930s must be mentioned: the impact of Mussolini's colonial ambitions and especially the war in Ethiopia. Observers have long noted — and here I cite the early work by Luigi Preti, *I miti dell'impero e della razza nell'Italia degli anni '30* (1965) — that the policies implemented in Libya in the 1920s and in Ethiopia after the conquest of that country in 1935-36 were closely linked to the evolution of official anti-Semitism later in the decade. It is, for example, difficult to describe the Fascist "pacification" of Libya, in which tens of thousands of Libyans were wiped out or relocated, as anything short of systematic genocide. And the racial policies imposed both on Italian soldiers and on the indigenous population of Ethiopia after the conquest — decrees against miscegenation, and the growing fears of Mussolini and Fascist ideologues about mixing of the races there — were bound to be connected to anti-Jewish thought.

In retrospect, then, Mussolini's decision in 1938 to adopt anti-Semitic measures must be seen not only in the context of his diplomatic break with the Western powers over Ethiopia, the formation of the Rome-Berlin Axis, and the search for a formal military alliance with Germany — in other words, in the context of the Hitler's influence — but against the larger backdrop of a decade-long "turning point" in the internal history of the Fascist regime. Domestic programs and totalitarian ambitions combined with foreign and colonial enterprises to move Mussolini in the direction of Fascist racial policy, and the roots of those policies were to be found, if not in Italian culture or "character," then certainly in deep-seated geopolitical concerns and social tensions that Fascism claimed to want to resolve for the Italian nation. In doing so, Mussolini and the Fascist ruling class made many Italians, and the mechanisms of the Italian state, complicit in one of Italy's darkest hours.

In the broad context of the Holocaust, Italians as a whole may well have been *"brava gente,"* but let us not as a consequence go to the extreme position of editing modern Italian history so that the record reads as we would like it to have read. Italians created Fascism. Mussolini was not an Italian hero to Hitler's villain, and Italian Fascism was not morally or politically "better" that German Nazism.

PHILIP V. CANNISTRARO

Queens College

NATIONALISMS AND INTERNATIONALISM: THE RESPONSE OF ITALIAN JEWS TO FASCISM

There have never been large numbers of Jews in Italy in absolute terms but nonetheless their history provides important insights into Italy's broader history. This is not just because Jews have played important roles in many fields of Italian life but because their position has acted as a political barometer for a whole series of other aspects of Italian society not necessarily directly related to Jews. This paper is part of a wider study of Italian nationalism in which the Italian state's relationship with the Jews of Italy and the Jews' own relationship with the state are crucial.

For most of *Risorgimento* the Jews of Italy supported the unification of the country and the governments which followed unification and indeed many took an active part in both. In the first years of unified Italy, there was little real political choice for an Italian Jew. The Risorgimento was a mix of liberal, secular movements which promised emancipation for the Jews and political and economic equality for the social classes to which most Jews belonged. Perhaps some were indifferent to unification but none were against it. By the end of the century there was a greater political choice for all Italians, including Jews. On the one hand, the liberal establishment of the *Risorgimento* had spawned an authoritarian nationalism which led to fascism and on the other there were the various forms of socialism and liberalism. For some Italians there was also the possibility of organized political Catholicism. For the Jews there was Zionism.

Using memoirs, community records and contemporary Jewish publications as well as published sources, this paper will present the choices which were made by Italian Jews as individuals, families and communities and will describe the tensions that these choices engendered as well as the differences over time or due to class or regional provenance. The aim is to see how Jews reacted to fascism rather than how they were treated by the regime.

Jews in Italy between World War I and the Racial Laws of 1938 were for the most part like their non-Jewish fellow citizens, only more so. They were more politically active; compared to the population at large more were either actively fascist or anti-fascist. The fascists were more patriotic and more devoted to Mussolini, the antifascists: communists, socialists and liberals, were more dedicated to whichever group they belonged. Obviously Jews were not going to work within organized Catholic politics but they could become Zionists and few were lukewarm on that topic; opinions were strongly held in favor or against.

These choices sometimes coexisted in single families. In a fictionalized memoir, Umberto Scazzocchio describes one sister as a socialist, a brother as a nationalist who becomes a fascist and his own character as following his elder brother only to become disillusioned long before the racial laws.[1] There were no Zionists in the account but the real world was not short of examples of families which crossed various divides; the most remarkable were the Sereni brothers in Rome, Enzo a dedicated Zionist and Emilio a leader of the Italian Communist Party.

Although the mold of Italian politics was breaking before 1915, it was Italy's participation in World War I and the world events which accompanied the war which finally destroyed the Risorgimento set-up.

The Effects of World War I on Italian Jews

The patriotic nationalism which swept the European middle classes enveloped Italian Jews as well. The only Jews who showed any hesitation towards the war were some of those who were socialists but as socialists not in any way as Jews. Institutionally, Jewish Communities were extremely patriotic and took up the war aims of *Irredentismo*, the "redemption" of those parts of Italy still in the Austrian empire; there were prayers and sermons for victory like this one given by the rabbi of Milan:

> Thou denizen of the Heavens, look with compassion upon our country, Italy, which is a fatherland so dear to us children of Israel and which with such magnanimity has taken up arms to redeem and liberate a great part of its people from centuries of oppression, to shatter the iron yoke and to give them the national liberty which is so desired. May You, King of Kings, bless our beloved monarch Victor Emmanuel III, symbol of loyalty towards all citizens without distinction.[2]

Two weeks after the major Italian defeat at Caporetto, *Il Vessillo Israelitico* was not only patriotic but very nationalistic and perhaps even un-Jewish or anti-Jewish:

we give our readers, Italian Israelites, a single word — which is an exhortation: save the fatherland! Drive out the foreigner from our land which has been profaned. Out with the barbarians now and forever. And if, in order to reach the aim, we must make sacrifice of our loved ones — or of our most beloved ideals — or ourselves if necessary, then we all know how to make the sacrifice.[3]

In all the patriotic rhetoric throughout Europe in the Great War, few people even considered sacrificing ideals for the nation. Most presumed that there was unity between "most beloved ideals" and the "fatherland."

The *Vessillo* refers to the war as the "war of redemption" meaning the conquest of the "unredeemed" parts of Italy, *le terre irridente*, Trent and Trieste for all, and for many, Dalmatia.

At the end of the war, the victory speech and sermon at Ferrara on 8 December 1918 by the president of the community, Leone Ravenna ("Oh! Fulgidissima sorte della nazione italiana" Oh! Most dazzling fortune of the Italian Nation), and the chief rabbi, Gustavo Castelbolognesi ("this Israelite Community where the burning love of the native soil is traditional") presaged the support for Fascism by Ravenna and many other Ferrarese Jews described by Giorgio Bassani in his Ferrara stories.[4]

Two major events of the war affected Italian Jews, the Russian Revolution and the Balfour Declaration, which for communists and Zionists brought their goals one step closer, while the effects of the war itself provided the foundations for the growth of the fascist movement.

Fascism

It is safe to say that most Italian Jews accepted and supported the status quo of Italy and of themselves within Italy. Even before Mussolini took power in 1922, there were Jews who supported the nationalist and radical right. One, Oscar Sinigaglia was an industrialist in steel who supported and funded D'Annunzio's expedition which in practice annexed Fiume[5] in 1919 while there were a number of Jewish volunteers who were recognized as such while the action was taking place.[6]

There were five Jews at the founding meeting of the fascist party in March 1919 (one of whom, Cesare Goldman, booked the room), three Jews were killed in the fascist struggle for power and earned the title of 'fascist martyrs' and the banker Giuseppe Toeplitz was apparently a major contributor.[7]

One of Mussolini's closest early collaborators was the nationalist, Aldo Finzi. He was an airman and later became Undersecretary at the Ministry of the Interior. He had been one of D'Annunzio's companions in his propaganda flights over Vienna during the war and then went on to be a committed fascist, on occasions pushing Mussolini into action. Already in August 1922 he went to Alberto Albertini, owner of *Corriere della Sera* and representative of the Milanese upper middle classes saying that there would soon be a coup d'ètat.[8] During the so-called March on Rome, it was Finzi who apparently convinced Mussolini to hold out for the prime ministership rather than a mere post in the government.[9] Finzi was closely involved in the murder of Matteotti at least to the extent of knowing about it if not of having organized it and he was almost the only person to lose his job after the murder. There can be no doubt of his strong commitment to fascism until 1925. Michele Sarfatti has argued that Finzi was not Jewish as far as the later fascist persecution was concerned though he was perceived as such. There were other Jews who were senior and influential fascists; like Guido Jung, Minister of Finance from 1932 to 1935 and figures like Margherita Sarfatti, Mussolini's mistress and first biographer.[10] There was also Carlo Foà, physiologist, editor of the Fascist review *Gerarchia* along with Sarfatti "in which capacity he did a good deal to mold the party's opinions and policy."[11] There were some like Ettore Ovazza in Turin who were patriotic nationalists during the war and became ardent fascists afterwards combining party positions with official functions in the Jewish Community.[12]

The percentage of Jews who were members of the Fascist Party was higher than the national average. Before the March on Rome there were 739 of whom 216 took part in the march.[13] This was probably around 3 per thousand among the members of the party (the Jews were around one per thousand of the total population) in 1922, reaching a maximum of 4.1% or 5,800 in 1933.[14] The figure corresponds more to the predominantly middle class and white collar, often civil service composition of Italian Jewry, rather than necessarily an ideological commitment to fascism. In fact, Rome, with a poorer and more working class community had fewer Jews who were early Fascists than the rest of country: with more than 12,000 members of the community, only 120 joined the Fascist Party (PNF) in the difficult periods: at the beginning in 1919-20 or the second semester of 1924 (just after the murder of Matteotti), compared with 146 in Trieste (less than 5,000 members) and 129 in Milan (just over 6,000 member).[15] A joke

The Response of Italian Jews to Fascism

at the time went that PNF, Partito Nazionale Fascista actually stood for 'per necessità familiare,' 'for family necessity,' and there were opportunistic fascists in the Jewish communities as well as among Italians at large. Some members of the Di Veroli family in Rome joined the Fascist Party "mainly because it was easier to work and raise a family with a party card than without one."[16]

Others considered politics like the weather, something to be enjoyed or put up with but certainly not changed; the group of brilliant young physicists around Enrico Fermi who worked in via Panisperna and which included a number of Jews was like that:

> As far as they were concerned, politics simply did not exist. And the fascist regime was considered a natural phenomenon, inevitable, a bit tiresome and vulgar in some of its manifestations, but nothing more. Obviously Fermi was a fascist, he was a member of the Italian Academy, and like all the others, put his black shirt on when it was necessary.[17]

For many of those who grew up under fascism, the question was not even posed; for Dan Segre, born just after the March on Rome, "those years were for me a period which was so regular, normal and carefree, and without any yardstick to make comparisons with that I would not be able to say what fascism had which was peculiar. I considered fascism a natural form of organizing society."[18] A young student from Emilia, Aldo Ascarelli, born in 1916 went further, "I was a fascist, my father wasn't but I was, and for a very simple reason: I saw the good things that Mussolini had done."[19]

The 'normality' of fascism was accentuated in the early '30s when the organization of the communities was reformed. The Piedmontese and then Italian states had already given the Jewish communities a special status; this was confirmed and revised in 1931 giving the communities and National Union of Jewish Communities the authority of law. This was particularly relevant in a country where there was no pluralism among the Jews. All were and indeed are, 'orthodox.' In the earlier years of fascism, before their form was introduced, the community authorities had some reservations about Mussolini and the regime. By the end of the '20s most hesitation had disappeared. Not surprisingly, despite the earlier considerable debate within the communities, most of them worked with the government and the governing councils were fascist. They were referred to dismissively by the present Chief Rabbi of Rome, Elio Toaff, as "spineless men who declared themselves 'Italians of the Jewish religion'."[20] In the north, some synagogues modified the prayer for the king by adding "Mussolini, head of the government and Duce of fascism" or that the king reigned "with the enlightened cooperation of the Duce."[21]

When in 1935 the government asked citizens for gold to combat League of Nations sanctions after the Italian invasion of Ethiopia, the queen and thousands gave their wedding rings. The Roman community gave the gold key of the tabernacle, a gold scroll indicator and a silver chandelier. The action was justified by saying that:

> the law only allows the use of sacred objects to be changed if the new use increases their sanctity; thus the community has given these sacred objects, because they could not be destined to a more sacred purpose than the defense of the fatherland.[22]

The patriotism of Italian Jews transcended fascism and later, even persecution. During the Second World War in 1941, the Roman community commemorated Jewish war dead[23] and despite the persecution, when the young Elio Toaff was not allowed to do his military service, he was upset: 'the words "Italy does not need you" wounded me deeply.'[24]

But if the Jewish establishment supported the fascist government and most individuals had a profound loyalty to the country, it was the anti-fascists who for obvious reasons were the most noticed during and after fascism.

The Anti-fascists: Socialists, Communists, Liberals

However one measures Jewish acceptance or support of fascism, it is safe to say that a high proportion of anti-fascists were Jewish right from the beginning. Of the nine Jewish deputies in Parliament in 1921, only one was fascist while none of the 18 senators was.[25] Benedetto Croce's anti-fascist manifesto of 1925 had about 10% Jewish signatories and more than 10% of the contributors to the socialist *Critica sociale* were Jewish. Leaders of the Socialist party like Claudio Treves were Jewish as were many militants.[26] *Giustizia e Libertà* was a liberal socialist antifascist movement, one of whose founders, Carlo Rosselli, was Jewish; in Turin it had such a high proportion of Jews that when Sion Segre Amar was introduced to the group, Carlo Levi exclaimed, only half in jest, 'oh no, another Jew.'[27] The preoccupation was justified; when a number of them were arrested at Ponte Tresa on the Swiss Italian border trying to smuggle anti-fascist material into Italy in 1934; eleven out of the 15 were Jewish so the immediate reaction by the state media was to emphasize the group's' Jewishness.

The event brought a strong reaction from the Turinese establishment, particularly Ettore Ovazza even if he mixed Zionism and GL's socialism into a single bundle. He criticized them at the time and when the Racial Laws were passed, he put some of the blame on the antifascist Jews:

> "Dear coreligionists. You will all remember because it only happened yesterday that it was from Turin, from our city which has borne such merit in the history of the fatherland and of fascism in particular, that the spark came which gave rise to the first sign of antisemitism. This, it must be said, was immediately quashed through the Duce's personal intervention. Whose fault was it? You all know the answer; of a group of young madcaps poisoned by false ideologies. If I bring this up when it would be easier to remain silent, it is because those anarchoid left-wing ideologies are entwined with a proclamation of Zionist faith. Zionist and therefore anti-national.[28]

Although one member of GL, Vittorio Foa, has said that "There were many Jews in the Resistance with me, but I always felt their commitment was not so much an expression of their Jewishness as a sign of their integration"others were very conscious of their complex identity. In a speech to the Jewish Youth Congress in Leghorn in 1924, Nello Rosselli, Carlo's brother, declared:

> I am a Jew who does not go to the Temple on Sabbath, who does not know Hebrew, who does not observe any religious rites. Nonetheless, I hold my Jewishness dear to me and I want to defend it from any deviation.[30]

Among the Communists, the Jewish contribution was no less than in other movements though not surprisingly, the party identity took precedence overall else. They were the least "Jewish" of the antifascists and neither emphasize or rediscover it like the Zionists or play it down like the fascists. For many, it is by their own accounts, irrelevant. For Giuliana Pontecorvo, the sister of Bruno, the physicist who defected to the Soviet Union and wife of a Communist Party militant Duccio Tabet "politics and the party came first, even before the children. Even though we were Jewish, we didn't feel it."[31]

Emilio Sereni began as a Zionist but went on to become a leader of the Communist Party. Another senior communist who was Jewish and whose militancy began in the '30s was Umberto Terracina.

Zionism

The Zionists were a minority within Italian Jewry and were treated with suspicion and fear by those Jews who were loyal to the regime or those who wanted to be considered such.[33] Nonetheless despite the reaction of the rest of the Community, for most of the 20 years between World War I and the Racial Laws, Italian Zionists were strongly patriotic and many combined action in favor of a Jewish State with a strong attachment to Italy, sentiments which of course were and are found in other western countries where Jews are well integrated.

Zionism, the aim of creating a Jewish State, was for other Jews, not Italians. There was no contradiction between being loyal Italians and wanting a Jewish State. On the contrary, the two aims could be complementary; *Il Vessillo Israelitico* was very clear in its position; in an editorial on the London Zionist Conference in 1919, they agreed with Nordau's proposal for a Jewish state in the future and accepted that it would take time. They criticized "the fanaticism of some" who considered the proposal too modest and explained their own position:

> We keep faith with the principles which we have put forward in this journal for a long time and declare that for us, it is a beautiful and generous act to render the sacred land of the prophets into a safe haven, a center of free life for those of our brothers in faith who *do not have a fatherland*. But for Italian Jews, the natural fatherland is Italy which has given us and gives us the most perfect equality with all other citizens and for whom we too fought with a filial heart. The publication of the roll of honor listing the part taken by Italian Jewry in this war will be an open affirmation of Italianess which we are proud of. [emphasis in original].[34]

The *Zionist Rassegna Mensile di Israel* started in 1925; most issues faced specifically Zionist problems, the law in Palestine, the League of Nations and the Mandate. It reprinted Achad-Ham (Asher Ginsberg)'s 1889 article analyzing nationalism and Jewishness.

Most Zionists felt not only that there was nothing incompatible between being patriotic Italian and working for the foundation of a Jewish state but that the two positions reinforced one another. The strongest exponent of Italian Zionism at this time, Dante Lattes, made an implicit link between Zionism and Italian unification "it is the desire of all Jews that Italy take part in the resurgence [*risorgimento*] of the Orient."[35]

Only a few expressed doubts at this early stage; Emanuel Segre, father of Sion Segre Amar, was one of the earliest to see possible contradictions between fascism and either Zionism or socialism and to express his doubts clearly. Just before he died in 1923 he wrote a letter saying:

> I have always been a fervent Italian like all my family which has also given shining proof of the fact, and I have always acted as such. But as a true Jew, because I consider it an honor to be one, long before Fascism rose, I was a Zionist. I see and feel the whole beauty of the ideals of Fascism; I share the aspirations to make best use of all the best forces of this our Italy, including those of the proletariat for whose well-being I have always had a lively sympathy. But it is with real pain that I perceive a tendency in fascism to go against Zionism.[36]

In fact very few Italians actually moved to Palestine in these years. The first clearly Zionist move was apparently that of Neomi Levi Mortara who went in 1925, followed by the Spagnoletto family in 1926 and then Enzo Sereni in 1927.[37] Sereni and his wife Ada are certainly the best known of Italian Zionists because of their joint commitment to the idea of Israel expressed practically by their foundation of a kibbutz, because of Enzo's death after being parachuted into occupied Italy in 1944 where he was captured and killed, and finally because of Ada's work in organizing illegal immigration into Palestine before 1948.[38]

By the end of the 1920s, there was also a revisionist Zionist movement in Italy; their strongly nationalist and anti-British point of view which was close to that of the fascist Jews.

But some Jews, both from the right and from the left, were very anti-Zionist. Already in the first months of fascism, the President of Turinese Community, Ernesto Ovazza rejected an appeal for aid to Zionism:

> As President of this Community I have received your... petition in favor of creating a Jewish national homeland in Palestine. While I consider with faith and sincere pleasure every effort and every generous act to-

ward the suffering and persecuted Jewish masses, I must with equal sincerity affirm that I cannot as an Italian participate in a program of such extreme consequences, particularly now in this moment, when we have a greater duty to participate in the front lines of the reconstruction of our country. In few nations in the world does the Jew enjoy such consideration as in Italy. We do not believe that in order to feel intimately connected to our fellow Jews suffering unjust persecutions it is necessary to create a second Fatherland. It is not selfishness that stimulates my firm stand on this point, it is the higher sentiment of the Fatherland which, from the ranks of the Thousand to the soldiers of Vittorio Veneto, so many of the purest heroes of Jewish blood have died for.[39]

It is possible to find similar remarks from upper middle class Establishment Jews in other countries at the time, but Ernesto's son, Ettore went much further in his anti-Zionism founding *La Nostra Bandiera*, and after the Racial Laws organizing a raid to destroy the Florence Zionist monthly, *Israel* and beat up its staff.

On the other side of the political divide, Claudio Treves accused the Zionists of being pawns in the hands of British imperialism "This is not the way to found the new Jerusalem."[40] Obviously Zionism was used as a stick with which to beat all Jews: it was a kind of crypto-antisemitism which questioned Jewish loyalty to Italy. When this happened as in Nov. 1928 with an article apparently by Mussolini[41] himself entitled "Religione o nazione," there was a rush to show how patriotic Italian Jews were. The government used Zionism as a double edged weapon: at home to attack all Jews and abroad to push Italian interests against either the British or the Arabs depending on the moment. Again in 1933-4 there was a campaign of anti-Zionism which elicited another wave of protestations of patriotism from the Jewish establishment.

Conclusions

The way in which Jews reacted to fascism corresponded to their stronger commitment to Italy and the Italian state than the non-Jewish population. Most Jews were northern or Tuscan and middle class; in general terms this meant that they had a higher than national average match with the regions and classes which supported fascism. On the other side, these same social and regional characteristics combined with some essentially Jewish features meant that there were also many highly committed Jewish antifascists. Some of them, like the Rosselli brothers were actually children or grandchildren of people strongly committed to Mazzinian democracy, others had been influenced by transalpine and Italian concepts of socialism. And even though Italian Jews had fewer of the internationalist qualities that are found in Jews in other countries, many were still strongly imbued with a distrust of too much nationalism and therefore accepted and supported either a socialist internationalism or Jewish nationalism. Institutional Jewry was very patriotic and establishment and therefore very fascist (in some cases even after the laws). During the First World War, they were certainly no more nationalistic than other Italians of similar class and regional background, with the exception perhaps of a decreasing number of Catholics who were still opposed to an Italian state.

The split within the Jewish communities was made much more severe by fascism and the results much more dire. The physiological differences of political choice open to Jews in Italy were accentuated by the presence of a regime which sought to be totalitarian; the Jewish supporters of the regime were therefore forced into positions which were much more extreme than those in Britain or France, say, who supported this or that government. This division became all the more apparent when the Racial Laws were passed and made cooperation between all shades of Jewish opinion that much more difficult.

In theory, there was also the religious option; avoiding active politics which in theory was open to Italian Jews as much as it was to Jews in other countries. In practice it was not taken up apart from very small numbers who followed the post World War One movements of religious revival which struck Christians as much as Jews.

By the beginning of the '30s, divisions had hardened with the Jewish establishment and community organizations declaring open and strong support for the regime, while the antifascists too became more convinced in their opposition. Regional differences too, reflect the overall Italian picture with northern communities showing both much stronger opposition and support of fascism than Rome. Naturally in the final phases of fascism, Jewish opposition did grow, manifesting itself in a high proportion of members of the Resistance.

Nonetheless, the attachment of Jews to Italy and to their single cities remained and was borne out by their behavior after World War II. It is hardly surprising that the relation of mutual advantage between Italy and her Jewish citizens was seriously damaged not only by the persecution but by the fact that the post-war settlement left a religious party holding most of the power and that therefore their contribution to public life became almost zero; the surprise was that so many remained in Italy or came back and continued to contribute in other fields emphasizing the commitment to Italy.

JAMES WALSTON
Rome International University

---

[1] Scazzocchio 1974.
[2] Quoted by Tullia Catalan 1997: 1287. For a general picture of Italian Jews and World War I, see Toscano 1990.
[3] *Vessillo Israelitico* 15-30 Nov. 1917: 485.
[4] *Vessillo Israelitico* 15-28 Feb. 1919: 54-60, Bassani's *Storie ferraresi*.
[5] Caviglia 1996: 167, Clarke 206.
[6] *Vessillo Israelitico* LXVIII 15-31 May 1920
[7] De Felice 1977: 89.
[8] Alberto Albertini cit. in Tasca 1995: 392.
[9] Tasca 1995: 509.
[10] Sarfatti 1997: 1633. De Felice (1977: 492), however, points out that by 1942 Finzi "had again moved closer to [Jewish] community life."
[11] Roth 1946: 510.
[12] For the story of the Ovazza family see Stille 1993: 17-90.
[13] Segre 1997: 257.
[14] Sarfatti 1997: 1632 and 1654.
[15] Caviglia 1996: 198.
[16] Stille 1993: 179.
[17] Mafai 1992: 64.
[18] Segre 1990: 63.
[19] Pezzana 1997: 35.
[20] Toaff 1987: 4
[21] Toaff 1987; 16, Segre Amar 1987: 61. For a general discussion of the reform, see De Felice 1977: 123-32.
[22] *La Comunità Israelitica* UV December 1935 (2) p. 2 cit. Caviglia 1996: 209.
[23] Caviglia 1996: 211.
[24] Toaff 1987: 17.
[25] Segre 1997: 257.
[26] Sarfatti 1997: 1633-4. With underground organization which obviously did not note member' Jewishness, comparable figures to the PNF are not possible.
[27] Stille 1993: 99.
[28] Segre Amar 1987: 132-3.
[29] Stille 1993: 323.

[30] De Felice 1977: 108.
[31] Mafai 1992: 112-3.
[32] For an account of the development of Emilio and Enzo Sereni see Emilio's daughter Clara's memoir of the family, Sereni 1993.
[33] Toaff 1987: 4.
[34] *Vessillo Israelitico* 15-28 Feb. 1919: 45.
[35] Quoted in De Felice 1977: 103. Lattes' book *Sionismo* was published in 1928.
[36] Quoted in *La Rassegna Mensile di Israel* Feb. 1926 I (4-5): 184
[37] Segre 1997: 253.
[38] Sereni A. 1994.
[39] Stille 1993: 45 quoting a reprint of the letter *la Nostra Bandiera* 1 May 1934.
[40] *Resto del Carlino* 23 May 1920, quoted in De Felice 1977: 69.
[41] De Felice 1977: 116.

Works Cited

Philip Cannistraro, Brian Sullivan. *The Duce's Other Woman*. New York: Merrow, 1993.

Tullia Catalan. "Le communità ebraiche dall'unità alla rima guerra mondiale" Corrado Vivanti (Ed.) *Storia d'italia. Annali 11. Gli ebrei in italia* Vol.II Dall'emancipazione a oggi. Turin: Einaudi, 1997. Pp. 1245-90.

Stefano Caviglia. *L'identità salvata. Gli ebrei di Roma tra fede e nazione*. 1870-1938. Bari: Laterza, 1996.

Martin Clark. *Modern Italy 1871-1982*. London: Longman, 1984.

Renzo De Felice. *Storia degli ebrei italiani sotto il fascismo*. Milan: Mondadori, 1977.

Miriam Mafai. *Il lungo freddo. Storia di Bruno Pontecorvo, lo scienziato chescelse l'URSS*. Milan: Mondadori, 1992.

Angelo Pezzana. *Quest'anno a Gerusalemme. Gli ebrei italiani in Israele*. Milan: Corbaccio, 1997.

Cecil Roth. *The History of the Jews of Italy*. Philadelphia: The Jewish Publication Society of America, 1946.

Michele Sarfatti. "Gli ebrei negli anni del fascismo" Vivanti Corrado (Ed.) *Storia d'italia. Annali 11. Gli ebrei in Italia* Vol. II *Dall'emancipazione a oggi*. Turin: Einaudi, 1997. Pp. 1623-1764.

Umberto Scazzocchio. *Uomini e donne solamente*. Bologna: Cappelli, 1974.

Dan Vittorio Segre. *Storia di un ebreo fortunato*. Milan: Bompiani, 1990. (*Memoirs of a Fortunate Jew*. Bethesda: Adler & Adler, 1987)

———. "Saggio Storico" in Pezzana Angelo *Quest'anno a Gerusalemme. Gli ebrei italiani in Israele*. Milan: Corbaccio, 1997. Pp. 249-99.

Sion Segre Amar. *Il Mio Ghetto*. Milan: Garzanti, 1987.

Ada Sereni. *I clandestini del mare*. Milan: Mursia, 1994. (First Ed. 1973)

Clara Sereni. *Il gioco dei regni*. Florence, 1993.

Alexander Stille. *Benevolence and Betrayal*. London: Vintage, 1993.
Angelo Tasca. *Nascita e avvento del fascismo*. Florence: La Nuova Italia, 1995. (First Ed. 1950)
Elio Toaff. *Perfidi giudei. Fratelli maggiori*. Milan: Mondadori, 1987.
Mario Toscano. "Gli Ebrei Italiani e la Prima Guerra Mondiale (1915-1918): Tra Crisi Religiosa e Fremiti Patriottici" in *Clio* I (1990). Pp. 79-97
_____. *Identità e integrazione. L'esperienza ebraica in Germania e l'Italia dall'illuminismo al fascismo*. Milan: Franco Angeli, 1998.

CHILD OF THE GHETTO

"The opposite of love is not hatred: it is indifference."
Eli Wiesel

When I was invited to be part of a Symposium on the Italian Jewish Experience, my instinctive reaction was to respond negatively. I knew that the prevailing belief is that the Italian people in general, and the Catholic Church in particular, had done the utmost to come in aid of the Italian Jews during the darkest period in the modern history of mankind; this theory is somewhat in conflict with my own experience, and I feared that my little voice would be drowned in the ocean of this nearly one-sided chorus.

Eventually I caved in. Direct testimony of that period is dwindling down rapidly and I came to the realization that it was my duty to contribute my knowledge of the facts as I have witnessed them.

I don't mean to posit that Italy was in the same league as Germany where virtually no one came in succour of their Jewish fellow citizens. In my first written assignment as a student at Columbia University on the subject of the Holocaust, I emphatically asserted that the generous behavior of the Italians stood out when compared to that of almost all other Europeans. If I am here to recount my story, I owe it, at least in part, to those people of good will who shared their food and shelter with us, sometimes at grave risks to their own lives.

I simply wish to put into perspective the facts as recorded by one child, born in the Jewish Ghetto of a small village called Pitigliano, as she grows into an adolescent and becomes an adult. The child is endowed with the acute spirit of observation of an artist, an incisive memory, and a keen sense of justice. Ultimately it was the latter, more than any other consideration, that compelled me to accept to be part of this Symposium and to talk also for those who are no longer here to speak for themselves. However, my emphasis will not be on the Holocaust per sè. Most people, by now, know more or less accurately of the atrocious, gruesome reality of the annihilation camps. Very few know of the years that preceded the actual deportation and destruction.

Our suffering as Italian Jews, on Italian soil, during the years between 1937 and 1943, and the ambiguous, neurotic aftermath at the end of the war, the still present feeling of alienation that had accompanied us for so many years, the marginalization, the lack of direction, which rendered impossible a full return to normalcy, are all things that must be heard. From 1937 to 1943 the Italian Jews, absolutely not guilty of any crime, and in the whole exceptionally worthy people, were offended, tyrannized, scoffed at and wounded in their pride, deprived of their employment, thrown out of schools and of the Army, denied the ration card without which one could not buy provisions, and the youngest of us felt gripped by shame and destroyed in our right to life. During the year 1943 concentration camps proliferated throughout Italy, and two of them were indeed death camps.

The majority of Italians and the Vatican still remained silent.

The revisionist approach embraced by most, the distortion of facts, through ignorance or malice or both, is what I must counteract.

How facts have been distorted, will be better illustrated with a joke made up by my brother Gino. "Do you know," he asks a friend, "how many Jews there are in Italy?" The friend hesitantly answers, "twenty, thirty thousand perhaps?" "No," replies my brother: "at least 50 million." The friend is puzzled. "Yes," says Gino, "if it is true what every Italian Catholic claims that he or she saved at least one Jew, then there are at least 50 million Jews in Italy!"

This is a joke, of course; but like all jokes it has its basis solidly grounded in reality. The people who claimed to have saved one or more Jews proliferated soon after the end of World War II, even in my small village where we knew one by one who had been sympathetic with our plight (very few), who had shown indifference (the majority), and who had been downright hostile.

Today, in addition to accepting this type of distortion as reality, from the part of most people, there is a general tendency to want to forget. Also among the Jews I have heard people say, "Why dig into the past? Let bygones be bygones." But in the sage words of Catholic philosopher George Santayana, "Those who cannot remember the past are condemned to repeat it."

A fact is that when Mussolini started his hateful campaign against the Jews, it was immediately adopted by all of the press, with not one voice of dissent. The Jesuit magazine 'Civiltà Cattolica,' that was traditionally close to Vatican thinking, went a step further by writing that "the Christian world must defend itself against the Jewish threat by suspending the civic rights of Jews and returning them to the ghettos." When in 1938 the many months of anti-Jewish campaign did culminate with the onset of the hideous racial laws which abolished one by one all our civic and human rights, only a rare private individual expressed his distaste for such horror. I can recall only one, in fact. In Livorno, a Catholic friend of one of my cousins told him, "Today, I am ashamed to be an italian."

A rare individual indeed. The majority of Italians — when not verbally and physically abusing their Jewish fellow Italians — remained silent. If it is true that a few clergy members helped some Jews, the majority of them kept a convenient silence as well — as did the bishop and all the priests in our village; when not engaging in virulent anti Semitic attacks from their pulpit — as did the parish priest of Latera, a small village a few kilometers from Pitigliano, where the only Jewish family living there was well known for its philanthropic deeds toward its fellow villagers, of course all of them Catholics.

I hear all too often that the Vatican, in the person of Pius XII, had no choice but to remain neutral. That it could have taken a firm stand denouncing the brutalities perpetrated against the Jews, is evidenced by the fact that in the early 40s it did indeed come out of its strict policy of neutrality to condemn Germany for its violation of neutrality of Holland, Belgium and Luxemburg; and long before then, as soon as Hitler came to power on the platform of anti-Semitism, the then Secretary of State Eugenio Pacelli took it upon himself to stipulate and sign a Concordat between the Vatican and the Third Reich. When in 1939 Pacelli was elected Pope assuming the name of Pius XII, Mussolini rushed to rejoice with Hitler that they could then act without fear of the Church's reprisal as regard to the Jews. I seem to remember seeing a newsreel during WWII, showing the Pope on the balcony of Saint Peter blessing the *gagliardetti*, the black fascist pennants, and the Nazi red-and-black banners, and to augur and look forward to the victory of the Axis. And I certainly do remember hearing, in 1957, a long and passionate speech of Pius XII condemning Russia for her invasion of Hungary which was broadcast on national radio. So much for Vatican neutrality.

It is said that eventually Pius XII, albeit unofficially and behind the scenes, left Catholic institutions free to help people in danger regardless of their race or religion, and it appears that a few Jews were indeed saved this way. But it was too little and too late, when the machinery of destruction had already decimated Italian Jewry. The only people I personally know who were sheltered by the Church were my three first cousins in Rome, ranging in age from 5 to 10. They were converted to Catholicism, and the youngest, a female now 60 years old, spent most of her adult life teaching Catechism in Sunday schools. So much for the salvation of Jews.

As a contribution to the historical perspective of those times, here is my story and my experience as an Italian Jew.

I was born in 1926 in the Ghetto of a small village in Tuscany, at a time when Fascism had held sway over the Italians for about 4 years. The Ghetto had ceased to function as such three quarters of a century earlier, when the Statuto Albertino emancipated the Jews, giving them equal rights as all other citizens, and since then the Jews had moved out of those quarters to go and live wherever they pleased or could afford. The reason we still lived there was that Father, being the Rabbi of our exiguous community like his father and his grandfather before him, enjoyed the privilege of living in the same house adjacent to the Temple as his ancestors had. Mother also came from a distinguished Jewish family in Rome. They both had a long line of ancestors who had been living on the Italian soil since antiquity, perhaps, according to historian Cecil Roth, since before the advent of Christianity. Given this background, my identity as an Italian Jew was clearly defined.

Both my parents relentlessly impressed upon us the notion that we must be tolerant, must respect and show compassion for all people no matter how different they might be from us. And we treasured their teachings. Very early on in my life, however, I had the displeasure to realize that whereas we truly respected everybody, from the humblest and poorest to the richest and noble, we were not equally respected by a large segment of the Catholic population. True, it was generally the poorest and most ignoramous of the children that hurled at us anti-Semitic epithets and curses, such as *ebreaccio* and *Amanne per un'ora*, (meaning that the wicked Haman of biblical notoriety, should come back for an hour and destroy all of us — this long before the coming to power of Haman/Hitler). But it is equally true that I never heard an adult stop or reprimand them. The opposite might be the case. Here is but one example. I was standing outside the pharmacy (I was about 4) waiting for my father to come out when a boy, a couple of years older, passed by and yelled in my direction, *ebreaccia*, something like dirty Jew. Instinctively I yelled back, *cristianaccio*. Two steps from me was a Catholic, very tall man. Having witnessed the scene, this "old" man (he might have been in his thirties!) came closer and frightened me by scolding me (not the provoker and initiator) for having called that boy *cristianaccio*.

Episodes of this kind punctuated my early childhood. However, after the government made anti-Semitism legal, it was no longer the street urchins, albeit encouraged or condoned by adults, who harassed us, but adults themselves.

The title of this paper is taken directly from the title of my memoir book, Child of the Ghetto — Coming of Age in Fascist Italy. This refers to an episode that occurred when I was 11 years old and was taking piano lessons from a Catholic friend 5 years my senior. One day, in the middle of my lesson, her mother stormed into the house cursing the principal of the middle school for words they had had regarding problems with her son. The woman, heedless of my presence, began to relate to her daughter the discussion she had had with the principal, yelling that he had no right to treat her like that. "I am a respectable person," the woman sputtered, "I am not *figlia di Ghetto!*" But I was the child of the Ghetto which that "respectable" person was so proud not to be; and even though I was really proud to be one and to have been taught to respect all people instead of being like those children that vilipended us, those words, coming from an adult, really hurt!

It is of the same period another episode I will never forget for as long as I live. My father's younger brother, a distinguished, well-groomed and well-loved gentleman of 40, who had served in the elite corps Bersaglieri during the First World War, meeting a friend in the middle of Piazza del Duomo, attempted to greet him by shaking hands with him. The "friend," however, responded by slapping my uncle in the face, with many people witnessing the scene. Nobody reacted, nobody showed disapproval of this ignominious act, perhaps from fear, more likely from indifference.

A year after these occurrences, the Italian government, satisfied that months of anti-Semitic propaganda had sufficiently poisoned the ears and hearts of the majority of people, began to promulgate and immediately enforce the so-called *leggi razziali,* the racial laws against the Jews aimed as it were at depriving us of all civil and human rights. The voices of our fellow Italians were conspicuously mute.

Then, after 6 years of these material and psychological abuses, came the Shoa, the deportation and physical destruction proper, when between October 1943 and August 1945 approximately 8 thousand Italians of Jewish faith — male, female, babies, pregnant women, the young and robust, the elderly and sick — were transported thousands of miles from their homes in hair-raising conditions to be murdered. (This number does not include those who perished as partisans, nor those who committed suicide or ended up in mental hospitals, unable to cope with such an unjustifiable and brutal reversal of their position in the Society they had served so well.)

During the terror of October 16, 1943, in the first round-up of the Roman Jews, practically under the eyes of Pius XII, we lost our only living grandmother, and many other members of my mother's immediate family. However, even at this late stage, we in Pitigliano were not only unaware of the fate of the European Jews, but not even of the tragic Roman deportation. Had the ecclesiastic authorities openly condemned the atrocities of the death camps as soon as they became aware of them (at least since the beginning of 1942, according to sources close to the Vatican), even if the horrible design to annihilate all Jews could not be stopped, many more lives would have been spared. Ironically, the only voice my family heard of the bad things the Germans were doing to the Jews, came from a German soldier, who just by looking at me had hopelessly fallen in love, and even after I told him that I was a Jew, he held on to his dream of marrying me "when this madness will be over"! But with all the people with whom our father had been always on good terms, including the bishop and all the clergy of our village, and a deputy at the Fascist parliament, a friend since grade school, why had he not heard anything? Why listen to the young soldier, who was not more specific than that his fellow Germans were doing "bad" things to the Jews?

A month and a half after the Roman terror, it was again a foreigner, a Russian lady, who came to our house to warn us of the "impending danger." (Again, no more specific that that.) Nobody ever mentioned the death camps. This time, however, we listened and tried to take measures. But for Father, a soldier who had distinguished himself during the First World War, earning two medals — a bronze one first and later also a gold one — the concept of legality was indisputable, and like many unaware Jews, remained at home to be taken by the fascists, together with Mamma and 9-year-old Mario, to a transshipment camp near Siena. The more "mature" of us, two girls and two boys ranging in age from 13 to 21 years, ran to the woods and joined the partisans.

During the ensuing 7 months, with scanty, if any, news of our beloved prisoners, we roamed the countryside in all kinds of horrible weather, begging like stray dogs, gripped by the terror of being caught, and often personae non grate among the partisans themselves, who feared that because of us the Fascists would be after them more rigorously. (Or was it not their atavistic anti-Semitism that surfaced even at these moments of badly-needed unity against the common enemy?)

Many farmers, when we knocked at their doors, yelled at us to go away, threatening to hand us to the Germans, but a few did show compassion, and despite facing reprisals from the Fascists, helped us to come out of the ordeal alive.

Had the truth come openly out, would our father volunteer to be taken to a concentration camp with Mother and Mario knowing that they would then be sent to their oblivion?

For a series of fortunate and fortuitous circumstances my parents and Mario were among the lucky 14 (of a total of 84 inmates in the camp of Roccatederighi) who were spared deportation. Among the 70 who were destroyed was a lovely family of 4, our not-too-distant relatives, taken in Pitigliano together with our family. My parents lived until a relatively ripe old age, and Mario is a Senior professor of Mathematics at the University of Parma, Italy. Also the four of us came out of the inferno alive. But as I mentioned earlier, a return to a "normal" life was impossible and an uneasiness that is too difficult to put into words still lingers on and will accompany us for the rest of our lives.

I have written extensively about the beautiful as well as the less beautiful feats of the interaction between Jews and Catholics in Italy in my three books. However I must here conclude that without denying the fact that there were good souls among the religious and laypeople who stood up to the Fascist Laws and helped Jews to survive, many more Italians would have taken this stance were it not for the fact that they were imbued with the bi-millenarian negative teachings of the Church, and were it not for the conspiracy of silence that prevailed, during those horrible years, among those who knew the fate of the Jews and had the authority of mitigate it.

EDDA SERVI MACHLIN

Bibliography
John Cornwell. *Hitler's Pope, The Secret History of Pius XII.* New York: Viking, 1999.
Liliana Picciotto Fargion. *Il Libro della Memoria (The Book of Memory).* Milano: Mursia, 1991.

Guenter Lewy. *The Catholic Church and Nazi Germany.* New York: McGraw-Hill, 1964.
Rosetta Loy. *La Parola Ebreo (The Word Jew).* Torino: Einaudi, 1997.
Edda Servi Machlin. *The Classic Cuisine of the Italian Jews I.* Croton-on-Hudson: GiRo Press, 1981.
_____. *The Classic Cuisine of the Italian Jews II.* Croton-on-Hudson: GiRo Press, 1992.
_____. *Child of the Ghetto, Coming of Age in Fascist Italy.* Croton-on-Hudson: GiRo Press, 1995.
Cecil Roth. *The History of the Jews of Italy.* Philadelphia: The Jewish Publication Society of America, 1946.
Susan Zuccotti. *The Italians and the Holocaust.* New York: Basic Books, 1987.

Racial Laws and Internment in Natalia Ginzburg's *La strada che va in città* and *Tutti i nostri ieri*

Biographical background: Natalia Ginzburg followed Leone, her husband, to the Abruzzi in 1940. Leone Ginzburg had received orders to leave Turin for Pizzoli, a small village ten miles from Aquila in the Abruzzi, on 11th June 1940, a day after Italy's declaration of war. He had lost his University post in Turin in 1934 because he had refused to swear allegiance to the regime. Between 1934 and 1936 he had been convicted in Civitavecchia for his political activity as an anti-fascist, and was therefore known to the police. His predicament had seriously worsened in November 1938 with the introductions of Racial laws: as a Jew born in Odessa, he lost his Italian citizenship, even though he was a resident in Italy since the age of five. Like other 'foreign Jews' he would have been interned at the beginning of the war even if he had not been antifascist, but since he was, police files labelled him "internato politico". He arrived in Pizzoli on 13th June 1940. He was supposed to appear before the Podestà every day and not to leave the village. Ginzburg requested and obtained permission for Natalia and his children to join him and they arrived on 13th October 1940. From 1940 to 1943 they lived in Pizzoli except for a short visit to Turin and a short period spent at the Hospital in Aquila, where Natalia gave birth to their third child around the end of March 1943. On the 26th July 1943, the day after Mussolini's fall from government, Leone Ginzburg went back to Turin and then to Rome, where Natalia and the children joined him in early November. On 20th November 1943 Leone Ginzburg was arrested by the Italian police and taken to the German section of Regina Coeli, the local prison, where he was tortured and died on 5th February 1944.[1]

The experience of internment surfaces time and again in Natalia Ginzburg's writings, both in her fiction (*La strada che va in città*, *Tutti i nostri ieri* and *Lessico famigliare*) and in her essays, and her gradual openness in disclosing traumatic autobiographical material seems important both from a human and from an historical point of view. The human side is the parable of a healing process, of a sorrow that cannot be healed but can at least begin to be voiced, even if faintly and tentatively; while the historical side lies in the communicative process that as a writer she established with her readers, so that even from her strategic self censuring, it is possible to infer how the author expected her readers to react to her story. The increasing degree of openness in her writings might also reflect her perceived judgement on their ability to face the legacy of their past anti-Semitism.

The first of her novels *La strada che va in città* was begun in September 1941 and published in 1942, whilst Natalia Ginzburg was living in Pizzoli. The spatial reference in the title echoes the last few words of the biblical epigraph: "Le fatiche degli stolti saranno il loro tormento, poiché essi non sanno la strada che va in città"[2] [The labour of the foolish wearieth every one of them, because he knoweth not how to go to the city. Ecclesiastes, 10.15] thus referring directly to the moral metaphor underpinning the narrative. The main character and narrator of the story is Delia, a sixteen-year-old proletarian girl whose main aspiration is to leave her family home and live in the nearby city. Her teenager attitude is a mixture of shortsightedness, materialism and laziness. She does achieve her goal of living in the city, but loses her chances of happiness by contributing to the destruction of the one man for whom she felt any real affection: though in love with Nini, a poor and somewhat idealistic character, she expects someone else's baby and is therefore assumed to marry the father. While the plot is not autobiographical, the descriptions of places and the tone of the narrative owes much to Natalia Ginzburg's newly imposed surroundings, particularly in the description of the tiny rural village where Delia is sent to hide her pregnancy before the wedding.

> La casa della zia era grande, con delle alte camere vuote e gelate. C'erano dappertutto dei sacchi di granturco e di castagne, e ai soffitti erano appese delle cipolle. La zia aveva avuto nove figli ma chi era morto e chi era andato via. In casa c'era solo Santa, che era la minore e aveva ventiquattro anni. [...] Lei piangeva ogni volta che sua madre andava per qualche affare in città, anche sapendo che prima di sera sarebbe tornata. In città Santa non c'era stata che due o tre volte. Ma diceva che si trovava meglio al paese. Pure il paese loro era peggio del nostro. C'era puzzo di letamaio, bambini sporchi sulle scale e nient'altro. Nelle case non c'era la luce e l'acqua si doveva prendere al pozzo. Scrissi a mia madre che dalla zia non ci volevo più stare e mi venisse a riprendere. Non le piaceva scrivere e per questo non mi diede risposta per lettera, ma fece

dire da un uomo che vendeva il carbone di avere pazienza e restare dov'ero, perché non c'era rimedio. Così restai. (*Opere* I, p. 41.)

The main feature of the house is its almost total lack of comfort. The narrator records the emptiness of the house, its lack of electricity and of running water; the only furniture mentioned in this section of the novel is a fireplace, one bed, stools and chairs. The austerity of this rural home is reinforced by the wintry weather, so that even the kitchen garden outside, planted with tomatoes and cauliflowers when Delia arrives, is soon covered in snow.

The observation that, throughout the text, Ginzburg's descriptions in general, and of places in particular, are extremely economical, almost scanty, was later explained by the author as a desire to please her mother's literary tastes:

> Cominciando a scrivere, temevo che fosse, di nuovo, solo un racconto breve. Però nello stesso tempo temevo che mi venisse troppo lungo e noioso. Ricordavo che mia madre, quando leggeva un romanzo troppo lungo e noioso diceva "Che sbrodolata". Prima d'allora non mi era mai capitato di pensare a mia madre quando scrivevo. E se ci avevo pensato, sempre mi era sembrato che non mi importasse niente della sua opinione. Ma mia madre adesso era lontana e io ne avevo nostalgia. Per la prima volta sentii il desiderio di scrivere qualcosa che piacesse a mia madre. Per non sbrodolare, scrissi e riscrissi più volte le prime pagine, cercando d'essere il più possibile asciutta e secca. Volevo che ogni frase fosse come una scudisciata o uno schiaffo. (Nota 1964, *Opere* I, p. 1125)

In becoming the favorite reader or addressee of the narrative, by dictating the style of the novel, the author's mother became a fictional co-author[3], and the authorial comment encouraged the reading of the text as an artefact bridging the geographical gap between her and her mother. Ginzburg herself and many of her critics have often pointed out how her awareness of family links is active both as creative stimulus and a recurrent motive within her work.[4] Distance in space is not very different from distance in time and this very novel, beginning with Nini's joining the narrator's family and ending with the narrator's realizing that his loss is irrecoverable, confirms that memory and nostalgia are indeed Ginzburg's inspiring muse[5]. Such appraisal is undeniably true, but it is also limiting in that it fixes Ginzburg's contribution well within the boundaries of an autobiographical, self-reflective genre which is often only part of her narrative. Yet the personal and the political do overlap, and it is also the case that, in particular, the way in which space is represented in this novel can be construed as politically active.

For, significantly, spatial or temporal co-ordinates are completely erased from the text: whilst most characters are named, places are not, and dates figure only as names of months[6]. The only place mentioned in the novel is Milan, the place where, according to her, the narrator's mother went in a short lived attempt to escape the tyranny of her family, whilst the rest of the community chose to interpret her transgression as an extra-marital escapade. Within the text, Milan points only to a big, distant city, but it seems significant that it represents distance itself within the restricted world of the narrator.

As the book was written in a location forced on the author and had to be published under a pseudonym because the racial laws would have stopped its publication otherwise, this lack of specificity is probably to be linked with a resistance to acknowledge such shameful oppression. Interestingly, the later authorial comment quoted above, when observing the lack of specific names of places in the text, recalls her earlier difficulty on the issue of national identity:

> La città era insieme Aquila e Torino. [...] Non diedi nessun nome né al paese, né alla città. [...] Non so se ancora in me giocasse il rammarico d'essere nata in Italia, e non sulle rive del Don. Ma credo piuttosto che allora io sentissi come una spinta a cercare un mondo che non fosse situato in un punto speciale dell'Italia, un mondo che potesse essere insieme nord e sud. (Nota 1964, *Opere* I, pp. 1126-7)

The author's perspective does not differentiate between this particular facet and the general problem of identity in her early writing, but this is no reason why the critic should not try to do so, particularly in view of the fact that all of her works written after the end of Fascism, the very works that could finally be published under her own chosen name[7], show that this referential uncertainty has disappeared. Moreover the link between identity and names of places in the narrative is also suggested by the choice of the author's pseudonym: her fictional surname, Tornimparte, is the name of a village near Pizzoli. The choice of a place name as a surname might also have been dictated by the wish to evoke the very Jewish identity outlawed by the regime. Moreover, Tornimparte may be stretched to mean "a partial comeback" or "come back in a role."

Ginzburg's account of her desire to create a fictional space that could be located both in the North and in the South seems to be reduced once again, to the undercurrent of nostalgia in her writing. On the other hand, it may be argued that her utopian attempt to bridge the distance between North and South is dictated by a strong idealistic determination to reduce the polarity between the two. Certainly because of the referential vagueness[8] of the text, the representation of the South in *La strada che va in città* is underplayed, and the poverty of the Abruzzi limited to the description of the village where Delia is sent to hide her pregnancy. Yet Ginzburg's sidestepping the issue of economic and cultural disparity between North and South, significantly known as the "questione meridionale", allows a picture of national integration in which the South might be blurred, but at least it is not characterized as Other, as often happens when the wri-ter is a Northerner.[9] The desire for integration goes even further: the narrator's language is modeled partly on the language of the place in which the writer was interned.[10] Subtly but clearly the voice of the oppressed writer resonates through the accent of the economically disadvantaged South.

As to the "Jewish question" and racial laws, the text is obviously completely silent: there are no allusions to race and all allusions to religion point towards Catholicism. Yet the temptation of reading Nini as a Jew is very hard to resist: the narrator's introduction of this character as a persecuted orphan, her insistence on his 'difference' from the rest of the family, on his generous and progressive moral stance, on his passion for self improvement and reading, on both his zest for life and his defeated despondency, on his stylish dowdiness, Bohemian attitude and finally on his powerless wisdom; all of these qualities, remarkably unlike those of the other characters in this novel, signal a hitherto concealed Jewishness, because some of these qualities will be identified with Jewish characters in her future writings.

The concern for a representation of national integration is even more explicit in *Tutti i nostri ieri*. This long novel was published in 1952 in a political climate which favored a greater degree of openness. It provides an extended portrait of the last few years of Fascism to the immediate post-war through the vicissitudes of two bourgeois anti-fascist families from Turin. Written in the third person, the novel retains autobiographical connotations through the similarity between the experience of the author[11] and that of a female character, Anna. But despite the autobiographical dimension, Ginzburg constructs the narrative so as to create a choral representation, and reach a vision of national unity through and despite the displacements, migrations and forced residences caused by the regime and the war. Like Ginzburg, Anna moves from the confined boundaries of her family home in Turin, spends the war period as a married woman in the South, and goes back as a widow to the same family home in Turin after the war.

The avoidance of the first person narrator is the vital element in this narrative and the focalization through the eyes of the youngest amongst the members of the two families allows for the novel to be read as a modern Entwicklungsroman, with all the surviving characters emerging from the experience of the war and the end of Fascism as more mature individuals and yet fully conscious of their shortcomings in facing the new reality.

The practice of restricted residence, both on political and racial grounds, appears in the narrative but it is not related to Anna.[12] This allows Ginzburg to portray the interaction between villagers and the restricted newcomers as a dispassionate witness, in a sympathetic but unsentimental way. The vulnerability and dignity of the displaced Jews on their arrival in small villages makes them interesting at first, but the initial curiosity is short-lived because of their poverty, mildness and compliant behavior.

> Un giorno vennero da Cenzo Rena a dirgli che a Borgo San Costanzo stavano per arrivare gli ebrei. La questura sparpagliava gli ebrei di qua e di là nei piccoli paesi, per paura che stando in città facessero qualche danno alla guerra. Ce n'erano già a Masuri, a Scoturno, solo San Costanzo sembrava fosse stato dimenticato. Adesso invece stavano per arrivare. Per un poco la gente di San Costanzo sperò negli ebrei, a Masuri e negli altri paesi erano arrivati degli ebrei molto ricchi, che spendevano tanto denaro. Ma gli ebrei che arrivarono a San Costanzo erano ebrei poveri, tre vecchiette cenciose di Livorno con un canarino in gabbia, e un turco che tremava di freddo in un soprabito chiaro. Le vecchiette di Livorno si misero subito a mostrare che scarpe avevano ai piedi, con la suola bucata fino alla calza. Il segretario comunale accompagnò il turco alla locanda che era proprio in piazza, al piano di sopra dell'osteria, e le vecchie le prese il sarto in una specie di granaio che aveva. Il canarino delle vecchiette morì subito, la Maschiona l'aveva predetto che quello non era paese per i canarini.

A poco a poco il turco e le vecchiette diventarono facce del paese, tutti s'erano abituati a vederli e avevano saputo ogni cosa di loro, e adesso tutti dicevano che gli ebrei erano gente come gli altri, chissà perché la questura non li voleva più nelle città, chissà che danno potevano fare. E questi erano anche poveri e bisognava aiutarli, chi poteva gli dava un po' di pane o un po' di fagioli, le vecchiette andavano in giro a chiedere e tornavano con il grembiule pieno. In cambio facevano dei rammendi, così ben fatti che non si vedeva niente, rammendavano non col filo ma con i loro capelli, era un uso di ebrei. Sovente salivano su alla casa di Cenzo Rena e la Maschiona le faceva sedere in cucina e gli dava il caffelatte, erano vecchie e lei pensava a sua madre, se fosse dovuta andare attorno a mendicare. Soltanto aveva schifo a pensare a quei rammendi che facevano coi loro capelli. (*Opere* I, pp. 433-434)

The seriousness and potential tragedy of their predicament is known and feared, and Cenzo Rena's recurrent mention and thought of *treni piombati* (sealed trains), in its concise yet evocative image, is palpably nightmarish.

At the textual level the best link between *La strada che va in città* and *Tutti i nostri ieri* is the plight of the main characters. Like Delia, Anna is pregnant when she is only seventeen and single; the only difference between the two emergencies is that Delia marries the father of her child, even if she is not in love with him; whereas Anna contemplates having an abortion but then marries Cenzo Rena, who offers to act as a protective friend and husband. Interestingly, Ginzburg describes the attitude towards the family's loss of respectability as the same both in Anna's North and in Delia's more likely South, with concealment and code of silence surrounding both events.

Once again, for the protagonist displacement comes as a consequence of pregnancy. But in this narrative North and South are distinct and in describing Anna as a Northerner in exile, Ginzburg has to confront the cultural division and the stereotypes which she had managed to avoid in her previous book. Her strategy is double: on the one hand she makes Cenzo Rena, a Southerner, the uncontroversial hero in the novel; on the other she underlines the fictional nature of stereotypes.

Anna is the main focalizer of the entire narrative, but whilst in the first part of the novel, set in the North during her adolescence, the story is filtered through the actions of a great variety of characters, the focalization becomes more perceivable in the second part, which is set in the Abruzzi. Ginzburg's description of Anna's feeling of alienness when she arrives in

Cenzo's village is clearly marked through a humorous perspective which makes everything appear disproportionate:

> Così era Borgo San Costanzo, il paese di Cenzo Rena, e il giorno che arrivarono Anna e Cenzo Rena sulla piazza del municipio, tutta la gente era fuori a guardare che moglie s'era presa Cenzo Rena, e rimasero male di quella piccola moglie, spettinata e con addosso l'impermeabile di Cenzo Rena che le arrivava fino alle caviglie. Trovavano che assomigliava alle figlie del negoziante di stoffe, ma in peggio, e trovavano che non c'era bisogno di andare lontano per prendersi una moglie così. E anche la vecchia marchesa era affacciata a guardare dalla sua carrozza, con la faccia grassa e incipriata e con gli occhi tinti d'azzurro alle palpebre e tutt'intorno, e a Anna parevano tutti contadini del Sud, anche la marchesa e il commerciante di stoffe, in piedi sulla porta del suo negozio con le dita infilate nel gilè. E dopo un minuto lei aveva una voglia terribile d'essere di nuovo a casa sua, alle "Visciole" o nella casa della loro piccola città, con Giustino e la signora Maria e senza contadini del Sud, e appena s'era trovata sulla piazza del municipio anche Cenzo Rena le era sembrato un estraneo, anche lui qualcosa come un contadino del Sud, e lui a un tratto pareva averla dimenticata e s'era messo a parlare fitto fitto con un uomo su un asino, erano molto amici e concertavano chi sa cosa insieme, una cosa che riguardava il demanio. (*Opere* I, p. 430)

By representing the different behavior within the couple towards the local people — with Cenzo able to protect and criticize the peasants, whilst Anna is uncomfortable with his friendliness, as an unconvincing breach of class barriers — Ginzburg signals another initial set of obstacles and difficult crossing of boundaries, which displacement brings about.[13]

Whilst most of the main characters in *Tutti i nostri ieri* belong to the educated bourgeoisie from the North, they are also clearly keen on taking an anti-fascist, progressive stance towards the needs of the lower classes and towards the Southern question. Their learner's zeal is gently teased throughout, but especially when it manifests a facile reversal of attitudes towards the poverty of the South, in the behavior of Emanuele, as a well-meaning visiting Northerner:

> E anche Emanuele era intimidito e felice a vedere tutti quei contadini, tutti quei contadini del Sud, sedeva molto serio e rosso in viso e arrischiava domande sul grano e il vino e i maiali e il demanio, con una

voce incerta e sottile e con una gran paura di fare delle domande sbagliate. E Giustino chiese sottovoce ad Anna se non pareva un provinciale snob che si trovi per la prima volta in salotto pieno di duchesse. Anna disse di sì e scoppiò a ridere forte e allora si avvicinò Cenzo Rena e chiese di che cosa ridevano, e lo dissero e rise forte anche lui e Emanuele guardò verso di loro con sospetto, ma subito riprese le sue domande sulle cose dei contadini. (*Opere* I, p. 452)

The first comments and reactions of visiting family and friends from the North are just another way in which Ginzburg exposes the feeling of cultural distance and makes fun gently of their parochial attitude. The mockery is very light touched and the comments of the visitors are completely inoffensive; they signal their alienness and the limitation of their views, but above all it is a sensitive portrayal which reinforces the feeling that it is harder to interact with stereotypes (North/South but also Gentile/Jewish) than with circumstances.[14]

Amongst the main characters the only Jew is Franz, an anti-hero. He enters the narrative as guest of Anna's neighbors in Turin. In the first instance Franz claims that he is a German baron, emigrated because he disapproves of the Nazis, although he does not seem very interested in politics, but rather in sport and women. He has affairs with both his female hostesses, stepmother and stepdaughter, and marries the daughter as soon as she inherits on her father's death. Only some time after the wedding, Franz sends his new brother-in-law a letter informing him that he was not a baron, but the son of a Polish merchant and that his mother was of Jewish origin.

> Franz nella lettera diceva a Emanuele che lui non era tedesco e non era un barone, aveva mentito sempre. Era cresciuto a Friburgo, dove suo padre un tempo vendeva impermeabili. Ma suo padre e sua madre erano polacchi, e ora abitavano tutt'e due a Varsavia. E sua madre era d'origine ebraica e i tedeschi l'avrebbero ucciso. Se l'Italia entrava in guerra chi sa cosa sarebbe stato di lui, che aveva in tasca un passaporto polacco. Se l'Italia entrava in guerra a fianco della Germania per lui era tutto finito. Qualcuno diceva che forse l'Italia poteva ancora allearsi all'Inghilterra e alla Francia. Pregava Emanuele di fargli sapere se poteva succedere così. Ma sarebbe stato troppo bello, non poteva succedere. Chiedeva perdono d'aver sempre mentito, non aveva mentito per malizia, ma proprio come un bambino che racconta una favola. Pregava Emanuele di p rendersi c ura d 'Amalia s e a l ui s uccedeva qu alcosa.

> Pregava di mandare un po' di soldi perché non aveva quasi più niente. Emanuele si strinse nelle spalle, era vagamente commosso ma gli venne anche un po' da ridere, per quegl'impermeabili che venivano fuori così tutt'a un tratto. Chi sa perché qualcuno doveva vergognarsi d'essere polacco e d'aver venduto impermeabili, confessarlo ad un tratto tra i singhiozzi. Mandò un assegno intestato ad Amalia, solo dopo s'accorse che non l'aveva intestato a Franz, pensò che dunque ancora diffidava di lui. (Opere I, p. 328)

Gradually Franz admits that both his parents are Jewish, and at the beginning of the war he is also interned in a village in the South, and manages to join Anna and Cenzo Rena at Borgo San Costanzo. Both before and during the German occupation, Franz appears as a weak, hunted character, completely lost in his terrifying predicament and a burden to the politically aware and mature Cenzo Rena. Yet in the end, when a German soldier is killed and Cenzo Rena gives himself up to avoid a massacre, Franz in a mad and heroic frenzy follows him to the very end, since he is quickly recognized as an interned Jew and executed with Cenzo.

Why did Ginzburg choose to represent the most prominent Jewish character in this novel as an anti-hero? My guess is that by making Franz such a weak (and in the beginning frivolous) character, Ginzburg was stressing that in order to be a victim, one does not need to be a hero, that being human is more than enough. Perhaps she was also going against a generalizing philosemitism which tended to over-idealize Jewishness. At the same time the circumstances of his death point unequivocally to another reading of his character as the reverse of Cenzo Rena, both his double and his other half, so that their joint execution extinguishes both the courage and generosity of the political activist and the fear of persecution of the victim.

Clearly Ginzburg's choice to represent all the Jews in the novel as weak and politically inactive characters appears strange, defeatist and above all completely inaccurate.[15] Her decision might have been determined by the need to allow the majority of readers to identify with a progressive stance that could otherwise have seemed minoritarian and less accessible. Inevitably we would then have to conclude that Ginzburg's implied reader retained an element of latent antisemitism.

CLAUDIA NOCENTINI

University of Edinburgh

[1] See: Maja Pfluig, *Natalia Ginzburg. Arditamente timida* (Milan: La Tartaruga, 1997); Alessandro Clementi, "I Ginzburg in Abruzzo", *Paragone*, XVII, n.s., 29, October, 1991, pp. 66-82; Laurent Béghin, "Leone Ginzburg, dal confino di Pizzoli", *Nuova Antologia*, 133, January-March, 1998, pp. 8-20. For general information about the racial laws, see Paola Di Cori, "Le leggi razziali", in *I luoghi della memoria: simboli e miti dell'Italia unita*, edited by M. Isnenghi, (Rome-Bari: Laterza, 1996) pp. 461-476 and for a study of racial laws in Turin, see *L'ebreo in oggetto* edited by Fabio Levi, (Turin: Zamorani, 1991). For information on internment, Gianfranco Porta, "Il confino" in *I luoghi della memoria*, op. cit., pp. 439-460, and also Leonardo Musci, "Il confino fascista di polizia. L'apparato statale di fronte al dissenso politico e sociale" in Adriano Dal Pont and Simona Carolini, *L'Italia al confino 1926-1943*, (Milan: La pietra, 1983), pp. XXI-IC.

[2] Natalia Ginzburg, *La strada che va in città* (Turin: Einaudi, 1942). All quotations from Ginzburg are taken from *Opere, raccolte e ordinate dall'autore*, 2 vol. (Milan: Mondadori, 1986 and 1987) (from now on *Opere*).

[3] See Cesare Segre, *Avviamento all'analisi del testo letterario* (Turin: Einaudi, 1985), p. 10.

[4] " Her desire to achieve such a sparseness of style in the interest of clarity derives from her conviction that although creative composition is a source of personal fulfilment it does not exist in a void, but ultimately, reflects one's relationship with fellow human beings [...]" in Alan Bullock, *Natalia Ginzburg: Human Relationships in a Changing World* (Oxford: Berg, 1991), p. 27.

[5] See Giovanni Tesio, "Natalia Ginzburg" in Giorgio Bárberi-Squarotti, (ed.) *Gli eredi di Verga*, (Randazzo, 1983), pp. 133-151. See also Bullock, *op. cit.* and Sharon Wood, "Memory and Melancholy in Natalia Ginzburg" in *Italian Women's Writing 1860-1994* (London: The Athlone Press, 1995) pp. 134-1151.

[6] Whilst there are no historical references within the text, a few details point to the years near the actual composition of this work: particularly female shoes with cork soles, *Opere*, 1, 10, became fashionable during the summer of 1941, according to Miriam Mafai, *Pane nero: Donne e vita quotidiana nella seconda guerra mondiale* (Milan: Mondadori, 1987 and 1989), p. 108. The description of Santa's fiancé mentions the term "podestà" (local administrator) used during the Fascist regime: Il suo fidanzato era il figlio del podestà del paese ed erano fidanzati da otto anni. *Opere*, I, p. 40.

[7] Natalia Ginzburg's very early work was published in her own family name, Levi. The choice of using her late husband's surname, Ginzburg, is very likely to be a tribute to his memory.

[8] It is worth mentioning that vagueness between the representation of city and village life informs Marchionne Picchione's elegant reading of the novel. Her account of the tension between the two is not entirely convincing, especially since very little village life features in the novel. On the other hand, the analysis of the representation of city life is very relevant: " [...] le articolazioni del romanzo tendono a scompigliare i limiti distintivi tra città e paese, associandoli entrambi a una realtà instabile e balord-

a. L'osmosi dovuta alle loro reciproche interferenze produce un impasto strutturale che nella caotica, scettica famiglia di Delia anticipa la città e di quest'ultima fa un insieme paesano, in cui i caffè, le donne abbigliate elegantemente, le vetrine, non impediscono gli incontri familiari e (campagnoli) fra le solite poche persone, circoscrivendo la diffusività alienante del clima cittadino." Luciana Marchionne Picchione, *Natalia Ginzburg* (Florence: La nuova Italia, 1978) pp. 29-30.

[9] In very subdued fashion, echoes of this representation are perceptible in "Mio marito", the first short story written by Ginzburg after her arrival in Pizzoli. The narrative describes a love triangle in which the narrator is the legal middle-class wife whose husband cannot stop loving a poor subproletarian girl. In this story, the North-South antithesis is mainly pared down to class division. Mariuccia's extreme poverty and ignorance, though, her primitive, almost animalesque behaviour point in the direction of the standard, orientalised representation of the Southern landless peasant girl.

[10] See the recurrence of words and idioms like: "[...] ancora non m'avevano chiesta" (Opere I, p. 5), "Avrei avuto vergogna [...] and "Mammà" (Opere I, p. 7), "[...] le strillava dietro[...] (Opere I, p. 41), "[...] fa l'amore da otto anni e non le riesce di farsi sposare" and "Provati un po' [...]"(Opere I, p. 42), "[...] da un metro lontano", "[...] lo portavo in collo" and "[...] fa peccato pensarci" (Opere I, p. 43), etc. My scrutiny suggests that Southern idioms are more common in Elide's speech. By contrast see also the restricted use of Tuscan variants more common in literary writings: "leticava" (Opere I, p. 6), "cascava" (Opere I, p. 8) "seggiola" (Opere I, p. 76). Since Ginzburg was from Piedmont it is to be expected that Northern idioms are also strongly present in this novel, the best recognisably North-Western feature is the recurrent use of a definite article in front of a masculine name, i.e. "il Nini".

[11] In "Inverno in Abruzzo", written in 1944 and republished in *Le piccole virtù* (1961), Ginzburg offers a straight autobiographical report. It is a narrative which can be read independently as a very concise summary of her years in internment, but on another level it is also explains what was fictional and what was real in *Tutti i nostri ieri*. As a reflection of her tragic experience it is powerful and moving. It is also very honest; the feelings of alienness at her arrival in Abruzzo are conveyed much more intensely than in her third novel. She discloses how her nostalgia for Turin and the anger for the inevitability of their exile are the unjust reason why she sometimes hated everybody and everything, and how she hid her hatred because she knew that it was unfair. In Freudian terms this hidden hatred would be called displacement and it is my impression that both in Carlo Levi's *Cristo si è fermato a Eboli* and Cesare Pavese's *Il carcere*, written after the same experience of internment, the extreme and exaggerated feeling of alienation is a consequence of Freudian, rather than geographical, displacement.

[12] A friend from Turin, Danilo, an anti-fascist activist, is dispatched to a small village in Sardinia when Italy enters the conflict, and as Anna moves to Borgo San Costanzo, the police force starts scattering 'foreign' Jews around the villages. Towards the end of the war, another acquaintance from Turin, Franz, a Polish Jew

who had married Emanuele's sister and had been displaced to the South, turns up in Borgo San Costanzo, and meets his death at the hands of the occupying Germans.

[13] Anna's comment can be seen to indicate the author's reluctance to embrace the postwar intellectual backlash in which the left-wing rhetoric celebrated the working class or the peasantry in a populist fashion. See Marchionne Picchione's discerning and clear remark: "Il bisogno di aderire prudentemente, nello scrivere, alle esperienze intimamente e direttamente condivise mantiene la Ginzburg lontana, anche nell'immediato dopoguerra, dalla tentazione di farsi ostinata portavoce di classi sociali umili, con l'intento di evidenziarne i problemi secondo un filone narrativo polemico o moralistico. Pertanto gli operai o contadini non arrivano a sostenere un protagonismo prolungato nelle sue opere; se prima di *Tutti i nostri ieri* si sono inseriti nella concentrata prospettiva del racconto o romanzo breve (*Mio marito, La strada che va in città*), in questo romanzo sono colti nella loro dimensione di gruppo, più che in rilievi di primo piano, e seguiti nelle loro abitudini di vita e reazioni alla guerra con documentarismo sobrio e non didascalico, percorso saltuariamente da intonazioni garbatamente caricaturali, che investono del resto anche il borghese nella riconosciuta, paziente adesione alle imperfezioni dell'umano." *Op. cit.* pp. 46-47. See also Italo Calvino, 'Natalia Ginzburg o le possibilità del romanzo borghese' (1961) in *I saggi* I, (Milan: Mondadori, 1995), pp. 1087-1094.

[14] Ginzburg portrays this laborious process also by creating internal references within the text, so that, for example, after the war Emanuele teases his brother, Giuma, who has recently inherited his own progressive zeal: "E Giuma disse che voleva far vedere a sua moglie tutta l'Italia del Sud, e a sua moglie che avrebbe potuto far molto per l'Italia del Sud, per esempio se andava a San Costanzo chissà quante idee le venivano di cose da fare. E Emanuele soffiava e sbuffava e disse che andassero pure nel Sud a psicanalizzare i contadini." (*Opere* I, p. 573)

[15] Textual links with *Lessico famigliare* or biographical notes would quickly establish that the entire Turinese milieu, including their progressive and antifascist stance, is modelled on the author's family.

JEWS, CATHOLICS, AND POPE PIUS XII

The Holocaust was both anti-Jewish and anti-Christian. Far from Christian in origin, Nazism was pagan and racist. In the *Introduction to Atlas of the Holocaust*, Martin Gilbert states that "in addition to the six million Jewish men, women, and children who were murdered, at least an equal number of non-Jews were also killed, not in the heat of battle, not by military siege, aerial bombardment or the harsh conditions of modern war, but by deliberate, planned murder."[1]

The Vatican document, "We Remember: A Reflection on the Shoah" issued on March 16, 1998, received mixed reviews in the media. On May 15, 1998, Edward Cardinal Cassidy, Chairman of the Pontifical Commission that issued this document responded to the reactions of Jewish leaders at the 92nd annual meeting of the American Jewish Committee taking place in Washington, D.C. He condemned as myth the accusation that Pope Pius XII did not do enough to stop the Holocaust: "It is our conviction that in recent years his memory has been unjustly denigrated. ...Monstrous calumnies... have gradually become accepted facts especially within the Jewish community." He reiterated that the "anti-Semitism of the Nazis was the fruit of a thoroughly neo-pagan regime with its roots outside of Christianity, and in pursuing its aims it did not hesitate to oppose the Church and persecute its members also."

Examples abound to document Cardinal Cassidy's contention. In 1940, in a letter to be read in all churches entitled *Opere et caritate* ("By Work and by Love"), Pope Pius XII instructed the Catholic bishops of Europe to assist all people suffering from racial discrimination at the hands of the Nazis.[2]

Two years later, on July 26, 1942, the day after the Dutch bishops ordered — in all Catholic churches — a strong denunciation of the Nazi deportation of Jews, the Nazi occupation officers met in The Hague. The record of the meeting clearly states that because the Catholic bishops interfered in something that did not concern them, deportation of all Dutch Jews would be completed within that week and no appeals for clemency would be considered.[3]

Among those sent to the Auschwitz gas chamber at that time was Edith Stein, a distinguished intellectual who, after her conversion from Judaism to Catholicism, became a Carmelite nun. On October 11, 1998, Edith Stein, known as Sister Teresa Benedicta of the Cross (1891-1942), was canonized by Pope John Paul II. To both Jews and Catholics, Edith Stein's life and death should be a source of inspiration. William Cardinal Keeler of Baltimore, the episcopal moderator for Catholic-Jewish relations at the National Conference of Catholic Bishops, stated that emulation of Edith Stein should lead Catholics to a deeper appreciation of the spiritual richness and integrity of Judaism, the faith to which God has called the Jewish people.

The Holocaust has always occupied some corner in newspaper articles, magazine stories, and ads. Papal protests were made 60 years ago as was recorded by *The New York Times* front page article on October 28, 1939. Its title was in large print and bold type: "POPE CONDEMNS DICTATORS, TREATY VIOLATORS, RACISM; URGES RESTORING OF POLAND."

Undoubtedly this *Times* article was a powerful attack on totalitarianism proclaiming the Pontiff's determination to step forward boldly in defense of the rights of the individual and the family and to fight the enemies of the Church. The entire encyclical was printed on pages eight and nine of *The New York Times*.

The front page of *The New York Times* of March 14, 1940, states: "Pope Is Emphatic About Peace: Jews' Rights Defended." Describing Pius XII's confrontational meeting with German Foreign Minister, Joachim von Ribbentrop, the story reads: "Twice in two days Pope Pius XII has gone out of his way to speak of the necessity for justice as well as for peace, and Vatican circles take this as an emphasis of his stern demand to Joachim von Ribbentrop, that Germany right the injustice she has done before there can be peace.... It was also learned today for the first time that the Pontiff, in the burning words he spoke to Herr von Ribbentrop about religious persecution, also came to the defense of the Jews in Germany and Poland."

The best tribute to the spirit of Germany's Christians was printed on December 23, 1940 in *Time*. It came from a Jew and agnostic, the great physicist Albert Einstein: "Being a lover of freedom, when the Nazi revolution came in Germany, I looked to the universities to defend it, knowing that they had always boasted of their devotion to the cause of truth; but, no, the universities immediately were silenced. Then I looked to the great editors of the newspapers, whose flaming editorials in days gone by had proclaimed their love of freedom; but they, like the universities, were silenced in a few short weeks....

"Only the Church," Einstein concluded, "stood squarely across the path of Hitler's campaign for suppressing the truth. I never had any special interest in the Church before, but now I feel a great affection and admiration because the Church alone has had the courage and persistence to stand for intellectual truth and moral freedom. I am forced thus to confess that what I once despised, I now praise unreservedly."[4]

Today there seems to be a great deal of space devoted to Pope Pius XII. Incredibly, despite the documentation available, countless inaccuracies and accusations continue to dominate the media. It is difficult to understand the criticism and false statements of contemporary "experts," who undoubtedly fail to consult the 12 volumes of Vatican documents printed between 1965-1981, four of which deal exclusively with the humanitarian efforts of Pope Pius XII. Indeed, it is time to right the injustice toward Pope Pius XII who saved more Jews than any other person, including Oscar Schindler and Raoul Wallenberg. Vatican records indicate that Pope Pius XII operated an underground railroad that rescued European Jews from the Holocaust. He used all possible diplomatic means to condemn Nazi atrocities and aid the persecuted Jews.

It is a known fact that both the International Red Cross and the World Council of Churches agreed with the Vatican that relief efforts for the Jews would be more effective if the agencies remained quiet. When the Catholic hierarchy of Amsterdam spoke out vigorously against the Nazi treatment of the Jews, the Nazi response was a redoubling of deportations. Ninety percent of the Jews in Amsterdam were deported to the concentration camps.

On the morning of October 16, 1943, the Nazis started a roundup of Rome's eight thousand Jews who were marked for elimination: one thousand were captured. The Jews of Rome disappeared into Rome's monasteries and convents, where they were safe until the war was over. There is documentation about an official, personal protest through the papal secretary of state. He delivered it on Pope Pius XII's orders that same fateful morning. The operation was suspended.

If Pope Pius XII had protested, not only would he have been unsuccessful in halting the destruction, but he would have endangered the lives of thousands of Jews hidden in the Vatican, convents, and monasteries.

On May 8, 1945, Germany surrendered unconditionally to the Allies. More than 11 million civilians had been murdered since the German invasion of Poland.

In the book, *Yours is a Precious Witness: Memoirs of Jews and Catholics in Wartime Italy* (Paulist Press, 1997), many survivors and rescuers express their solidarity. The stories link people together with love and compassion. They help to bridge differences; not perpetuate the tragic horrors of the Holocaust.

Many Jews and other refugees were saved by the Vatican "underground railroad." The doors of convents and monasteries were opened at the direction of Pope Pius XII. One survivor, Emanuele Pacifici, recently gave a eulogy in the Vatican, for Sister Esther of the Franciscan Missionaries. These Sisters saved him and his brother Raffaele, age twelve and five. With their mother the boys escaped to Florence. The Nazis captured their father, the Chief Rabbi in Genoa, who would not desert his post. He was tortured by the Nazis, but would not reveal the names of other Jews in Genoa. Later he was seen entering the gas chamber in Auschwitz.

The boys were sent to a school where their name was changed to Pallini. Their mother was later deported to Auschwitz with 50 other women captured by the Nazis and sent to the gas chamber.

Emanuele Pacifici stated that the Sisters respected the Jewish religion. While the other boys were told to kiss the crucifix on her ring before going to bed, Sister would cover it for them and quietly remind them to say their Hebrew prayers.

Enrico Modigliani, now a professor at the University of Rome, has this childhood memory of learning Catholic prayers. His parents had taught him these prayers in order to avoid being sent to a concentration camp. Though but six years old, he remembered that, one evening, some peasants visited them. Enrico was saying his Hebrew prayers — the *Shema Israel* — when the door of his bedroom opened. He noticed a stranger. He knew he had to conceal his Jewish heritage. Unruffled, he shifted from the *Shema Israel* to the *Ave Maria*. After this visit, the Modiglianis realized that the Nazis and Fascists were searching for them, so they took refuge in a convent. On June 5, 1944, young American soldiers came to their rescue, smiling and helpful, distributing chewing gum and chocolates — the first Enrico had in his life.

"We were young," Sister Maria Pucci said when interviewed. "In the Spring of 1943, we opened our doors for 25 men, women and children who lived in the auditorium which we closed to the public. What a scene that first day! They were desperate. We gave them what they needed, especially blankets to keep warm. Children were crying, hugging their mothers. During air raids the Jews fled with us. Everyone was frightened. Our prayers were mixed with tears."

When asked, "Why did the Sisters protect Jews?" Sister Maria answered: "Why, these were our neighbors. We respected and loved them. We responded to the Pope's plea to open our doors."

In the town of Cave, near Rome, Sister Lelia Orlandi vividly recalled the bitter night during one of those terrible storms that occur in November. It was about 9:00 p.m. Clara Coen-Capon had a one-year-old infant in her arms. Her husband Luciano knocked on the convent door. Fully aware of the risk that, by protecting them, they too would be shot, Sister Lucia welcomed them. When she was 100 years old, she told this story on national Italian TV.

At the end of the war, in gratitude for having been "rescued," a group of Jewish women presented a beautiful five-foot statue of the Madonna to the Religious Teachers Filippini who, in Rome, saved 114 Jews. The statue stands today in a place of honor in the very wing where 60 Jews were hidden for more than a year.

In October 1994, the Jewish congregation in Rome presented a lovely document to the Sisters, "recalling those who risked their lives to save Jews from Nazi-Fascist atrocities."

During this ceremony, Rabbi Elio Toaff said: "We do not want to forget the good that was done by many Italian citizens who saw the persecuted Jews not as people to abandon. They saw them as their brothers."

One story of compassion and love appeared in the November 1, 1943, issue of *Life Magazine*. It began in 1941, when 150 German Jews fled from Germany armed with visas for the United States. In order to obtain transportation, they sought refuge in Italy. But soon, the war had become a World War. The Jews were immediately chained and arrested.

For three years they were interned in the town of Campagna, near the Bay of Salerno, living in a monastery and enjoying the loving care of the local residents. When the Allies bombed the monastery, the Jews fled to the mountains. Within days the Nazis took control of the town and they began shooting the Italians.

When the Jews learned that the Italians were without medical assistance, four Jewish surgeons, returned to the town to care for the many casualties. These Jews knew the Nazis were searching for them; if caught, they would have been shot or deported. Yet, they did not hesitate. Without medical equipment, they performed 40 major operations in two days and saved the Italians.

At the end of World War II, Dr. Joseph Nathan, representing the Hebrew Commission, addressed the Jewish Community and expressed heartfelt gratitude to those who protected and saved Jews during the Nazi-Fascist persecutions. "Above all," he stated, "we acknowledge the Supreme Pontiff and the religious men and women who, executing the directives of the Holy Father, recognized the persecuted as their brother and, with great abnegation, hastened to help them, disregarding the terrible dangers to which they were exposed."[5]

It is a sad but indisputable fact that the official publications of the Holy See, documents of the Nuremberg Trial Proceedings, state papers of the warring countries, and published Vatican War Documents have been largely ignored by those who would impugn the Pope's integrity. The twelve volumes of *The Acts and Documents of the Holy See* demonstrate the close collaboration between the Holy See, Jewish representative bodies, the international Red Cross, and allied governments. No one can deny that numerous protests were made by Pius XII. Elie Wiesel, who was a child when he was sent to Auschwitz, said: "Not all victims were Jews, but all Jews were victims.... They were doomed not because of something they had done or proclaimed or acquired but because of who they were."[6]

The Shoah "Reflection" of the Catholic Church is the most significant statement in support of the truth of the enormity of the Holocaust which resulted in the extermination of six million Jews, only because they were Jews. However, the tragedy of their death is not diminished when we remember the millions of others who were also victims of the Nazis.

Repeatedly, Pope John Paul II has defended Pope Pius XII, recalling "how deeply he felt about the tragedy of the Jewish people, and how hard and effectively he worked to assist them during the Second World War."

In the words of the Jewish-Hungarian scholar, Jeno Levai, it is a "particularly regrettable irony that the one person [Pope Pius XII] in all of occupied Europe who did more than anyone else to halt the dreadful crime and alleviate its consequences is today made the scapegoat for the failures of others."

Golda Meir and so many Jewish leaders world-wide recognized the greatness of Pius XII — the Pope who had saved the lives of so many thousands of people without distinction of race, nationality, or religion.

In February 1945, Chief Rabbi Isaac Herzog of Palestine stated: "The people of Israel will never forget what His Holiness and his illustrious delegates, inspired by the eternal principles of religion, which form the very foundations of true civilization, are doing for our unfortunate brothers and sisters in the most tragic hour of our history, which is living proof of Divine Providence in this world."

SISTER MARGHERITA MARCHIONE
Villa Walsh

---

[1] New York: William Morrow and Co., 1988, p. 11.

[2] Joseph L. Lichten, *A Question of Judgment: Pius XII and the Jews*, Washington, DC: National Catholic Conference, 1963; reprinted in *Pius XII and the Holocaust*, Catholic League for Religious and Civil Rights: Milwaukee, Wisconsin, 1988, p. 103.

[3] *Inside the Vatican*, Rome, October 1998, p. 11. Official records give August 9, 1942 as the date that Edith Stein (the Carmelite, Sister Teresa Benedicta, who was canonized by Pope John Paul II on October 11, 1998) and her sister Rosa died in Auschwitz.

[4] Time, December 23, 1940, pp. 38-40

[5] Osservatore Romano, September 8, 1945

[6] Ridgefield, CT: *Sursum Corda!*, Summer 1998, p. 49.

Judaism and Manhood in the Novels of Giorgio Bassani

While historical accounts of the forces at work during certain periods of the past may serve to pinpoint some of the "causes" of events as they unfolded, there is no exhaustive or objective answer to the question of what makes certain events possible at any given time. Ultimately, why something happens, what it is that really catalyzes certain historical conditions to produce a specific reaction, remains a mystery. A large part of the answer to the question "why" is to be found, however, in the human heart, and it is this frequently unspoken and certainly elusive dimension of history that the work of Giorgio Bassani attempts to recapture.[1] His goal as a narrator has been to suggest if not the causes, then some of the "conditions of possibility" that led to the expulsion of the Jews from the very "civil society" they had contributed to building and of which they had appeared to be, since the Risorgimento, such an integral part. In that sense, Bassani's writings can be said to be part of the implicit project of "working through" the horrors of civil war and Fascist violence that occupied so much of the energy of Italian intellectuals in the post-war years.

Once exemplary patriots, with the passing of the race laws in 1938 the Jews became enemies of the state almost overnight.[2] As a Jew, born in 1916 and growing up in a well-to-do family in Ferrara in the years between the two world wars, Bassani experienced this sudden change in status at a particularly important point in his life — as he was about to embark upon manhood, at the end of his university years. Forced to set aside the professional goals he had set for himself, he joined the Resistance and took part in the struggle for the liberation of Italy from its Fascist and Nazi oppressors. How he came to make this decision, and the internal obstacles he had to overcome in order to do so are, I believe, the true subject of the trilogy of first-person novels I shall be discussing here, *Gli occhiali d'oro* (1958; *The Gold-rimmed Eyeglasses*), *Il giardino dei Finzi-Contini* (1962; *The Garden of the Finzi-Continis*) and *Dietro la porta* (1964; *Behind the Door*).[3]

All three novels are set in the pre-war years in the author's native Ferrara, a town known for the prominence of its Jewish community and the vestiges of its once-teeming ghetto. His account differs from a historical one not only because of its esthetic and personal dimensions, but also because as "fiction," it deliberately underscores a truth that traditional historians have had some difficulty accepting — that the past can only be evoked as filtered through the hearts and minds of those who lived it and of those who attempt to recreate it. Witnesses and historians alike are at the mercy not only of their own foibles, failing memories, and unconscious fantasies and conflicts, but also of linguistic, narrative and historical conventions.[4] To emphasize that all reconstructions are subject to these mediating influences, in each of the three novels Bassani has the same unnamed but clearly autobiographical fictional narrator recall a different significant relationship from the past as it appears to him now, transfigured by time, memory, hindsight, rationalization and the lingering conflicts he has about it. Using an implicit Freudian framework and the potential for irony provided by the device of the "unreliable narrator," Bassani exploits his considerable powers of analysis and suggestion not to describe the Holocaust as such, but to capture the subtle and elusive ways in which it continues to live in the mind of his tormented narrator many years later. He challenges the reader to find, in the conflicts and contradictions of the narrative present, as well in its leitmotifs and recurring patterns, in its particular combination of "blindness and insight," clues as to what the past reality might have been.[5]

The premises of Bassani's work are that the integration of the Jews in post-Unification Italy was actually somewhat of a myth, subscribed to by both Jews and Gentiles, who colluded in sustaining it as long as it suited them both; the Jews' "fall from grace" was really just a "return of the repressed," the lessons of the past coming back to haunt those who would be blind to them, with a vengeance no one had dreamt possible. The primitive human need to belong, the difficulty of tolerating separateness and difference, in oneself as well as in others, after the war determines the desire of many to bury the horrors of the recent past and to return to a state of "normality" as quickly as possible. Bassani's short story "Una lapide in via Mazzini" depicts this phenomenon in a haunting account of one's man's return from the dead — Geo Josz, presumed dead in Auschwitz and commemorated in a plaque on the wall of the synagogue, returns to Ferrara to confront Jews and Gentiles alike, who nonetheless try to carry on as usual, refusing to pause and acknowledge where he is coming from for fear of having the past, freshly buried in its hastily improvised grave, come to life again. The same fear and wilful blindness create havoc for the Jewish characters depicted in these novels set before the war. Bassani's skill lies in the subtlety with which he evokes this dynamic of self-delusion as it manifests itself in a specific historical context, in conjunction with complex issues of class, race and sexual orientation.

The first of the three novels, *Gli occhiali d'oro*, published in 1958, recreates the parallel between the fate of the homosexual and that of the Jew in Western society. It presents us with a very subtle portrayal of a young Jew's not-so-unwitting contribution to the marginalization and eventual suicide of a formerly respected homosexual physician, Doctor Fadigati. Both are struggling with persecution at the hands of a society to which they once belonged, and it is this shared experience which causes Fadigati to consider the young Jew an ally, and to turn to him for support. But the young Jew is unable to respond to him sympathetically, and shuns him just as he himself is being shunned by his own Gentile cohorts. His failure to recognize the doctor's plight as similar to his own still haunts him twenty years later, as an adult and as a Holocaust survivor. For reasons unknown to the reader at first, he now feels compelled to tell Fadigati's story — the story of his fall from grace in the eyes of the bourgeois establishment of Ferrara, once he inexplicably abandons the mantle of discretion and publicly displays his homosexual relationship with the young, vulgar and sadistic Eraldo Deliliers. Slowly, however, Fadigati's story turns into the young Jew's story, or at least they become intertwined, as the adult narrator's account of the events of those months unwittingly betrays his sense of guilt, by displaying the parallels between their two situations without ever explicitly recognizing them as such. For example, in one chapter Fadigati finds himself faced with the protagonist's obtuse obliviousness to his anguish, in the next chapter the young Jew himself complains of the same indifference to his plight on the part of a close friend who happens to be a Gentile: the analogy is clear but is never addressed.

There are many other failures of memory, contradictions and paradoxes in this account, but none is as striking its glaring omission of any direct reference to the events of the intervening twenty years, the events of the Holocaust itself. In this first of the three novels they remain "unmentionable" and their absence testifies to the fact that Bassani's focus here is not merely what happened then, but what is still going on at the time of narration: denial. The inconsistencies in the narrator's story, and particularly in his telling of it, are the real subject of Bassani's interest, inasmuch as they provide clues to his as yet unresolved conflicts. For example the narrator is hostile to the bourgeois society of Ferrara, both Gentile and Jewish, and yet cannot bring himself to express any real solidarity with the unfortunate doctor. The result is a constantly shifting voice: one moment he speaks as outsider, the next as an insider, one moment as victim, the next as persecutor. He darts back and forth between expressing bitterness toward Fadigati's — and his own — tormentors and sounding just like them, as when he smugly congratulates himself for not having contributed actively to Fadigati's humiliation, though he did absolutely nothing to defend him. The problem the reader has in pinpointing the narrator's allegiances are signs of his continuing ambivalence to Fadigati, twenty years after the Doctor's death and fifteen years after the revelation of the horrors of the death camps. This first novel ends with the account of his discovery of Fadigati's death from the newspaper. The day before he had failed to keep an appointment with him, claiming, even now, to have simply forgotten it. The newspaper, in deference to the official policy of maintaining appearances, reported the death as an accidental drowning rather than as the suicide the protagonist instinctively knows it to have been.[6]

The next and most famous novel of the trilogy is *Il giardino dei Finzi Contini*, which picks up where *Gli occhiali d'oro* leaves off — 1938, the race laws are in place. Just as Fadigati was dismissed from his position as the chief of his division at the Hospital shortly before his suicide, so our protagonist finds himself expelled from both the public library where he was researching his thesis and the exclusive tennis club where he and the rest of Ferrara's young elite spent much of their leisure time. The narrator has made a little headway — he is able to speak openly of the Holocaust. However, he approaches the subject indirectly, through the account of his relationship with Micol Finzi-Contini, whose proud and wealthy Jewish family uncharacteristically opened the doors of its secluded garden and tennis courts to the young people suddenly excluded from their usual haunts by the race laws.

The novel opens in the present, in an Etruscan cemetery in Umbria, with the narrator creating a parallel between the Etruscans and the Finzi-Continis: the Etruscans are now extinct and there are no vestiges of their existence save in their tombs and artifacts. So too the Finzi-Continis are now extinct and there are no traces of their past save in their ancestral tombs and in the ruins of their once-magnificent home — except for what remains in the minds of those who knew them. There is also a difference however, which is obfuscated by the more obvious similarities: the Finzi-Continis with whom our narrator associated — Micol and her family — have no tombs, having been deported by the Nazi occupiers as a result of their passivity in the face of approaching doom.

The archaeological reference also suggests that what is about to take place is another kind of archaeology: a digging into the past with all the pitfalls of any reconstruction on the basis of the recovery of a few selected objects or memories, examined out of context and eroded by time. Again, the workings of the narrator's mind as he evokes his relationship with the beautiful and elusive Micol serve to elucidate the issues that persist for him now as well as the issues that may have existed then.

Self-styled aristocratic Jews who chose passive resistance and denial as their weapon of choice in the struggle for narcissistic self-preservation, the Finzi-Continis had always considered themselves different and better than other Jews as well, constituting themselves as a sort of Jewish upper class in a world which failed to grant them entry into its highest social echelons even at the best of times. Their stately home and garden, their silent, faithful servants, their tennis court, their private library, all are part of an enclave that points to their hubris, their refusal to embrace the reality of their outsider status and their paradoxical turning of this "outside" into an "inside" — the ultimate refuge of the helpless, a sort of adaptation to circumstance which turns a disadvantage into an advantage. Their children were privately schooled at home, the family occupied a separate section in the synagogue, Micol and her brother Alberto even have their own private language, *finzi-continico*, which consists of changing the usual emphasis in a word or sentence so as to confuse the outside listener. Their habit of keeping themselves at a distance even from their own community has earned them the diffidence of other Jews including the protagonist's father, but the protagonist himself is prey to lingering childhood fantasies about their superiority, nurtured by the memory of a few fleeting glimpses and brief encounters, during which he was both fascinated and intimidated by the aura of self-confidence and mystery that seemed to emanate from them. The protagonist's relationship with this proud and misguided family now that he finds himself and his own family pushed to the margins of society bears all the markings of a retreat into the fantasy world of the Freudian Family Romance.

The Family Romance as described by Freud involves a rejection of one's real parents, and hence one's identity, for the fantasized acquisition of origins worthier of one's imagined self.[7] By attaching himself to this family at this very difficult time Giorgio takes a detour into unreality which allows him not only to postpone the narcisisstically painful confrontation with his newly degraded status as a Jew and nothing but a Jew, but to fulfill many contradictory fantasies as well. Micol's blond good looks, her skill at tennis and her general aura of relaxed self-confidence make her a sort of Aryan Jewish princess, more desirable than any other Jewish girl could be at this time. Through the Finzi Continis our hero can be both Aryan and Jewish, both aristocratic and Jewish, both an outsider and insider, at the same time: in this paradise there is no contradiction between the two, there are no choices to make.

Or so it seems. Just as in *Gli occhiali d'oro* he is forever circling around the truth about his failure to defend either Fadigati or himself, what remains an obsessive preoccupation here is why he was unable to come out of his passive adoration of Micol and declare his feelings to her at the opportune moment in the evolution of their friendship. One of the key scenes in the novel takes place in the closed carriage, the vestige of a past long gone, which he and Micol climb into in the stables of the estate. Here he fails to take his cue, to profer the kiss that might have been the declaration of his feelings to her at the appropriate time. In his recollection this failure to come forward remains the turning point in their relationship, after which Micol gives up on him as a potential suitor and he begins his descent into despair, as she casts him out of paradise and he is forced to return to his own family. He finally does make an awkward advance, in the wrong place and at the wrong time, and suffers the humiliation of rejection. The narrator recreates all these events in detail and even provides what seems to be an accurate analysis of the other characters in this drama, but fails to draw the obvious conclusions about his own behavior. In both novels we are dealing with the protagonist's inability to act, to reach out at a crucial time, to establish a connection that would involve confronting the truth about another person and about himself and accepting it. The truth he would have had to accept about Fadigati was the truth of his homosexuality and of their common plight as outcasts in their own land, while the truth he would have had to embrace about Micol was the truth of her sexuality, that is to say of her existence as a flesh-and-blood woman, which would entail the acceptance of his own adult sexuality and of the difference between them. This was impossible because it ran counter to the entire spirit of his sojourn in the garden of the Finzi-Continis, clearly presented by the author as a metaphorical excursion into the fantasy world of pre-oedipal narcissism, in which the comforting mirroring of the child by the mother shields the infant from the harsh realities of a hostile world. Having been cast out from the society that once accepted him as one of its own, he refuses to accept that his beloved Ferrara has lost its once "maternal face" ("volto materno") and joins the Finzi-Continis in the ghetto/paradise they have created to mirror the image of themselves they so desperately sought and that the Gentile world would never quite yield up to them. Just as he is unable to accept the regime's hostility to the Jews, the difference between himself as a Jew and the Gentile world in which he lives, so too he is unable to embrace the difference between himself and Micol, the reality of her sexuality as a woman and his own adult masculinity.

But all is not lost. In literature, whenever a hero is captivated by a beautiful woman and drawn into her lair, he is in fact being waylaid on his journey to another destination, he is being distracted from his real mission, like Ulysses and his men by Circe, like Aeneas by Dido, like Rinaldo by Armida in Tasso's *Gerusalemme Liberata*. So too, the protagonist's attraction to the world of the Finzi-Continis and to Micol is a "battuta d'arresto," in this case an illusory escape from a difficult place and a difficult time in the life of a young protected Jewish male having to negotiate his entry into manhood at a time when the society into which he seemed naturally destined to be integrated has just slammed its doors in his face.

It is important to emphasize that this is an issue which is never confronted directly in these novels, and that does not emerge clearly unless each novel is read in the context of the other two. But the whole is greater than the sum of its parts. The three stories were conceived as a trilogy, as a self-referential body of texts which gesture back and forth to each other, in the process producing an additional level of meaning which none of the stories alone allows us to grasp. It is at this level that we can find answers to the questions that interest us here: "what are these novels really about? How do the stories of an unfortunate homosexual, of a love affair that never was and, as we shall see in the third novel, of adolescent male rivalry, fit together and what do they tell us about the specific experience of a young, privileged Jew in Ferrara at this time? What questions are still bothering the author about this time in his life and in the life of his community? What is it that he is trying to come to terms with?"

In *Gli occhiali d'oro* we already see the protagonist's contempt for his own father, who retreats into denial and passivity as he refuses to acknowledge that the Jews, in spite of their "patriotic virtues," have now become enemies of the state. As that novel draws to a close the young man is caught between two equally unpalatable possibilities: embrace his Jewishness and identify with his father, or reject his Jewishness and identify with the enemy. Fadigati's solution as a homosexual enemy of the state is the result of his choice of the second alternative: Fadigati embraces the regime's hatred of the homosexual and saves it the trouble of ridding itself of him by commiting suicide. Our hero is unwilling to do either and withdraws into an illusory paradise, the garden of the Finzi-Continis, where he finds slowly a way out of his predicament. Having adopted the Finzi-Continis as his own family he discovers, sadly, that this golden Jewish ghetto offers no positive male role models either. Unable to identify with his own father's denial and passivity in the face of persecution, he is equally stymied by the attitudes of the Jewish men he finds here. Micol's father is an old man preoccupied with Jewish genealogy and cemeteries: death and the past. It is he who has created this artificial atmosphere and he who has condemned his own family to death. His son Alberto is the inheritor of this legacy. A sickly young man who withers away in the face of his family's denial of his illness, he is a passive lifeless latent homosexual, doomed to live out his sterile destiny as the carrier of his family's defective male gene. Both of these characters are more symbolic than real, actor's in the hero's own dilemma of identity at this difficult time. The only viable role model in this doomed paradise is, perhaps not surprisingly, a Gentile, Giuseppe Malnate, a college friend of Alberto's and the incarnation of "health" in a diseased environment. An anti-Fascist who works as an engineer in a local factory and belongs to the outlawed Communist party, he offers the model of an active, engaged masculinity which contrasts sharply with the passive demeanor of the Jewish men, our hero included. Appropriately, it is Malnate who gives our hero the impetus to work his way out of his impasse. In a desperate attempt to remain connected to Micol after she has asked him to stay away, he begins to befriend Malnate and, on the basis of a few elements concludes, or rather fantasizes, that Malnate is Micol's lover. It is this traumatic suspicion that finally provokes the oedipal crisis and its resolution. Bassani uses the oedipal crisis and its resolution as a metaphor not only for the acquisition of male gender identity but also for the process of acceptance of racial and ethnic difference, as well as for the recognition of the existence of evil in the world. As the protagonist begins to withdraw from the make-believe universe of the Finzi-Continis, he gradually mends fences with his own family and particularly with his own father. I would add — although all this remains unsaid in the novel — that it is at the point at which he re-embraces his own family that he also realizes that he must find a "third way." Not his father's way, desperately clinging to the post-Risorgimento idea of Jewish integration and acceptance in spite of all the evidence to the contrary; not the Finzi-Contini way, creating one's own artificial reality to avoid the narcissistic injury of exclusion and marginality; but Malnate's way, a Gentile's way. He relinquishes Micol and takes his place next to Malnate, the positive male figure in his Family Romance gone awry and accepts that the only way to be a Jew and a man at this time in history is join the Resistance and to fight. By refusing to bring the relationship between Micol and Malnate into the "real world" so to speak — all we know is what the narrator knows to be true and, more importantly, what he imagines to be true — Bassani emphasizes that its importance exists at the level of fantasy, as the protagonist's way of working through the fears which have driven him into the narcissistic passivity of the garden of soon-to-be-horrors. The "maternal face" of Ferrara, as of the Garden and of Micol, is an illusion : the world is not made in our image and must be dealt with as such.

The third novel in this trilogy, *Dietro la porta*, was published in 1961. While the two earlier novels go forward in time — *The Gold-Rimmed Eyeglasses* is set in 1936-37, *The Garden of the Finzi-Continis* in '37-'38 — and deal directly with the Holocaust years, *Behind the Door* takes place in 1929, suggesting that Bassani sees the answers he is seeking through the fictionalized exploration of his own experience as lying in the condition of the Jews previous to the events of World War II. The novel's title alludes directly to what Freud termed the "primal scene" — the child's imaginings of what takes place behind his parents' closed door.[8] Here Bassani takes us back to another important transitional moment in his character's development: a young Gentile classmate of inferior social extraction leads our protagonist to an unwelcome and traumatic awakening that coincides with the onset of puberty, the acceptance of one's sexuality and the recognition of the sexuality of one's parents. Adolescent male rivalry is complicated by issues of class and race, in a narrative which attempts to address the reasons for the protagonist's choice of the vulgar, opportunistic, hypocritical and academically mediocre Luciano Pulga as a best friend and deskmate, when in reality other classmates such as the brilliant, well-bred young Carlo Cattolica would certainly have been more seemingly appropriate. Questions raised obliquely and metaphorically in the two earlier novels here return to the fore in their crudest and most explicit terms. Not coincidentally, the relationship between the protagonist and Pulga reproduces the sado-masochistic victim/oppressor dynamic between Fadigati and his lover Eraldo Deliliers, drawing the parallel between Fadigati and the adolescent protagonist that the adult narrator worked so hard to deny in the earlier novel. Why did Athos Fadigati, a respected member of the professional upper middle class choose to take as a lover, openly, the young, vulgar and opportunistic Deliliers? Deliliers' openness about sexual matters not only contrasts sharply with Fadigati's demeanor but also makes the repeated public humiliation of Fadigati by his lover the hallmark of their relationship. In *Gli occhiali d'oro* the narrator is fascinated and mystified by Fadigati's passive submission to his lover's sadistic behavior; in *Dietro la porta* the narrator describes a similar dynamic between himself and Pulga, with Pulga doing everything in his power to provoke and humiliate the sexually repressed, passive over-protected mama's boy who has chosen to befriend him in spite of the social, economic and intellectual differences between them. In an adolescent comparison of penis size provoked by Pulga, Pulga accuses him of homosexuality, and this trauma is clearly meant to be at the origin of the protagonist's profound ambivalence to Fadigati later on. But his difficulty as an adult narrator in dealing with Fadigati's story has at least as much to do with his intense discomfort at Fadigati's passivity in the face of his tormentors. Repeatedly he makes reference to Fadigati's apparent complacency and even enjoyment of the humiliation being inflicted upon him, both by the society at large and by his own lover, who mercilessly assaults, robs and deserts him during their vacation at Riccione. Fadigati's seeming masochism still strikes a raw nerve in our narrator, who returns to it over and over again, as he does to the image of his father as a lamb about to go to the slaughter, evoked by the older man's exasperating denial of the degradation of the Jews. Both are examples of passivity that raise difficult questions similar to those he is now seeking to answer, specifically about his own reluctance to speak up as a Jew to his Gentile friends and neighbors supporting the regime, as well as the real and unspoken question of the entire trilogy — why did the Jews not fight back more energetically?

This last novel provides no clear answers: as always the reader is forced to weed out those hints of the truth that can be gleaned from the narrator's rationalizations and pseudo-self-awareness. Clearly though, the young protagonist is more comfortable with the inferior Pulga than with his social and intellectual equal Cattolica. Pulga's marginality, both social and academic, mirrors the protagonist's marginality as a Jew, while at the same allowing him to feel superior and powerful, to deny his feelings of inferiority and exclusion by acting the role of generous benefactor to the less privileged "outsider". But this is just one aspect of things. Like Fadigati vis à vis Deliliers, so our protagonist is clearly drawn to precisely what repulses him in Pulga, the macho bravado and vulgarity that contrast so sharply with his own naive and precariously budding masculinity. When the protagonist finally is approached by Carlo Cattolica, the Gentile golden boy to whose inner circle he had never hoped to gain access, it is only to be told that Pulga has been humiliating him behind his back, particularly by making reference to his mother's sexuality. The protagonist is invited to Carlo's home, and eavesdrops from another room while Pulga does indeed make the offensive remarks, hence the novel's title *Behind the Door*. While this episode marks the end of his friendship with Pulga, it also leads to an oedipal awakening. He suddenly realizes that a favorite photograph of his, showing him in his mother's arms as a small child, was not just about the two of them. His mother's dazzling smile and sparkling eyes were not for him, but for the invisible photographer, his father home on leave from the army, in anticipation of their sexual reunion.

This last novel conflates the issues addressed far more indirectly in the first two novels by tracing back his own ambivalence to Fadigati and passivity vis à vis Micol to a precarious masculinity deriving from an unresolved oedipal crisis further complicated by his traumatic adolescent relationship with Pulga. To this he attributes the blocks he had to overcome in order to stand up and fight at a time when that was the only acceptable way, in his mind, to be a Jewish male. This suggests that the question of the so-called passivity of the Jews vis à vis their persecutors is somehow linked in Bassani's mind to the problem of Jewish masculinity, itself at least partly a function of Jewish history and of the difficulty Jewish men had in defending their families since they were always outnumbered.[9] This legacy, combined with the pampered and protected upbringing of Jewish boys of the middle and upper middle classes such as himself, amply described in *Dietro la porta*, must have made it all the more difficult to confront the harsh realities of official anti-Semitism. In his fictional works Bassani never addresses the question of his role in the Resistance and of how he came to make the decision to fight, and the protagonist of these novels is never seen to be grappling consciously with that possibility, while the narrator of *The Garden* makes only one oblique reference to the time he spent in prison during the war years. And yet this is clearly the unspoken subject of these novels: the internal blocks that needed to be overcome for him to make what appeared to him as a most un-Jewish decision in his particular milieu: the decision to give up the mantle of privilege and passivity and to embrace the common underground struggle for freedom being waged in all of Europe.

LUCIENNE KROHA

McGill University

---

[1] See Marilyn Schneider, *Vengeance of the Victim. History and Symbol in Giorgio Bassani's Fiction* (Minneapolis: University of Minnesota Press, 1986) 9.

[2] For a specific treatment of the subject of the Jews under Fascism see Renzo De Felice, *Storia degli ebrei italiani sotto il fascismo* [1961] (Turin: Einaudi, 1972). For an account of Italian Jewish writers which includes a chapter on Bassani see H. Stuart Hughes, *Prisoners of Hope: The Silver Age of the Italian Jews, 1924-1974* (Cambridge, Mass. and London: Harvard UP, 1983).

[3] For a complete listing of Bassani's works and their English language translations see Schneider 233-34. Both *Gli occhiali d'oro* and *Il giardino dei Finzi-Contini* have been translated twice: by Isabel Quigley as *The Gold-Rimmed Spectacles* (London: Faber and Faber, 1960) and *The Garden of the Finzi-Continis* (London: Faber and Faber, 1965) and by William Weaver as *The Gold-Rimmed Eyeglasses* as part of the volume *The Smell of Hay* (New York: Harcourt Brace Jovanovich, 1975) and *The Garden of the Finzi –Continis* (New York: Harcourt Brace Jovanovich, 1977). *Dietro la porta* was translated by William Weaver as *Behind the Door* (New York: Harcourt Brace Jovanovich, 1976). For critical studies of Bassani's work and detailed critical bibliography see, in addition to Schneider, Massimo Grillandi, *Invito alla lettura di Giorgio Bassani* (Milan: Mursia, 1972); Giusi Oddo De Stefanis, *Bassani entro il cerchio delle sue mura* (Ravenna: Longo, 1980); Douglas Radcliff-Umstead, *The Exile into Eternity: A Study of the Narrative Writings of Giorgio Bassani* (Rutherford, N.J.: Farleigh Dickinson UP, 1987).

[4] For an illuminating discussion of these and related issues see the Introduction to *Rediscovering History: Culture, Politics and the Psyche* (Essays in honor of Carl E. Schorske), edited by Michael S. Roth (Stanford: Stanford University Press. 1994). I owe the title of this essay to this volume.

[5] Integral and essential to an understanding of the analysis that follows is the distinction in all cases between the protagonists of the three stories and their narrators, who are telling their stories years later. Bassani's concern is not to recreate what really happened, which in any case cannot be known directly, but to call attention to the potential problems in this account, which are signs of "truth".

[6] For a detailed textual analysis of this novel see my own "The Structures of Silence: Re-reading Giorgio Bassani's *Gli occhiali d'oro*," *The Italianist*, n. 10 (1990) 71-102.

[7] For a definition of this term and for an account of its appearance in Freud's writings see "Family Romance" and "Oedipus Complex" in J. Laplanche and J.-B. Pontalis, *The Language of Psychoanalysis,* trans. Donald Nicholson-Smith (New York and London: W.W. Norton and Company, 1973), 160-61 and 282-87.

[8] See "Primal scene" in Laplanche and Pontalis 335-36.

[9] On Jewish masculinity and some of the issues raised in this essay see Barbara Breitman, "Lifting up the Shadow of Anti-Semitism: Jewish Masculinity in a New Light" in *A Mensch Among Men. Explorations in Jewish Masculinity*, edited by Harry Brod (Freedom, Ca.: The Crossing Press,1988) 101-117.

Italy: A Fond Remembrance

It may be a good first step to explain how we (my parents and I) arrived in Italy at all. It was not our first choice, nor indeed an initial choice at all. After all, Italy was a member of the Axis, an ally of Hitler's Germany. Would that be a country where Jewish refugees, fleeing for their lives from that inferno, would choose to go?

So let me begin with what admittedly lies somewhat outside the advertised topic of these meetings, requesting your indulgence and with the promise that we shall be in Italy within a very few minutes.

I was born in Vienna, as were my parents, and after Hitler invaded and annexed Austria in March of 1938, we stayed on for nearly three years, not, once again, by choice, but continually attempting to obtain entry visas into countries likely to offer refuge, above all the United States. A long and eventful history goes with that period, but that belongs elsewhere. Suffice it to say that, as a last resort, we left "Greater Germany" in late January of 1941, emigrating legally, but entering what was then Yugoslavia illegally (another story for some future occasion). After a few weeks of uncertainty — and considerable danger of being shipped back to Germany — we were placed into a refugee camp called *Draganiçi* (near Karlovaç) by the Jewish organization HIAS, and my father was appointed one of three camp administrators. Living conditions were scarce and food even more so, but we felt safe at last.

Our security there was of brief duration: in April of 1941 Germany invaded Yugoslavia and our camp, within the newly created German puppet state of Croatia, was once again enemy territory for us. It so happened that, while we were within the zone of so-called Croatian sovereignty, about 40 miles south of us lay that area of Croatia occupied by Italian military forces.

My father, suspicious (or, as he was dubbed by his two fellow administrators, paranoid) had little trust in the benevolence of the Croatian regime and its paramilitary outfit, the Ustase. A few days later, I forget under what pretext, he managed to enter the Italian-occupied zone and attempted to see the Italian military governor there. He succeeded and, to the surprise of both of them, found himself in the company of a brother officer from World War I, a Count Attems from Triest, which as you know was part of Austria until Austria's defeat. That noble and compassionate man, sharing my father's misgivings about Croatian benevolence, immediately offered temporary entrance visas to every refugee in our camp.

My father communicated this offer, generous beyond all expectations, to the assembled camp the next day, but, unexpectedly or otherwise, the other two administrators declared emphatically that leaving the camp was not a good idea. It was best to say put, they opined, within the "safety" of the camp; after all, the Croatians were not Germans, were they?

So it happened that the three of us, together with less than 10 others, took a train to Sussak (on the way, crossing form the Croatian into the Italian zone, the Croatian border guards sequestered all our worldly goods, but that, too, is another story). Within two weeks or so, the remaining 150 or so inmates were herded by the Ustase to a mass grave and shot or burned alive.

Sussak was a welcome refuge, a life saver, in fact. But despite the general benevolence of Italian authorities, it was not a place where we could expect to settle permanently. We were, after all, "enemy aliens," being Jews, and even the local Jewish community, headed by a brave young rabbi, though it assisted us financially to the best of its ability, could not obtain *permessi di soggiorno* — or resident permits — for us. Thus it happened that we had no other choice than to make a *domanda* — an application — to the Italian Ministry of the Interior to admit us to the Concentration Camp Ferramonti, Provincia di Cosenza, where we arrived roughly in December of 1941.

We did not yet know, at that time, of the extermination camps, but we were aware — partly from personal experience — of enough about German camps to be utterly amazed at our reception in Ferramonti. True, the living quarters assigned to us (together with another family) were primitive, and the food and climate left much to be desired. But imagine our surprise when, a few days after our arrival, the — presumably Fascist — camp commander invited us to dinner! Aside from the fact that he reproached me for my almost non-existent knowledge of Italian which, he said, was not what he expected of the children in his camp, he treated us with exquisite hospitality. During the following months, his sons played soccer and other sports with us, the children of inmates. In other words, apart from the modest and malaria-infested living conditions — which were shared almost fully by the camp guards — we led an almost "normal" life — and I learned Italian at the camp school; I still have my *pagella*, the report card.

My mother, an outstanding cook of Viennese pastries, created a small "café" where she would often sing Viennese songs, and I — the mind boggles — played the accordion. We earned little, but just enough to improve the scanty food situation a little.

Unfortunately, the climate severely affected my father; he lost a great deal of weight and his life was in serious danger. He therefore decided to submit another *domanda*, asking for us to be transferred to a *confino libero* farther north. A *confino libero* meant that one would be confined in what was usually a small village, or even an island, within which, however, one could move about with almost complete freedom, at least during daylight hours (there would not have been much to do after dark anyway). Incidentally, Italian citizens deemed to be inimical to the Fascist regime were also liable to such confinement. One of the more famous ones was Carlo Levi, physician, painter, and author of *Cristo si è fermato a Eboli*. Our application was approved and in June or July of 1942 we were transferred — under military guard as before — to Bomba, province of Chieti, in the Abruzzo region.

Bomba is the birthplace of the brothers Spaventa, the famous statesman Silvio and his perhaps less-known philosopher brother Bernardo. They were what during the last century were called liberals, though today they would probably be seen as conservatives. In any event, their descendants still lived in Bomba and formed the center of a daringly outspoken antifascist contingent, one part of which was represented by the D'Intino family, which received us and other confinees warmly and generously. I almost became an adoptive son, and their surviving two children, Maria and Rodolfo, have remained our dear and valued friends to this day. (For those of you interested in jazz, you may have heard of Peppino d'Intino, the drummer and founder of the Roman New Orleans Jazz Band in 1946; he was the oldest of the three children, and unfortunately died prematurely some years ago.)

You might wonder at this point why Spaventa and his followers suffered no reprisals by the government. I cannot answer that question, but one is inclined to surmise that Spaventa was regarded as either too important or too inconsequential a personage.

The overwhelming majority of inhabitants, whom we might fairly describe as politically indifferent, and even most of the — probably obligatory — Fascists, such as the mayor, "Don" Armando Ciarrapico, the village secretary, and the local *maresciallo* or commanding non-commissioned officer of the local police, never failed to treat us with every courtesy and consideration. Ciarrapico, also the highly respected owner of the local oil press, regularly favored us — secretly — with a bottle of Abruz-zo's delicious and nutritious olive oil (to this day, I and subsequently even my American-born wife Corinne, prefer an appetizer of Italian bread dipped into extra virgin olive oil to almost any other). Signora Pedretti, refined owner of the bakery, never refused us a loaf of — rationed — bread, still scalding hot from the oven. Contrary to most native inhabitants of the large cities, we, refugees and officially declared pernicious enemies of the State, never went hungry.

Our well-being, under the circumstances close to paradise, lasted about a year. On July 25, 1943, Mussolini was deposed and our antifascist friends and I marched down the main street, chanting the Garibaldi hymn. We rejoiced in the Allied advance into Calabria (incidentally, liberating the Ferramonti camp) and on September 8, Italy, under Field Marshal Badgolio, capitulated. We thought that the war was over for us. We were quite mistaken. The Germans had begun to occupy Italian military strongholds immediately after Mussolini's demotion, and, in fact, quickly liberated him from the Abruzzo mountain stronghold not far from us, where the new Italian government had imprisoned him. Following capitulation, German forces quickly occupied all the major cities.

From then on, matters rapidly deteriorated. A day or two later there appeared, on the main gate of the village hall, a proclamation by the commander-in-chief of the German occupation armies, Field Marshal Kesselring, ordering the immediate arrest and delivery to the Germans of all political and "racial" (that meant us) internees, as well as any Allied prisoners of war — who had been released by the Italian military after capitulation and were trying to make their way south to join the advancing British and American forces. A few days later, a battalion of the dreaded and murderous Waffen-SS took up residence in our village, in the vast home of Dr. Luce, one of the two village physicians and a well-known Fascist.

Our mayor and the *maresciallo* made it immediately, albeit very secretly, clear to us that they had no intention of following Kesselring's order, and it became generally known, through the grape vine, that villagers all over Northern and Central Italy were assisting in hiding confinees, as well as aiding the escaping Allied soldiers with food, clothing, occasional medical attention, and often hiding them for days, even weeks, fully aware that to be discovered in such acts of high treason meant instant death. Also, after the end of the occupation we learned that cases of handing over confinees of Allied soldiers represented no more than a minute percentage, and our village was an outstanding example of how not a single inhabitant, man, woman, or child, betrayed either us (once or twice someone would express surprise that we, who spoke German, evinced no desire to make friendly conversation with the German soldiery, but once the state of affairs had been explained, he showed full understanding) or the dozen or so Allied ex-prisoners who not only came through our village — many others did — but stayed for several weeks, hidden high up in the mountain and constantly supplied with food and clothing (it had gotten pretty cold by then). Not only did our mayor and our police chief condone this clandestine supply line from the village up into the higher hills, they organized and often took part in it. One night, when one of the soldier's leg, previously bitten by a dog, became infected, Dr. Luce, the same who was perhaps our leading Fascist and currently host of the SS battalion, was willingly escorted to one of the remote huts and administered medical aid to the — to us erstwhile, but to him presumably still present — enemy.

Our dilemma continued for several months. As some of you may recall, the Allied advance was halted for a long time near Cassino, south of Rome, on the western side of the boot. Abruzzo, and our village on the southern shore of the river Sangro, lie at about the same altitude, but on the eastern, Adriatic side. The Allied advance at the entire front, about halfway between Calabria and Lombardia, was held up for about three months. Indeed, we learned that only in late November the small town of Atessa, south of us on the other side of the mountain and only a few miles away, was already in the hands of the British Eighth Army, while Bomba, though the Germans had by then departed, was still a no-man's land, subject to occasional bombardments, or even (who knew) a German return.

The two d'Intino boys and I, after consulting with our Allied guests as well as the mayor and the *maresciallo*, decided it was time to make our move, and in the dark of night we and the soldiers crossed the mountain. On December 3, 1943 we were warmly received by an advance New Zea-land unit, to whom the soldiers we had escorted recommended us enthusiastically. A few days later, my parents followed.

Thus ended the years of immediate danger to our survival. A few weeks after our arrival in Atessa the British Army arranged for our transport to Bari, initially and briefly to a refugee camp. Both my father and I almost immediately found employment with that army, first as interpreters and later in somewhat more responsible positions, and we moved to a private apartment in Bari. I even did a brief stint as a "batman" in Foggia (no, not Robin's boss. A batman was the personal attendant to a British officer, but my boss, the Canadian major, soon discovered that my qualifications for personal servant and factotum were negligible, and I was promptly dispatched back to Bari). On May 9, 1945, Germany capitulated and soon thereafter we moved to Milan, where I enjoyed a happy adolescence as a permanent resident, until our emigration — finally — to the United States at the beginning of 1950. I held various jobs with Allied and Italian employers, and even earned a *maturità scientifica* certificate from the Liceo Vittorio Veneto. Above all, I made up, at least in part, for the years of my childhood and adolescence I had lost previously. Had it depended on me, I probably should never have left Italy, but to my parents it was still the Promised Land and for me, as an only child who had survived with them through countless dangers, there was no question of separation.

Finally, just two concluding remarks:

First, a personal note: It is now almost 50 years since I left Italy as a permanent resident. I have returned frequently, sometimes as often as twice a year, usually to deliver lectures or attend conferences, but also because my love for, and gratitude to that country and its people have remained a powerful magnet. I try to retain its beautiful language, reading and writing it as often as possible. I engage in conversation, too, but that is less easy here, and sometimes, to my embarrassment and chagrin, I find myself faltering. But I shall keep trying and cherish my affection for the country and the people who, even though I was supposedly their enemy, saved my parents' lives and mine many times over.

Secondly: as a social psychologist I know how foolish it can be to speak of "national characteristics." I know how different northern Italians are from, say, Sicilians and, speaking of Sicily, where I visit dear friends as often as I can, I also know that western Sicilians are quite different from eastern ones. Moreover, how can one even speak of ethnic generalizations when every single person is unique to himself? Still, Luigi Barzini did it and while I lay no claim to come close to his remarkable insights, I will venture a few words: It seems to me that much of what is commonly thought by outsiders of Italians is grossly distorted. They are neither a people constantly engaged in singing and merrymaking, nor are they deeply engaged in Mafia intrigues. There *is*, I believe, good reason to think of them as generally individualistic and anti-authoritarian. They — again speaking with all possible reservations — are likely to resent and be suspicious of constituted authority, having had grievous experiences, originating from outsiders as well as each other — remember the many wars among city-states — for may centuries. As a relatively young country, they tend to be contentious; were there room enough, most Italians might like to found their own political party.

Above all, however, they are humane and compassionate, particularly toward those they perceive as being persecuted by someone more powerful. It is sometimes said that, if you have so-and-so for a friend you don't need an enemy. I have always felt that, having an Italian for a friend, no enemy can harm me.

HARRY KAUFMANN, EMERITUS
C.U.N.Y.

The Coherence of Memory

I live in Rome but every summer I go back to Cagliari, capital of Sardinia, the city where I was born. My annual vacation is a time of solitary morning walks, in search of the places I associate with my childhood. The most important of all, because of that association with childhood and beyond, into adolescence as well, is the Castle. In ancient times, when Cagliari was a feudal town, it was the fortress. Today it is a residential quarter housing rich and poor alike. I only came to know and appreciate its history, at least part of it, much later. It's a real shame that families and schools don't teach us to understand the history of the place where we grew up. It was only recently that I came to understand something about mine.

Like this, for example.

The medieval house my family lived in stands in what was once the ghetto, reserved for the Jews and very close to the synagogue. Abandoned for centuries, today the synagogue is a museum. Beneath the arches and vaulted ceilings that survive, gather clusters of visitors, Jews and gentiles. Every now and then I join them, struggling to understand the mystery of my origins: a sizeable portion of my life lived in a ghetto without me having the slightest idea what that meant. Not to mention the most surprising stories that I still come to hear about today through the notes left by the visitors: a few of these notes have been framed and hang on the walls.

There's one that reads: "Thank you, Brother Sardinian, for letting me stand in a temple that was once the Glory of God. If you permit me, I would like to leave a testimony and I shall be sincerely grateful if you don't destroy it. I am a Jew of Italian origin and have lived in the United States for a long time. Among my most distant memories is one of a long journey in a railway cattle-car and of a small station with a wooden roof with writing on it that meant nothing either to my family or to me: DACHAU.

We got off the train exhausted, guarded by the SS with their guns pointing at us. All you could hear was the whimpering of the children, an occasional cry, and the shuffling of shoes on the ground. The sound of that shuffling still echoes in my ears and in my mind and I think I shall go on hearing it for the rest of my life. I can say no more, or maybe I don't want to: I'm sorry. On this island, separated from the rest of the world, in this enchanted place, I have found something that belongs to me: and I am very grateful to you for it." It is signed: B.P.

The lump in my throat breaks into a sob. My eyes come to rest on the floor where other notes lie, held down with a white stone, the lovely white stones from the beaches of my beloved Sardinia. There are more on the wall, that forgotten wall that has been turned into a new Wailing Wall. Other stories which I don't dare examine. Other stories that my imagination and my tears can merely skim.

I leave the synagogue, a place of prayer in ancient times, now transformed into a place of memory — both distant and recent. The sun blinds me, the coolness of a moment ago is immediately consumed by the stifling heat. A brief pause at a café for a glass of milk with a splash of mint, and I'm on my way again. I follow the same route I used to take years ago to go to school: I'm on a memory walk. I recognize the uneven stones, I even recognize the smells as I walk up and down the narrow lanes. Then, there it is: my school.

Yes, that was my school. At once I can feel the same fear I did then. I even recognize the fear. I want to run away, get away, forever. But flight won't help me overcome my fear. I must confront it, I feel like the time has come: to confront my story, my little, banal story, as I lived it when I was between six and ten years of age.

I'm over fifty now, a woman who has found fulfillment, partially at least, in writing — together with this friend I am with, Fabio Della Seta — a novel entitled, "Dear Sophie." It is not an autobiography but it does have a special meaning for me: it has helped me put into focus and to understand many of the fears I kept locked up inside for too long: fears linked to back then.

I am the daughter of an officer in the Italian Navy who served his country during the last war as captain of a submarine.

He was the son of a Catholic father and a Jewish mother. There were, and still are, important military bases in Sardinia. It was during one of his postings on the island that my father met my mother — a beautiful, charming girl with blond hair and blue eyes. Her fragile appearance didn't stop her from getting her new family to adopt her religion: she was a Protestant. Her brother was a minister.

And thus the autobiographical elements, apparently lost to memory, start taking shape. Needless to say how much memory is our very life. It dictates our understanding, our reasoning, our feelings, even our way of behaving. Life is not life without memory.

Right now I'm standing in front of the large entrance to my school. Differently to what usually happens with adults, I see it just as I did when I was a child. I see myself little again, my hand holding onto my mother while she talks to the teacher: "We are Protestants. I don't want my daughter attending the Catholic religion class." That sentence, so innocent-sounding today, marked the beginning of my problems, as I shall shortly explain.

First I'd like to recount the fearful days spent at my grandmother's villa in Lombardy. She was a hard woman with a huge heart. It was 1944 and the villa was near the Swiss border. My mother, my brother and I had taken refuge there.

My mother was terribly upset: they said my father was lost in action and she had no one she could talk to. My grandmother was a woman ahead of her time: she taught philosophy in a state school. Her origins were Jewish but she didn't practice her religion. Even so, before dinner in the evening she used to read to us from the Bible.

One evening, during the reading ritual, we heard a knock at the door. My grandmother told us to stay where we were and to go on eating while she went to answer the door. The knocks became more persistent as she made her way down the stairs. Crouching behind the bannister, I watched the scene from above. About a dozen people, young and old, were all talking at once at the top of their voices. I had difficulty making out what they were saying to my grandmother: "Alright," she replied, "I can put you up for tonight. The only safe place is the cellar. Follow me." At once the small procession disappeared into the kitchen.

We watched our grandmother as she returned to the dining room: she looked worried as she whispered something to my mother, explaining what had happened.

Later, my mother told me I would be sleeping with her, in her bed. It was the first time and the idea made me happy. It was a short-lived happiness. On the contrary, it marked the start of a nightmare I was destined to relive for a long time, at least until I was sixteen. All night long my mother repeated how I was not to tell anyone about what had happened. "Whatever they may ask you, you always say you don't know anything, you never saw anything."

That phrase: "I don't know anything, I never saw anyone" ...she made me say it over and over again, a hundred times.

My persistent questions were answered: obviously in a manner suited to a little girl of three years old. "They were friends of grandma being chased by bad men, very bad men, real devils. If you say anything they could kill your mommy, your granny and your little brother. You don't want that to happen, do you? Your granny is a very courageous lady and you must obey her...even if she hasn't seen the Light."

I didn't know what "Light" she was talking about, but I behaved myself just the same. To the extent that when German soldiers arrived and commandeered the villa for a few days, or a week perhaps, I transformed myself into a little deaf mute. I played the part so well that those strange individuals who walked around the house as though they owned the place, never even bothered to look at me. My brother was the center of their attention: blond-haired and fair-skinned, they adopted him as their mascot — perhaps because they thought he was a prize example of the pure Arian race.

The German soldiers left after a week without asking anyone for their documents. My grandmother's refugees could finally come out of hiding in the cellar and make their way across the border into Switzerland.

As I said, this episode remained in my memory for a long time because it coincided with another persecution — of which I was the victim. Racism, or rather, religious hatred, doesn't affect only Jews, but anyone who is labeled "different."

My mother called herself Protestant in an undeveloped nation like Sardinia where Catholicism, imposed by Byzantium and reinforced by the Spanish presence on the island, is part of an even older, primitive culture. The Inquisition happened in Sardinia too, persecuting the Jews there who had pretended to convert in order to avoid exile and the confiscation of their property: the so-called "marrani." Isolated as it is, Sardinia was more attached to age-old prejudices than the regions of northern Italy were.

Those prejudices no longer exist today, but when I was a child they were still strong. Protestants were considered rebels and heretics, to be combatted or converted. Moreover, the public school I attended was marked by a mentality that was not only Catholic but Fascist: which often resulted in the same thing.

In response to my mother's request, I was banished to the back bench, isolated from my companions. Whatever happened in class, I was the one who was blamed and duly punished by being made to kneel on some dried chick-peas behind the black-board for a period of time — an hour, say — that varied according to the crime of which I was accused.

The sound of the bell was my liberation. But when my mother couldn't come and fetch me, which happened quite often, I had to race home with my heart pounding: behind me I could hear the sound of my companions running to catch up with me. If they did it meant being beaten in the face and punched in the stomach and cursed: "Filthy priest-eater! Your mother's a witch!"

My parents' complaints fell on deaf ears, if anything they made matters worse. I learned to keep my fear to myself. At night, when I recited the "Our Father," on reaching the words "Thy Will be done...," I added: let me die. All that is over now, for me at least. But part of that fear still hovers inside me: it springs to life every time I read in the papers, or see on television, that some act of cruelty has been perpetrated in the name of tribal, racial or — yet again — religious hatred.

Today I'm overcome by a desire to see my old classroom again, with its wooden, black-painted benches — with the front that opened so you could put your books inside. Where are they? I ask the caretaker who listens to me in amazement.

"Why do you want to know? We piled them in the basement."

"I'd like to see them again, if I can."

He doesn't answer and continues looking at me curiously. Then he goes and gets a bunch of keys, walks down some steps and opens a small door. And there they are: all the benches from my elementary class. They're not piled up but laid out in rows. Maybe they were waiting for me. And here I am, looking at them one by one.

"What are you staring at? Looking for something?"

Yes, I'm looking for something. Here it is: I've found it.

"This bench is broken. Look, there's a piece on the floor. Can I have it?"

"I don't know what to say. Are you sure you feel alright?"

"It's a personal thing. This was my bench...Please?"

"But it's only a little piece of wood. You know what I think? There are some weird people in the world. Anyway, if you really want it, take it. They'll think it got lost."

"Thank you so much. That's very kind of you."

"Don't mention it. You take care of yourself, though..."

He puts out his hand, like he wants to feel my head.

I cast a final glance at the long corridor, the stairs — the same as they always were, only the furnishings have changed: more modern, more comfortable, and brighter. I leave happily clutching that little piece of wood in my hands: it's something which is mine and which contains the little story of my childhood with all its pain and fear.

I walk back home, happy, and find myself in front of the old synagogue again. I go in and put down my little piece of wood.

You suffered with me, now it's right that you find peace among these paper voices.

I write on the wood with a felt pen: "Sometimes pain can generate great happiness."

And I place a piece of my life on the ground.

There you have it: I have tried to explain — to myself, above all — how and why I collaborated in writing a story like "Dear Sophie."

M. SOFIA CASNEDI
Author

Contemporary Jewish Memorialists in Italy:
The Reasons of a Recent Literary Phenomenon

This paper is very much a work in progress, in that the entire field of Jewish memorialism in Italy is so fluid and so intensely productive, that it will take a long and protracted commitment of study and research before the canon of a critical discourse can be established. The raw material being produced right now is so copious and diverse that it is even impossible to delineate the criteria for the selection of a representative bibliography. What is certain is that we are observing a puzzling whose area of belonging, the famous and cherished Italian "appartenenza," in Italian literature is still elusive. My curiosity in the phenomenon can be summarized in a few simple questions: Why is so much written about Italian Jews today? Why are so many Italian Jews writing about themselves today? What is it about Italian Jews that makes them the object of so much attention today? What is it that makes Italian Jews the object of their own attention? Why are Italian Jews so interested in talking about themselves, in disclosing to other Italians and themselves who they are, how they think, who they think they are? Why this interest — and why now — in the past and the present, contemporary, living experience of Italian Jews?

Let me specify the boundaries of my own inquiry first. By "memorialists" I refer primarily to writers who described personal vicissitudes in exceptional circumstances, primarily those of the Lager. But under this term I started grouping other genres of texts, autobiographical in nature, that focus on the themes of the Jewish identity and the Jewish experience in general. Among them are books like "Essere ebrei in Italia"[1] and "Raccontalo ai tuoi figli"[2] by Stefano Jesurum. Or Elio Toaff's interview with Alain Elkann "Essere ebreo"[3] for instance. I also include in this group of works the book by Liliana Picciotto Fargion "Il libro della memoria,"[4] which is quite simply the encyclopedia, a monumental undertaking, with the names and essential biographical data of the Italian Jews deported to the Lager between 1943 and 1945. And even Angelo Pezzana's "Quest'anno a Gerusalemme,"[5] the book of a non-Jew who collected the autobiographical accounts of Italian Jews who emigrated to Israel in the last sixty-seventy years. But the bulk of my reading has been on autobiographical works such as "Cara Sophie"[6] by Maria Sofia Casnedi and Fabio Della Seta who are speaking at this symposium; Elia Springer's " Il silenzio dei vivi"[7]; Ada Sereni's "I clandestini del mare"[8]; Aldo Carpi's "Diario di Gusen"[9]; or Lia Levi's "Una bambina e basta."[10]

These represent a spectrum of experiences, of sensibilities and literary abilities that differ in scope, profundity and urgency. But they all share the Jewish perspective on events and — peculiarly — they all have been written in the last 10-15 years. Indeed, the amount of publications about Jewish subjects, which started as a trickle around the mid '70's, has dramatically increased in the last few years. Before that time, there was mostly silence. With the exception, of course, of Primo Levi.

And it was with Primo Levi that my critical inquiry began, and with it the first questions started forming in my mind. The questions that I was asking then, though, were the exact opposite of what I am asking now. Back then the main enigma was: Why is it that, with the exception of Primo Levi, basically no other Italian Jew had described and defined in autobiographical terms the experience of the Jewish identity in Italy, particularly after the *Shoa*? And why such experience of identity had not been committed to the literary form? Where were those who could talk about such dramatic aspect of the recent history of Italy as the racial laws and the deportations? Where were the Italian Jewish writers who could shed light on the contemporary reality of the longest continuous Jewish community outside of Israel, a community as old as the Diaspora itself? Of course history books were being written, but never, it seemed, the accounts came from the victims themselves. So, why didn't those experiences have the voice of the protagonists themselves?

I found myself confronting an even more puzzling question when, in 1989, I was offered by Mondadori Editore the opportunity to collaborate to the series "Guida alla lettura di..." I was asked to submit a list of three authors that fit my interests and expertise. In order of preference, I listed Primo Levi, Italo Calvino and Vasco Pratolini. To my great surprise, Primo Levi was eliminated by the editor. And even greater was the surprise when I heard the motivation: Primo Levi was, in the eyes of Mondadori's literary establishment, "un minore." I knew at that time that certainly in the United States and, dare I say, in the rest of the Anglo-Saxon world, Levi was definitely considered a "maggiore," whose fame and reputation at that time was rivaled only by Italo Calvino's, and whose work, in the recent years has shown an even longer shelf-life than Calvino's.

What was, or was not, in Levi's work that made him one of the most celebrated and respected *writers* in the United States but not in Italy? What was in his *writing* that made him marginal with respect to the canon of Italian literature? It couldn't be that Levi was a "minore" in Italy just because the subject matter of his work only concerned Jews and the Italian Jewish community is so small. His work, particularly "Se questo è un uomo," is not exclusively about Judaism or the Jewish experience, but rather about the Lager and the immensely vast questions on human nature that it raises.

As my study proceeded, I began to conceive Levi's work as the itinerary of discovery of an identity. In my analysis each of the writings fit within the notion of a macrotext, where the genre and the content of each single work could be seen as a chapter in the lifetime story of the definition of his Jewish identity, a psychological journey into the consciousness of a Jewish identity. In each of the works, I traced the evolution of this consciousness and the dynamic relationship with the permanence of an Italian identity, together with the process of integration of the two at levels that became progressively deeper and deeper both in the literary form and in the dimension of the autobiographical representation. And here I must make clear the distinction that Jean Starobinsky credits to the Italian language, the ability, that is, to distinguish between "autobiografia" and "autobiografismo," where the first is a conscious process, while the latter is the mere reflection of existence.

It became progressively clear to me that Levi's psychological and spiritual parable had to be seen in the context of a Jewish experience and could be understood in the context of the Jewish literary discourse. In the formulation of this hypothesis I found the key, or what I believe is the key, to the questions that had puzzled me. The perspective that I had adopted was to be inverted: the question of belonging was not to be asked of Primo Levi but of Italian literature. In other words, I should no longer ask what was missing in Levi's work that caused the exclusion from Italian literary discourse, but rather I should try to determine what was missing in the Italian literary discourse that didn't allow it to include Levi's work. If Levi's work belonged to the Jewish literary discourse, and if his work was outside the canon of Italian literature, I was now ready to entertain the notion that for the Italian literary discourse, the Jewish discourse was absent. For the transitive property, if the Jewish discourse doesn't belong in Italian literature, Levi's work is also excluded. Ergo, Levi is a "minore" notwithstanding the commercial success of his work. (Paradoxically, commercial success and recognition outside the literary establishment could be seen as further evidence of strangeness. We all know that in Italy commercial success is de facto an argument against the "letterarietà," the literary properties, of any work.)

I soon discovered that it was indeed almost impossible to assign Levi's opus to any category of "belonging" within Italian literature. With "Se questo è un uomo" and "La tregua," the most documentaristic of the texts, the obstacle is the *Shoa* itself, since the *Shoa*, as per the famous caveat by Theodore Adorno is itself outside any literary discourse. But if we were to remove the *Shoa* component, probably the realm of belonging would be that "war stories," autobiographical accounts of extreme situations describing how ordinary people behave in extraordinary circumstances. (See for instance Mario Rigoni Stern with "Il sergente nella neve"[11] or Giulio Bedeschi with "Centomila gavette di ghiaccio,"[12] about the disastrous Russia campaign by the ill-equipped ill-trained Italian mountain troops of the mythical "Julia" and "Tridentina" divisions.) Levi's narratives fit quite well within this group, and, as anyone who frequents Italian literature knows, this genre is always "minore." Just as 'minore' was "Perché gli altri dimenticano," an almost forgotten book about the Lager by Bruno Piazza, published posthumously by Feltrinelli in 1956.

However, when we include Levi's work in the overall discourse of the *Shoa*, and if we connect the strictly narrative texts to the later ones, a different picture begins to emerge. With "Il sistema periodico," "La chiave a stella," "L'altrui mestiere," to finish with "I sommersi e i salvati" the problem is how to account for it in the context of Italian literature? What use does Italian literature have for the moral aphorism, the moral allegory, the "dilettantismo" that attempts to define a cosmogony out of the details of everyday life in which chemical elements become the physical representations of the spiritual world of the Jewish soul? And what is the place of the self-effacing, unassuming, anti-heroic, auto-ironical autobiography that hides universal metaphysical meditations under the guise of the ordinariness of existence. If something similar is to be found in literature, Levi's identity leads us to search in the tradition of the rabbinical tales, the so-called "storielle ebraiche," a tradition that Levi studied intensely, and a tradition characterized by stories that have a moral but not an answer and almost never offer a completely satisfactory solution. A tradition, I shall submit, very far removed from the Italian.

Italian literature is ignorant of the Jewish discourse. As evidence, I will refer to a recently published collection of essays on the Jewish literary experience in Italy, with the quite significant title of "Appartenenza e differenza: ebrei d'Italia e letteratura." What emerges quite clearly in these essays, with particular regard to the 20th century, is the absence of *any* Jewish discourse, even in the works of Jews or half-Jews such as Carlo Levi, Alberto Moravia and Umberto Saba. Where Carlo Levi could be said to be basically a-Semitic, and Alberto Moravia sounds determinately un-Semitic, Umberto Saba pushes his rejection of the Jewish identity to an extreme that to any objective observer is simply anti-Semitic.

All this is particularly curious, in light of the fact that a significant portion of the Italian literary establishment, and particularly the publishing and intellectual world, had a very significant presence of Jews. It should be sufficient to mention the names of few of the important publishing houses between the two Wars: Treves, Lattes, Bemporad and Mondadori among them. The exception is the publishing house Adelphi, although this happened decades later.

Jews as writers have been silent. Maybe this silence has resulted both from the learned ancestral survival instinct not to attract attention, and the desire to belong. The first reaction is readily understood. After centuries of persecution, from the Middle Ages through the Reformation and the Counter Reformation, through the establishment of the ghetto, until the emancipation by Napoleon, the Jews learned not to raise their voice outside the walls of the compounds where they lived. They had learned to fear "being noticed," for being noticed, individually or as a community, eventually would draw the fire of the anti-Jewish elements always fanatically present.

The second aspect, the desire to belong, finds its most obvious manifestation in the ardent participation of Jews in the widespread movement to unify Italy that is known as "Risorgimento."

It could also be argued that the so called benign treatment of the Jews by Italians is more wishful thinking on the part of Italians than reality. This conclusion can be drawn from the observation that while in the rest of Europe, Eastern as well as Western, Jewish communities flourished until they amounted to hundreds of thousands if not millions of individuals, in Italy the number of Jews was always kept very small, and in reality has declined progressively as a percentage of the total population. Genocide and pogroms were not necessary in Italy, one could suspect, because there was always some subtle kind of population control mechanism at play. I don't believe necessarily in a vast anti-Jewish conspiracy to keep the number of Jews constantly low, but it is possible to envision a sort of "self control" implemented by Jews who had realized that once the community went beyond a certain size, they would suffer repercussions. So, each community learned what its organic size was, above which it could not go.

If attracting attention was a way to insure reprisals, one could also argue that writing about oneself attracts attention. But maybe another mechanism of self-censure was at work as well. Literature, unless you call literature the blatant propagandistic efforts of "regime authors" in dictatorial societies, is almost never about the positive, but rather about the harshest truth about oneself, one's own people or culture. It is in fact a denunciation of what is immoral, wrong, intolerable, hypocritical and corrupt. It lifts the veil, it allows discovery. In an editorial that appeared in *The New York Times Review of Books* a few years ago in response to the question about the paucity of Italian American writers, Gay Talese stated that the cause was the reluctance, the embarrassment, the "vergogna" to talk about private matters in public. Maybe this reason is also common to the Jews and explains why they are absent from the literary discourse in Italy. Because, whatever the reasons, collective, subjective, overt or subconscious, the fact remains of the absence of a Jewish discourse in Italian literature. More specifically, a Jewish discourse is absent in terms of themes, genres and topoi. Nor is there a framework of reference in a moral sphere, or an aesthetics, or a mythology. The exception of the Finzi Contini, is really no exception at all, in that the work's literary form, the novel, corresponds to all the expectations of the Italian literary canons. In it, the Jewish text, lacking a context, becomes almost a pretext.

Another argument could be made for this silence, and it is in a way what Haym Maccoby addresses in his remarks reported by Ron Rosenbaum in his very recent book "Explaining Hitler."[13] "Here the Jews are, for the first time for many centuries, able to speak out. Before we couldn't speak out because we are going to get killed if we speak out. Now supposedly, we must not speak out because it is bad taste to speak out. One way or another there is a gag on us (...) We can't speak out in times of persecution because we'll be persecuted. But in times when we are not persecuted, we must not speak out because that would show lack of gratitude to people for not persecuting us. So, when do we speak out? Never?"

"Never" is no longer the answer apparently, not even in Italy. Quite the contrary, the moment has come to speak out. But that also means to reveal, to disclose, to bare one's soul. And the books start coming: memoirs, stories, interviews, accounts, contemporary narratives, experiences of the camps, memories of the Shoa, genealogies, explanations, narrations, cookbooks....

Italian Jews are speaking out. They are writing, both those who have something to say, and sometimes even those who don't have much to say beyond their own personal stories. They write and they find publishers. And they find publishers because somebody buys their books. And there must be a lot of people buying those books because new books keep on coming out. So, suddenly there is this convergence of interest: Jews who write about themselves and non-Jews who want to learn about them.

What are the circumstances that make the phenomenon of current Jewish memorialists possible now? It is not, I argue, the narration of the event themselves, but the process of identity discovery of the people involved. The works we see in the bookstore are not simply about the *Shoa*, or about surviving the Lager. Of course the urgency to speak out is also a response to revisionist history that denies the *Shoa*, and the imperative to speak the truth. It is undoubtedly true that the few survivors that are left, as they get old, realize that once they are gone, no memories will be left. But for every person who wants to talk, there must one another one who is willing to listen. So why is it that Italians are willing to listen today? And why do they buy those books?

The question now is: What is the common ground where Jews and non Jews are meeting through the mediation of books? What do the Jews say now that they are speaking out that non-Jews want to hear?

My answer is both simple and, I think, complex, and it will require a careful analysis. I believe that the Jews are allowed to speak now because they found a proper context of belonging, not just in literary terms, but in terms of the society as a whole. This domain is the discourse of diversity. Simple and reductive as this may sound, the Jews speak out their diversity. A diversity the Jews themselves denied in the first part of the century, that was imposed upon them with the racial laws, that remained with them when the society denied that diversity in the period after WWII. Jews were an anomaly in the homogeneity of the Italian people, a small curiosity, a little bump.

A diversity that, until a few years ago, Italy was not able to hear and perceive, as if it were made of sounds so faint that the ear could not detect. But now Italy is facing a whole loud choir of diverse sounds. And literature, as a reflection of society is reverberating these voices and is making them its own. As far as the Jewish experience is concerned, diversity was always imposed upon Jews through history as a mark of guilt and shame. In the last one hundred years then, Jews sought to defy the notion of diversity by stressing "normality" and integration. But diversity fell upon Italian Jews again as a curse during the Fascist regime when the racial campaign began and later the racial laws were promulgated. Primo Levi is the term of reference when it comes to describing this sense of bewilderment and estrangement that befell the Jews, but it is a feeling shared by all the accounts one is given to read.

Diversity, of course, became very much part of the consciousness of the Jews after the horror of the *Shoa* became known. Yet Italy still did not have a context for its appearance, maybe also due to the fact that Jewish diversity would have been a reminder to all Italians of the racist nature of Mussolini's regime, something Italians are all too willing to forget or minimize. Italy probably could not accept the notion of diversity because for the dominant ideologies, Marxism and Catholicism, to admit its existence would have been an implicit admission of a complicity in creating it. Moreover, in the absence of the discourse of national identity and in the absence of a definition of what it is to be Italian — a discourse that has forever been suffocated both by the Marxist doctrine and the Catholic thought — there was no space for a definition of what is Italian and at the same time "other" than Italian. The universalism both of the Catholic church and the Communist party made it impossible for the discourse of diversity to emerge. So Jews were left in the peculiar position of having experienced diversity, of carrying within themselves the notion of this diversity, and yet of facing the impossibility to express it.

For the longest time there was no space in the consciousness of Italian for any diversity. It could be interesting to try to determine whether it was Italian Jews that imposed this discourse of diversity or if it developed in Italy out of other pressures. The timing of the circumstances is such that it is hard to resist the temptation to theorize that Jewish themes began to emerge at the same time as Italy, for the first time in recent history, confronted the phenomenon of diversity brought to its shores by immigration. Italy began to interrogate itself, questioning its attitude about immigrants, wondering if it harbored racist feelings. And almost with a sense of anxiety, Italy turned to the Jews as a mirror in which it could see itself. But in turning to them, it didn't only see itself, but it did see them in their diversity, it discovered in its own midst a people who felt differently, whose internal collective experience was different, who saw history in a different way, who lived religion and ethics according to a different perspective. And Italy started to listen.

At the very same time the Jewish leadership in Italy took a very clear position on the issue of diversity brought by immigrants: absolute rejection of any discrimination, pressure on the State to recognize the rights of the new minorities and pressure on the society to develop a new sensibility. Within the context of the discourse of diversity, the Jewish discourse could finally be articulated and, in this form, it found a way into literature. The little known genre of memorialism, or the account of diversity, began to appear in the bookstores. It wasn't Jews trying to explain themselves as a way to apologize for being different, but a way to assert an identity, a certainty that before could not be expressed. First of all, the need to take possession of their own history, by means of the accounts of the protagonists themselves, the victims of history that official history had somehow put in a corner and forgotten. Furthermore, literature offered the possibility to express the real-time experience of the discovery of that difference. One of the most significant accounts I read is by Stefano Jesurum, who, as a militant of the far left, much to the disapproval of his family and friends, embraced the Palestinian cause and became involved in a sort of celebrity tour of *Feste dell'Unità* and similar political gatherings where he was asked to debate, as a Jew, a Palestinian. He was the "good Jew" who bashed Israel, who felt dutifully remorseful and guilty, until the day when he shocked the audience, his comrades and the Palestinian partners in this representation, claiming an identity he had until then exploited but not abided by.

In the other texts I have been reading, I found the constant thread of trying to "educate" people about this diversity, about this thing we call the Jewish identity. There is no minimizing it anymore, as the trinity of Carlo Levi-Moravia-Saba were doing, but rather the intellectual equivalent directed to Italian of the famous slogan of diversity we hear here in the United States: "We are Jews, we are here, get used to it." This assertion of identity and diversity is the beginning of a substantial phenomenon and I anticipate that it will take time before we will be able to construct a hypothesis on the various aspects of this discourse and the specificity of the Jewish discourse within the discourse of diversity in Italian society and in literature. I think that it is inside society that we will see more and more the apparent signs of the affirmation of diversity from the Jews. The first example of this new consciousness are already in the history book. In 1994 when a political election was called, the date chosen for the election was a Sunday that corresponded with the first day of Pessach. The Jews demanded and obtained that the polling stations be kept open until after sundown on the following Monday so that observant Jews could vote without violating the commandment. It was a significant "victory" not against the State, but rather against the tendency of accommodation, the defensive attitude of not making waves in fear of retribution. But the most eloquent case of this affirmation of diversity, this determination to speak out, not to suffer in silence anymore, occurred on the occasion of the shameful verdict on Priebke, when the Roman community, the "ghetto," and I use this word with affection, rose up and forced the Jewish vision of justice on the cynical indifference of the State.

The phenomenon of the Jewish themes in the field of publishing is thus a result of the interaction of forces that converge at this particular point in history. A people with an identity finds in the changes in society an aperture for letting its voice come through. And this voice is heard because it has a function in society, it helps society cope with diversity, it teaches society that it has lived with diversity within itself for a long time and from those experiences, good and bad, something can be learned for the days ahead. Italians maybe are learning that diversity doesn't mean alienation, hostility, conflict. The Jews, despite all they had to endure, show how it is possible to be different while at the same time being the same. And in everybody's heart there is the hope that this model of diversity could work for all the other minorities, present and future, that will have to coexist under the same Italian sky.

FABIO GIRELLI-CARASI

C.U.N.Y., Brooklyn College

---

[1] Longanesi, Milano 1987.
[2] Baldini e Castoldi, Milano 1994.
[3] Bompiani, Milano 1994.
[4] Mursia, Milano 1991.
[5] Corbaccio, Milano 1997.
[6] Paolo Gaspari Editore, Udine 1996.
[7] Marisilio, Bari 1997.

[8] Mursia, Milano 1973, 1994.
[9] Einaudi, Torino 1993.
[10] Edizioni e/o, Roma 1994
[11] Einaudi, Torino 1962.
[12] Mursia, Milano 1963.
[13] Random House, New York 1998.

The Garden of Arturo Vivante

"Memory's images, once they are fixed in words, are erased," Polo said. "Perhaps I am afraid of losing Venice all at once, if I speak of it. Or perhaps, in speaking of other cities, I have already lost it, little by little."

Italo Calvino, *Invisible Cities*[1]

The short stories of distinguished American writer Arturo Vivante have appeared steadily in *The New Yorker* and various literary journals for more than three decades. Many of Vivante's tales describe the trysts of a meandering young doctor or the domestic problems of an older, somewhat embittered New England painter. The preponderance, however, centers on the Vivante family in Italy before and after the war, as well as their experiences as refugees in England. Though divided into short stories like terraced Tuscan farmland, Vivante's literary territory, when seen in its entirety, proves to be vast and fertile. It extends, in fact, across two continents and documents not only the seductive charm of sunny Italy but also the chill intransigence of the English speaking world.

Until viewed as a whole, like a panorama seen from a distant hilltop, the author's tentative style and his polite, self-deprecating point of view seem to have made it difficult for critics to visualize the enormity of the Vivante saga, and the diversity of the narrative 'landscape' he has been cultivating. "Most of [Vivante's stories] lack the shape, the tension, the nerve, of fiction," complains a Washington Post critic. "Their principal method is not scenic but synoptic: there is a quality of summary, of looking back from a safe distance, many years later."[2]

Vivante, being a modest gentleman, might not even disagree with this statement. Looking back at the past — a past, that encompasses World War II — from a safe distance is the only way any sane person would wish to look at it. "My writing is mainly a study of life as I've known it," he states in a published interview. "I write to know the mystery that even a small matter holds. Through my writing I have come on some of the calmest, clearest and brightest moments of my life."[3]

"It is all useless, if the last landing place can only be the infernal city, and it is there that, in ever-narrowing circles, the current is drawing us."

Italo Calvino, *Invisible Cities* [4]

At the outset, Vivante's destiny was weighted in favor of 'the good life.' Descended, on his father's side, from a line of affluent Venetian Jewish ancestors and, on his mother's side, from American Protestants and Italian poets and patriots, he was born in Rome on October 17, 1923.[5] When he was about five years old, his family moved to Chianti to an estate named *Solaia a Malafrasca*.

> [It] was three or four hundred years old, the house. Originally, it might have been a monastery. Later, until the time we bought it, it was in one family for two hundred years. We were there for forty-five. Compared to those who had it for two hundred, we were only sojourners there...But frivolous our sojourn had certainly not been. The Second World War was at the center of our stay, astride it, and the dramatis personae themselves were anything but fickle.[6]

The huge, rambling villa was surrounded by farmland, which, before the war at least, generated enough income to support the Vivante family and the people who worked for them. When Vivante's father, Leone,[7] a philosopher "was forty-three and a novice to agriculture" —

> ...with extraordinary energy he set himself to looking for spring water, of which the house was till then deprived, found it ("It was there," he said) ordered two hundred peach trees from a nursery in Pistoia and had them planted down on a fertile plain below the spring.[8]

Like all children who grow up on farms, Arturo and his siblings, an older brother Paolo,[9] his younger brother, Cesare, and their baby sister, Charis had the freedom to run and play in the haystacks and trees on their own property. Their playmates were children from neighboring farms. It was a happy childhood spent in a beautiful pastoral utopia, though outside those stately walls, and beyond those open fields, things were not so idyllic. In '*The Sound of the Cicadas*' Vivante describes a Fascist 'inspector' who came from Siena to his rural elementary school to sell party bonds. The following day, one child reported that his father, a farmer, had refused to give him the ten lire, the equivalent of a day's wages. Though the man swore and shouted at him ruthlessly, the heroic little boy "stood by his desk without saying a word. He didn't cry. He only flushed a little."

Illustrating the difference between country folk and the urban bourgeoisie, when Arturo attended middle school in Siena, he realized that his family's political views were in the minority. When the news arrived of the fall of Addis Ababa, his teacher, who was also a Catholic priest, rushed into the classroom, cassock flying, to bring the boys the exciting news. While the other boys cheered, the narrator, that is, the young Arturo, "watched with scorn, kept quiet and felt disappointed in the man." [10]

With the rise of Fascism came "The Manifesto of Italian Race" in 1938 that prevented Jews, like Arturo's father, Leone, from publishing articles and barred Jewish children from attending school.[11] The sun was setting on *Solaia da Malafrasca*, and chill winds, as if fanned by Satan in his icy domain, began to blow. After a few seasons of good harvest, came a deadly frost.

> Not for two more years was there a good season. By then, however, the Second World War had broken out, and he, being Jewish and alert to what might happen, had taken the family out of Italy to England, leaving the estate in the care of a bailiff. For the duration of the war, the peach trees were forgotten. For so long they had been the subject of so much conversation, and now suddenly, they didn't matter anymore.[12]

Had the Vivante family not been so thoroughly anti-Fascist, they might have risked riding out the Fascist storm, but external forces, the same forces that would uproot and destroy so many millions during the 1930's and 1940's were to draw young Arturo into the vortex. Vivante's mother, Elena De Bosis, a gifted painter and conversationalist, was a member of a non-Jewish but vigorously anti-Fascist family.[13] Her American-born mother, Lillian Vernon De Bosis,[14] widow of the well-known poet, Adolfo de Bosis,[15] had been arrested in December of 1930, at the age of 67 for her anti-Fascist activities. She had printed anti-fascist literature on behalf of a group headed by her youngest son, the young intellectual, Lauro, a poet and man of letters like his father.[16] Having been a sort of spokesperson for Italian culture in New York and at Harvard, Lauro de Bosis was by no means a leftist.[17] He was, in fact, attempting to rally moderates to join the Alleanza Nazionale to take a stance against Fascism, lest the Communists take power in what he perceived to be the inevitable collapse of Mussolini's regime. In October 1931, Lauro flew an old plane from Southern France to Rome dropping anti-fascist leaflets onto the rooftops and streets below. As he flew over his own home, near the Piazza di Spagna, his mother watched from her rooftop. Like Icarus,[18] he flew west into the sunset and, running out of fuel over the Mediterranean, was never seen again.[19]

As Arturo, the second oldest of the four Vivante siblings, recalls, "For children under ten — I wasn't quite eight at the time of my uncle's death — we were sharply aware of politics." With the arrival of the so-called Racial Laws, Vivante's father, Leone, though an impractical man in other respects, took his family to England where they were officially classified as war refugees. In a story called *"The Soft Core"* the elderly Leone, his memory impaired by a stroke, tries to recall this journey:

> "And you say we went to England?"
> "Yes, do you remember, in 1938? You took us there."
> "Yes, you children were so good on that crowded train."
> "And when we got to England you saw a sign that read, 'Cross at your own risk' and you said it was worth coming just to see that sign and that in Italy it would have said, 'It is severely forbidden to cross.'"
> His father smiled. "It was a sign of freedom."[20]

After a stay in London during the blackout[21], the Vivantes found a cottage near Oxford. The boys were now able to attend school again. Arturo's older brother, Paolo, a gifted classical scholar, won a scholarship to Oxford, while his youngest brother went to a nearby school. In January of 1939, Arturo, fifteen, arrived at a 'typical' English boys' boarding school — complete with icy showers, canings and upper classmen bullies — in Criccieth, North Wales. On June 10th, 1940, while listening to the radio in the common room, he heard that Mussolini had thrown Italy into war. "The other boys looked at me," he writes. "while my eyes shone with shame."[22] The next day, in the middle of class, Arturo was arrested and taken to the next town, Portmadoc, where he was locked in jail. "Silently, I wept and wondered where I would spend the night, and when the night came, where the next day. An internment camp in Liverpool, as it turned out."[23]

On July 3, 1940, Arturo Vivante was put aboard the Ettrick, a former Greek ocean liner, which was crammed with over 2000 men, twice her capacity. The others included 879 German prisoners of war (mostly downed airmen), as well as German and Austrian war refugees and 403 Italian civilians. The POWs, in accordance with the Geneva Convention, were given the best accommodations while the others were sent to the bowels of the ship. Putting "unprocessed" Italian refugees, especially schoolboys, on a transatlantic ship among prisoners of war, was an egregious error in judgement, a British decision made under duress.[24] Canadian authorities objected to the arrival of so many civilians[25] but bombardments of London had begun and England could not or would not undo its mistake. It was too dangerous to transport the refugees back across the Atlantic. Indeed, another ship full of internees, The Arandora Star, en route to Canada was torpedoed with a loss of 603 lives, all of whom were either Italian civilians or Jewish refugees.[26] (German prisoners of war commandeered the lifeboats and beat back others attempting to save themselves.)[27]

Young Vivante would spend a full year, until the summer of 1941, behind barbed wire in Camp "S" on St. Helene Island within view of the city of Montreal.[28] "Week after week, I proclaimed my anti-Fascism and hoped to be let out. At last, after a year, an American actress — a friend of my family — came to Canada for a Red Cross tour. In Ottawa, she met Prime Minster Mackenzie King and asked him if I couldn't be released. The next morning, I was free."[29]

Though Arturo Vivante would never write a story set inside the camp where he spent a year of his life behind barbed wire, the indelible effect of imprisonment can be felt in many of his stories:

> Time to forget — that is what I needed. Forget the caning to which, like most English schoolboys, I had been subjected and which broke something in me that mended very slowly or not at all. Forget, later, being pushed into a shower room full of naked men, forget my hair having been cut down to my scalp, forget the hideous prison clothes, the insults, the internees' despicable talk — forget and return to the years in Italy when I had known a certain ease with girls.[30]

While many of Vivante's stories are set in 'the past' there is an elipsis around events that took place inside "Camp S" which is not unlike the silence of others who had been unjustly imprisoned or interned during World War II. As he writes in the passage, above, what was needed was "time to forget," yet he has not forgotten what happened to him. If he speaks gently, or remains evasive, even when asked directly, it is because he knows he was spared the unspeakable horror of the *Shoah* and the suffering inflicted on civilians during the war. If his youth was taken from him, he knows, only too well, how the war indelibly affected everyone. Released in Montreal while the war was still raging and trans-Atlantic crossings were dangerous, Arturo, thanks to support from Ruth Draper and the Canadian International Refugee Committee, finished high school there and went on to complete his undergraduate degree at McGill University. At the end of the war, the Vivante family[31] all returned to *Solaia a Malafrasca*. As the post-war economy changed their former way of life, acreage was sold off and the huge villa became a profitable *pensione* for paying guests. At least this enabled the family to remain connected to the estate until the deaths first of Elena, Arturo's mother, and then Leone, his father, in the mid to late 1960's.

> *Those who know how rare it is ... to fashion a dream without resorting to escapism will appreciate these instances of a self-awareness that does not deny the invention of a destiny, or the force of reality which bursts forth into fantasy.*[32]
>
> Italo Calvino, *Italian Folktales*

Arturo Vivante ought to be regarded as one of this century's greatest writers. His contribution to literature has been formidable. According to Calvino's standard, he has managed to 'fashion a dream without resorting to escapism.' Not only has his influence on American writers has been enormous, but his work has also shed light on the long-range consequences of this century's greatest tragedy, World War II itself as well as the extermination and suffering of millions of civilians. "There is no manufactured drama," [in Vivante's work], observes a critic in the New Republic, "no exaggeration, no attempt at psychological analysis. The past can only be put into a larger perspective, and accepted. Again and again, in that acceptance, Vivante convincingly affirms life..."[33] As we have seen, indeed, it is life itself that Vivante celebrates, blessing the miracle of survival with a survivor's ambivalence. Reflecting on a moment when the Ettrick was pulling into Montreal harbor and he might have leapt overboard, his narrator in 'The Jump' observes, "Perhaps the body, with its wisdom had sensed death in those waters. Suddenly, he brought the back of his wrist to his lips and kissed it — his body, his life."[34]

Warren Hecht, head of the undergraduate Creative Writing Program at Michigan's Residential College, has been an ardent admirer of Vivante's work since the early seventies. "Vivante is the master of the sentimental reminiscence," says Hecht. " Writing mostly in third person allows him to reveal everything — and what he is revealing is himself." In Hecht's opinion, Vivante isn't egocentric enough to be called an autobiographical writer, for, while never entirely 'made up', his understated stories include fabrication and juxtapositions. Hecht recalls Arturo admitting that when he feels embarrassed about something he's revealed about himself, he knows he's onto a good story. These revelations, however, are not made at the reader's expense. "Even in his fiction, Vivante is a gentleman," Hecht observes, "inviting us in and doing his best to make us feel 'at home'. He's too polite to point fingers at wrong-doers, seeming almost uncomfortable on their behalf." In teaching narration, Hecht uses Vivante's stories as examples of the correct use of 'sentiment' in fiction writing. These stories show young writers that "it's ok to reveal, to look warmly, to look back lovingly on things of the past, not to discount the small but significant moments of their lives."[35]

Having served twice as a judge for the University of Michigan's prestigious Hopwood Writing Awards, Vivante's comments on student work provide insight into his approach to writing. In his notes, he invokes terms like *coherence, cohesiveness, unity, progression and conviction*. He deems one set of stories 'memorable' for its '*natural and telling*' dialogue; another is '*convincing up to a point — but somewhat melodramatic...* He criticizes other entries as '*inchoate — needs more form*' and another as "*too fragmentary*," while praising another for its "*spontaneity, immediacy, and robust language*," especially its "*right, inevitable yet unpredictable ending*." Indeed, it is the unity, the cohesiveness, the unaffected, natural, telling dialogue and the inevitable yet unpredictable endings that make Vivante's own writing so astounding.

When asked why Vivante, who has written so much about things that embarrassed or humiliated him, has never fully described his experiences in the Canadian internment camp, Nicholas Delbanco, head of the University of Michigan's M.F.A. in Creative Writing Program and director of the Hopwood Awards, observes that Vivante is anything but secretive and cautions against drawing any heavy-handed conclusions. "It must have been an experience where Arturo simply could not zero in on a '*defining moment*'" — a skill, which Delbanco identifies as the essence of Vivante's power and technique "— nor would it even remotely resemble anything from the vanished world that he endeavors to preserve." A *New York Times* critic, A. G. Mojtabai observed that in Vivante's fiction this vanished world "is evoked fragment by fragment, rather than delivered full-blown to a single steady gaze. The cumulative effect... with its sudden stops and starts, its restless hoverings, hesitations and searchings, is true to our sense of man as a temporal being, haunted by past and future, with an eye that is ever adrift between the two horizons."[36]

In speaking of Vivante's geographical vacillations and 'hoverings', Delbanco characterizes Vivante's work as highly evocative and painstakingly crafted. "Very few contemporary authors," he stated emphatically, "have evoked the poetry of displacement and sense of loss — loss of youth, loss of family, loss of place, loss of position — and longing for such an unrecoverable Eden with as such persuasive conviction as Arturo Vivante."[37]

Possibly, apart from the events and people he describes, Vivante's crowning achievement is his evocation of the nearly universal feeling of displacement, the spiritual loss from which we as a society suffer. In a sense most of us are 'immigrants' of some kind, from other countries, other regions, other value systems, other socio-economic groups, having become members of a society so mobile and materialistic that we as individuals have lost our bearings. Vivante's work is meaningful and moving because, in our heart of hearts, we share his acute sense of loss and of being lost. To describe this state of mind, an Italian might invoke the word, 'spaesato,' which means 'confused' but which literally means 'un-countried.' Fifty years after the end of World War II, long after the resettlement of displaced persons and refugees from that conflict, the mood of our society as a whole is, nonetheless, increasingly spaesato: leaderless, directionless, restless, joyless. Paradoxically, as his many stories attest, it is not Arturo Vivante but ourselves who keep asking, Where, if anyplace, is 'home'? Who, if anyone, is family?

CAROLYN FELEPPA BALDUCCI

University of Michigan, Ann Arbor

---

[1] Calvino, *Invisible*, p. 87.
[2] Gale Database, Contemporary Authors.
[3] Gale Database, Contemporary Authors.
[4] Calvino, *Invisible*, p. 165.

[5] "I will start by saying that I was born under the sign of Libra, so that in my character, equilibrium and unbalance mutually correct each other's excesses. I was born when my parents were about to come home after years spent in the Caribbean; hence, the geographical instability that makes me forever long for somewhere else." Calvino, *Uses of Literature*, p. 339.

[6] Vivante, *Conversationalist, Run*, p. 8.

[7] Leone Vivante, philosopher and aesthetician, was the author of several volumes including: Principii di Etica (1920), Della Intelligenza nell'Espressione(1922), Note Sopra La Originalita del Pensiero (1925), Studie sulle Precognizioni (1937), Il Concetto dell'Inderminazione (1938). La Poesia Inglese ed il suo Contributo alla Conoscenza dello Spirito was published in English as *English Poetry and its Contribution to the knowledge of a creative principle* with preface by T.S. Eliot.

[8] Vivante, The Orchard, *Run*, p. 15.

[9] Paolo Vivante, Professor Emeritus, Classical Studies, McGill, is the author of several books on Homeric lyric. Gale Database, Contemporary Authors.

[10] Vivante, *Sound of the Cicadas, Tales*.

[11] The question of the state's ability to identify race, even to benefit under-represented groups, is at the heart of recent debates about University Admissions. According to U of M Professor Carl Cohen, "Whenever the body politic — the state, the community — pursues its objectives using racial categories among its instruments, it must face the eventual need to formulate the principles of membership in this or that racial group. The objectives may be evil, they may be humane — but if some citizens are to get more because they are of this race and others less because they are of that race, the state must be able to determine with accuracy who are members of which race. The racial laws of Germany and Italy in the early 20th century were wholly rational in this sense given their aims. Our aims are very different, of course, but insofar as we, like them would reform by race we will need racial laws precisely as they did. Legislation relying upon racial categories entails racial adjudication; there is no escaping that. Cohen to CFB, "Reflections on Racial Laws," 10/14/98, quoted in its entirety.

[12] Vivante, Orchard, *Run*, p. 21.

[13] "Conversare con Elena era un diletto, le sue descrizioni di luoghi di persone di cose, i suoi racconti di avvenimenti piccoli or grandi, erano vive...una pittura che completava il quadro." Nissim, *Il Ponte*, p. 860.

[14] Lillian Vernon came to Rome at the age of 16 with her father, a New England clergyman who founded the first Methodist church in Rome. In a story, Arturo Vivante describes her forty years after her arrival in Italy as still looking like a tall Puritan girl, full of good will. Origo, *Testify*, p. 35. In a telephone conversation, 10/8/98 with CFB, Vivante mentioned that Lillian, who outlived 4 of her 8 children was a 'great optimist' who was close to her youngest son, Lauro. Years later, at the very end of her life, Signora de Bosis accepted a tribute for Lauro as a hero who had given his life for Italy's freedom. When they showed her the letter of thanks of the Comitato di Liberazione, she remarked, "Look, Lauro's leaflets are still falling, *Che ebbe mai al mondo si larga tomba?*" Origo, *Testify*, p. 78.

[15] Adolfo de Bosis was the author of Amori ac Silentio (sic) and translator of Homer, Shelley and Whitman. He founded the most interesting periodical of his time, *Il Convito* whose contributors, Carducci, D'Annunzio and Pascoli were family friends. Origo, *Testify*, p. 34.

[16] Lauro De Bosis was a young man with both great literary talent (translations of Antigone, Promethus and Oedipus) as well as scientific interests and skill(degree in Chemistry and Anthropology at the University of Rome). He translated the short version of Frazer's *Golden Bough*. He wrote a poetic drama, *Icaro*, which won the Olympic Prize for Poetry in 1929. His compilation of *The Golden Book of Italian Poetry* (Oxford, with forward by Trevalyan) is still regarded as definitive. He came to America and gave lectures at Harvard in the early twenties. In 1928 he was offered the post of Executive Secretary of the Italy-America Society of NY founded at Casa Italiana in 1920 for promotion of cultural good will. As Fascism became increasingly repressive, De Bosis' was unable to tolerate it. He wrote and published anti-fascist pamphlets in Italy. Eventually, he resigned his post at the Italy in America Society and sailed to Europe in late November, 1930. Upon landing in England, he learned that his mother, who had cyclostyled his pamphlets in her home, had been arrested. Origo, *Testify*, p. 33-78.

[17] "I remember him walking in the garden with my parents, his step much lighter and gayer than theirs...something about him winged...a great entertainer — handsome, cheerful, high-spirited." Vivante, *The Visit, New Yorker*, 3 July 1965. Cited, Origo, p. 44.

[18] Arturo Vivante, letter 9/24/98 to CFB, "My last play, 'Icarus' is about my mother's brother, Lauro de Bosis, who in 1931 flew over Rome and dropped anti-Fascist leaflets, then died at sea on his return to France."

[19] See, Vivante, *Sound of the Cicadas, Tales*.

[20] Vivante, *Soft Core, Tales*, p. 78.

[21] Vivante, *The Holborn, English Stories*.

[22] Vivante, *The First Kiss, French Girls*, p. 118.

[23] Ibid.

[24] When the war broke out, 76,000 German and Austrians lived in Great Britain, 85% of which were refugees. Draper, *Accidental*, pp. 1-2.

[25] "... while Canada agreed to accept prisoners of war and dangerous enemy alien internees requiring close scrutiny, there had been sent to this country a very large number of Jewish and other refugees...Approximately 2280 including 401 Italian internees ...are of the refugee type and include a large number of school boys, college undergraduates, priests, rabbis, etc." Draper, *Accidental*, pp. 2-3.

[26] Draper, ibid., p. 5.

[27] In his fictional version of that voyage, Vivante indicates that for many weeks his mother did not know whether or not he had been on that ship. See, Vivante, *The Jump, Run*, 53, cited in Addendum A.

[28] "I wrote a thesis (Ph.D., 1983, Ontario Institute for Studies in Education, U of Toronto called the *Accidental Immigrants*) in which Arturo Vivante's story is quite

prominent. A book on internments in Canada, focusing on the Italian Internments, U of T Press, Eds., Franca Iacovetti, Roberto Perrin) is just being completed... I did not know what happened to (Vivante) after his release." From an e-mail message, Paula Draper to CFB, dated 7 Oct, 1998.

[29] Arturo's release would actually take three months. Canadian immigration officials' feared establishing a precedent while refugee organizations hoped that resolution of his case would enable others to be released. See Paula Draper's Thesis, *Accidental Immigrants*.

[30] Vivante, *The First Kiss, French Girls*, p. 118-119.

[31] Arturo's father and older brother had also been interned, but they were transported to a British island. They were released fairly quickly, due to the intervention of friends. Paolo's enlistment in the British Air Force was another factor which should have strengthened arguments in favor of Arturo's release.

[32] Italo Calvino, *Introduction, Italian Folktales*, p. xxxii.

[33] New Republic, cited *Contemporary Authors*, Gale Database.

[34] Vivante, *The Jump, Run*, p. 53.

[35] Having heard about Arturo Vivante in 1974 from Ken Pfeiffer, (Purdue's Creative Writing Program), Warren Hecht has been 'teaching' Vivante since 1976. Warren and his associates published stories by Vivante in "Anon" as well as issues of "Periodical Lunch." As editor of Street Fiction Press, he published *English Stories*, a short anthology of Vivante's stories. (Ann Arbor, MI Interview with Warren Hecht, October 8, 1998, Ann Arbor, Michigan).

[36] Gale Database, *Contemporary Authors*.

[37] Interview with Nicholas Delbanco, October 1, 1998, Ann Arbor, Michigan.

Works Cited

Italo Calvino. *Invisible Cities*. Trans., William Weaver. New York: Harcourt, 1974.
Italo Calvino. *Italian Folktales*. Trans., George Martin. New York: Pantheon, 1980.
Italo Calvino. *The Uses of Literature*. Trans., Patrick Creagh. New York: Harcourt, 1986.
Carl Cohen. "Reflections on Racial Laws." Memo to CFB. Ann Arbor. 10/14/98.
Nicholas Delbanco. Interview with CFB. Ann Arbor. 10/1/98.
Draper, Paula Jean. *The Accidental Immigrants: Canada and the Interned Refugees*, Doctoral Thesis. University of Toronto, 1983.
Gale Literary Database: *Contemporary Authors*.
    http://www.galenet.com/servlet/LRC
Warren Hecht. Interview with CFB. Ann Arbor, 10/8/98.
Iris Origo. *A Quest to Testify*. London: J. Murray, 1984.
Arturo Vivante. *English Stories*. Edited by Warren J. Hecht. Ann Arbor: Street Fiction Press, 1975.
Arturo Vivante. Telephone interview. Wellfleet. October 8, 1998.
Arturo Vivante. Telephone interview. Wellfleet. October 7, 1998

Arturo Vivante. Letter to CFB, 9/24/98.
Arturo Vivante. *Run to the Waterfall*. Scribner, 1979.
Arturo Vivante. Unedited correspondence: 11/7/84; 2/10/85; 3/7/85 (re:1984-85 short story judging); 5/1990 (re:1990-91 judging). Hopwood Awards Collection, 1930 — University of Michigan Special Collections, Ann Arbor.
Arturo Vivante. *Tales of Arturo Vivante*. Edited by Mary Kinzie. New York: Sheep Meadow. 1990.
Arturo Vivante. *The French Girls of Killini*. New York: Little Brown, 1967.

Addendum

These excerpts from five of Arturo Vivante's short stories describe his experiences before and after his 'detainment' in a Candian Internment Camp (Camp S) on Isle St. Helene Montreal, Quebec.

(C.F.B.)

I was fifteen and I was going to an English boarding school. I entered it in January — an odd month to be entering a school. But it was January of 1939, and my family was in the process of leaving Italy, because of the Fascists, and, within a few weeks, was settling into a small cottage in the country near London. I had preceded them to England by a few months and had stayed with friends in Wales. These friends recommended the school.

The Cane, *English Stories*, p. 29

On June tenth of that year, listening to the radio in the common room of my boarding school, in Criccieth, North Wales, I heard that Mussolini had thrown Italy into war. The other boys looked at me, while my eyes shone with shame. The next morning, a policeman, gigantic in his uniform, came into the classroom and called me out. I followed him into a Black Maria waiting outside. There was no jail in Criccieth, and so I was driven to a neighboring town — Portmadoc — where there was one. A real old country jail — three cells off a small courtyard behind the police station. The cells were empty. With barred doors wide open, they seemed to be

The Garden of Arturo Vivante

waiting for someone to occupy them. I was locked up. I sat on a wooden bunk in the dimness. Silently, I wept and wondered where I would spend the night, and when night came, where the next day. An internment camp near Liverpool, as it turned out. After two weeks, I was shipped to Canada to a camp on a small island on the St. Lawrence, in full sight of Montreal.
The First Kiss, *The French Girls of Killini*, p. 118-9

It was in July, 1940, and he was on the Ettrick, a Polish liner taken over by the English when the Nazis invaded Poland. The ship was loaded with German prisoners of war — most of them airmen — and interned civilians: sailors from Italian freighters caught in British waters, and German, Austrian, and Italian refugees, and other Italians who had been living in England. Perhaps three thousand men altogether. He was sixteen then, and he had been picked up by the police in an English boarding school as an enemy alien, which he was only technically, his family having left Italy because of the Fascists. He still wore his school blazer, with a pair of blue-jeans he had bought from an Italian sailor for a few shillings when his own flannel slacks had torn. For a while after leaving England, none of the men knew where they were going...What was her destination? One such ship had gone to Australia; another — though at the time he wasn't aware of it — had been sunk, and the Germans and the Italians on board had fought each other in a mad scramble to be saved. Nearly all had drowned. For a long time, his mother thought he was on that ship. But the Ettrick kept sailing west, and it became apparent that they were going to North America — to Canada, probably.

It was nice on the ship. After the big internment camp where he had spent two weeks, he felt perfectly free. He was on the deck most of the time. Diminutive though the space allotted to them was, it seemed quite sufficient. Here he could feast his eyes on the sea's wideness. Even in the cabin, which he shared with a dozen others, he didn't feel cramped. But he knew it would soon be different — another camp awaited him in Canada. It would end, this interlude.

As for him, he didn't want to get to the end of the journey. He stayed up on the deck, sitting on the good wooden floorboards, his eyes on the [St. Lawrence] riverbanks, which now were dark shadows under the night sky...(He) had heard one of the German airmen commenting on his age — he was the youngest there — to an Italian sailor who knew a bit of German.

"*Jude?*" the airman said. "No, no," the sailor replied for him as he turned away... Why, Jewish or not, hadn't he replied yes to the airman instead of walking away? He hated himself for taking the easiest course.

The Jump, *Run to the Waterfall*, p. 48 to 53

Week after week, I proclaimed my anti-Fascism and hoped to be let out. At last, after a year, an American actress — a friend of my family — came to Canada for a Red Cross tour. In Ottawa, she met Prime Minister Mackenzie King and asked him if I couldn't be released. The next morning, I was free.

I found myself back with people my own age, first at Montreal High School, then at McGill. But two years in a strict boarding school, and one shut in an internment camp with four hundred men, stood between me and the other students. I was both older and younger than they were. Years ahead and at least three behind. Time to forget — that is what I needed. Forget the caning, to which, like most English schoolboys, I had been subjected, and which broke something in me that mended very slowly or not at all. Forget, later, being pushed into a shower room full of naked men, forget my hair having been cut down to my scalp, forget the hideous prison clothes, the insults, the internees' despicable talk – forget and return to the years in Italy when I had known a certain ease with girls.

The First Kiss, *French Girls of Kilini*, p. 118-9

In the summer of 1941, when I was seventeen, I was released from internment and I felt like a child who has been long in bed with a fever and finds that on getting up his legs are too shaky for him to go skipping around as he wanted.

In June 1940, my family and I were in England where we had gone from Italy as refugees. Being over sixteen, when Italy entered the war, I was interned — taken out of my boarding school and shipped to Canada to a camp near Montreal. Being anti-Fascist, I expected each day to be let out on the next. At last, after over a year, I was released.

Wholly unaccustomed to freedom, like a bird just set free from a cage, I found that the beautiful long flights I had dreamed couldn't be quite as readily accomplished as they had been in my dreams. Even the first moments of freedom weren't what I had hoped they would be. Time and again, I had imagined myself standing alone outside the gate, with walls and barbed wire behind me, at last able to choose any one of the several roads that led away from the camp to the marvelous world open to me. But that image was spoiled by one of the camp officers accompanying me into town and, once there, taking me to his home. I felt it was like having the internment prolonged. I remember something constantly urging me to leave, to go and walk alone in the city that for a whole year I had seen so tantalizingly close. I remember my impatience at last winning over my shyness, and awkwardly, very self-consciously rising while he was insisting that I should stay a little longer. But to me it seemed I was cheating my freedom of every moment that passed. I remember walking down the front steps of his house and feeling under his gaze until, having gone around a curve, I looked back, and, seeing there was no one behind me, I suddenly broke into a run that lasted till I was out of breath — and I had caught up with my freedom.

I remember wandering about Montreal a long time, climbing a hill and seeing, hardly discernible in the distance, the tiny island that had been my world for a year. I remember running down that hill and, halfway, saying to myself, You are free — you don't have to prove it!" This thought had the effect of a brake. It sent me at a slow pace toward the boarding house where a refugee committee had arranged for me to spend a few days. It wasn't so late — half-past eleven, I think — when I arrived, and yet the landlady, who had been expecting me, was worried and told me she was about to phone the police. The police...the police...Oh, but why? Just the thought of the police looking for me made me shudder and have visions of myself being taken back to the camp.

The Stream, *The French Girls of Killini*, 3-4

Arturo Vivante

Having been educated in Italian, British and Canadian schools, Arturo Vivante completed his medical studies at the University of Rome (M. D., 1949) and practiced medicine from 1950 to 1958. His first book, *Poesie*, lead to a Fulbright grant in 1952 that enabled him to visit the United States for the first time. (He has also won an Italian Communication Media Award, in 1976, and a National Endowment for the Arts grant, 1979 and other distinctions.) Between 1968 and 1992, Vivante taught creative writing at several American universities and contributed over seventy short stories to the New Yorker as well as about 50 stories to other fine literary journals. Vivante resides in Wellfleet, Massachusetts where he and members of his family established The Delphinium Press.

Major Works:
The Goodly Babe, Little, Brown, 1966.
The French Girls of Killini, Little, Brown, 1967.
Un caso d'amore, Garzanti, 1968.
Doctor Giovanni, Little, Brown, 1969.
English Stories, Street Fiction, 1975.
Run to the Waterfall, Scribner, 1979.
Writing Fiction, Writer, Inc., 1980.
Leone Vivante, *Essays on Art and Ontology*, Utah UP, 1980. (Translator)
Tales of Arturo Vivante, selected and with an Introduction by Mary Kinzie, Sheep Meadow Press, 1990.
Giocomo Leopardi, poems, translated with an Introduction by Arturo Vivante. Bilingual edition. Delphinium.
Italian Poetry, An Anthology, (Translator and Editor) Delphinium Press, 1996.
Icarus, a drama based on the life of Lauro de Bosis.

INDEX

Abbanascia, Rabbi Giuseppe, 68
Acts and Documents of the Holy See, The, 182
Acuña, Viceroy Ferrando de, 71-76
A.d.e.i. see Women's Organization
Adelphi, 217
Adorno, Theodore, 216
Aeolian Islands, 92
Aggiunta per gli Ebrei di Sicilia, n80
Agustus, 16
Albergati, S. Niccolo, 41
Albertini, Alberto, 144, n152
Albertine Statue; Article 24, 26, n36, 107, 158
Alberto, Carlo, 44
Alexander III, 19
Alleanza Nazionale, 227
All or Nothing, the Axis and the Jews occupied Territories, 1941-1943, n37
Altrui Mestiere, L', 216
Amar, Sion Segre, 146, 149, n153
Amendola, Giovanni, 121
American Armed Forces Club, n37
American Jewish Committee, 177
America Oggi, n126
Anacletus II, 19
Ancona 1 Novembre 1900, 100
Anzio, allied forces at, 31
Apostles, Paul 17, 18; Peter, 17, 19
Apostolic Nuncio in Munich, 30
Arabs, 51, 55
Aragon, 42; Aragonese, 51, 55, 58; mon-archy of, 67
Aragon, Charles of, 58
Arandora Star, 229
Ardeatine, Massacre, n36; Caves, 117, 118, 120, 123, n124, 131, 132
Arendt, Hannah, 74
Aristotelian, 20
Artom, Eugenio, 112

Artom, Isaac, n35, 45, 112
Aruch "The Ordained", 19; *see also Nathan of Jechiel*
Aryan, 190
Ascarelli, Aldo, 145
Ashtor, Aliyahu, n63
Asmorean Family, 15
Assimilation of Italian Jews, 10
Auschwitz, 10, 30, 32, 117, 123, 129, 180, 182, 186
Austria, House of, 43
Ave Maria, 180
Avviamento all'analisi del testo letterario, n173

Badoglio, Field Marshall, 202
Balfour Declaration, 143
Banality of Evil, 74
Banks, Banco Rosso 6; secure banking system, 20
Barbarossa, Frederick, 56
Baruch, *see Benedictus*
Barzini. Luigi, 205
Bassani, Giorgio, 143, 185, 186-188, 193, 196
Bassola, Moses, 100
Battaglia, Salvatore, n105
Beccari, Father Don Arrigo, 130
Bedarida, Guido, 39
Bedeschi, Giulio, 216
Bellarmino, Roberto, Church of, 21
Behind the Door, see Dietro la Porta
Bemporad, 217
Benedicta, Sister Teresa of the Cross, 178
Benedictus, 19
Benevento, Immanuel, 100
Benjamin, Walter, 110, n115
Bérard, Léon, n36

Berlusconi, Silvio, 121
Bible, 209
Bibliographic Center of the Union of Italian Jewish Communities, n35, n36
Birnbaum, Lucia Chivola, 88, n95
Black Sabbath, n124
"Black Shirts", 121, 135
British Eighth Army, 203
Bolzen Battalion of SS, 117, 203
Bonaparte, Napolean, 43, 98, 217
Bonavoglia, Rabbi Moses, 67-69, 76
Books of Macabees, 39
Bottai, Giuseppe, 120
"Breviaire de la haine – Le III Reich et les Juifs", n35, n36
British POW camp, 118
Buttitta, Antonio, n94
Byzantium, 56, 210

Caesar, Julius, 40, 131
Caligula, 16
Calvino, Italo, 214, 215, 225, 226, 230, n233, n235
Camera Regia, 53
Camerino, Aldo, 102, n106
Campanilismo, 79
Campidoglio, 132
Camp Without Walls, n130
Canadian International Refugee Committee, 230
Canepa, Andrew, 112, n114
Capistrano, Giovanni da, 20
Capitoline Hill, 24
Capogreco, Carlo Spartaco, n37, 128
Capon, Clara Coen, 181
Cara Sophie see Dear Sophie
Cardinal Caraffa, 42
Carpi, Aldo, 214
Carpi, Daniele, 134
Caruso, Pietro, 117, 118
Casnedi, Maria Sofia, 214

Cassa del Mezzogiorno, 80
Cassidy, Edward Cardinal, 177
Castelbolognesi, Gustavo, 143
Castelnuovo, Guido, 29
Castro, Nuccio Lo, 87, 89, n94
Catacombs, 117
Catechumens, House of, 43
Catholic, 8, 93, 110, 137, 141, 158, 167, 210, 220; Catholic Church, 20, 30, 49, 70, 89, 92, 119, 134, 155, 177-179, 220; Roman, 36,131; French, 36;
Monarchs, 52, 77
Catholic Lateran Atheneum, 29
Cattolica, Carlo, 194, 195
Caviglia, Stefano, 112, n114
Centomila gavette di ghiaccio, 216
Chaplin, 28
Charles V, 21; *see also Reubeni, David*
Charles VI, 68
Chiave a stella, La, 216
Child of the Ghetto-Coming of Age in Fascist Italy, 159
Christ Stopped at Eboli, 32, 98, 103, n175, 201 see also Levi, Carlo
Christianity, 18, 53, 77, 89, 177; Christians, 17; relations w/ Jews, 18; hagiography, 99; anti, 177 *also Jesus Christ*
CIA, 123
Ciarrapico, Don Armando, 202
Ciano, Galeazzo, 138
Cicero, 40, 131
Cisalpine Republic, 43
Citone, Rabbi Angelo, 107, 108, n114, n115
City-States, in Italy, 1
Civiltà Cattolica, 157
Civil War, 185
Clandestini del mare, I, 214
Clement VII, 21
Codice Diplomatico DCCCXIV, 75; DCCCXV, 74; DCCCXVI, 75;

INDEX 243

DCCCLXXII, 73; DCCCLXXIV, 73; DCCCXCV, n81; DCCCCLXXI, 75; DCCCCXIII, 76; DCCCCXXIII, n81; DCCCCXXVII, 75; DCCCCXXXI, 75; MX, 76; MLXI, 73
Coeli, Regina, 163
Coen, Guido, 27 *see also the Rome School*
Cold War, 118, 121
Colorni, Eugenio, 29
Columbia University, 155
Columbus, Christopher, 52
Communism, 117, 147, 121, 192, 220, 227; Italian Party, 142
Concentration camps, 103, 156, 180, 200; camp Roccatederighi, 161; camp Ferramonti, 202
Constantine, the Great 18, 40 *see also Constantinus, Flavius Valerius*
Constantinople, 61
Constantinus, Flavius Valerius, 40
Contrada dell'Unione, *see ghetto*
Cori, Paola Di, n173
Corinne, 97
Cornwell, John, n162
Corriere della Sera, 144
Corriere Israelitico, Il,, 109
Corte Cassazzione, 123
Council of Ministers, 133
Council of Trent, 21
Counter Reformation, 21, 217
Crime Against Humanity, A, n124
Cristo si è fermato a Eboli, see Christ stopped at Eboli
Critica Fascista, 120
Critica Sociale, 146
Croatia, 33; Regime of, 199
Croce, Benedetto, 146
Croniche, 107, 108
Crusades, 19, 40
"Cum nimis absurdum", 42

Cuneo, Sabina, n95, n96

D'Anjou, Charles, 57
D'Annunzio, Gabriele, 143, n234
Dante, 20
Dear Sophie, 34, 208
Death camps, 32
Death in Rome, n124
DeBosis, Adolfo, 227
DeBosis, Lauro, n234
DeBosis, Lillian Vernon, 227
Decline of the West, 136
DeFelice, Renzo, 134, n152, n153
Delbanco, Nicholas, 231, 232, 235
Delphinium Press, The, 240
Denmark, King of, 30
Deutsch, Helen, 129
Diario di Gusen, 214
Diaspora, 17, 47
Dienchelele, 68
Dietro la porta, 185, 193-196
"Difesa Della Razza", 46
D'Intino, Peppino, 201, 203
Dionysus, 88
Doge's Palace, 2; Doge of Venice, 21
Donaldson, Sam, 119
Donati, Angelo, 33
Don Felice, 24
Doniach, N.S., 90, n95,
Draper, Ruth, 230, n234, n235
Dubnov, 17
"Duce", *see Mussolini, Benito*

Easter, 4, 83, 84, 86, 90
Ebraismo, Sionismo, Halutzismo, n36
Ebrei(1931), 97, 101, 102, n105, n106
Ebrei D'Italia. 39
Ebrei in Sicilia, Gli, n62
Ebrei nell'opera del Belli, Gli, n36
Educatore Israelitico, 108
Einstein, Albert, 28, 178, 179

Eliahu, Kibbutz of, n36
Elkann, Alain, 213
Emanuele, Vittorio, 108
Emanuele, Vittorio II, 109, 111
Emmanuel Victor III, 133, 142
Emperor Claudius, 17
Emperor Frederick II, 54, 56, 57
Emperor Licinius, 40
Empire of Freedom, 114
Encyclical, *Cum nimis absurdum*, 22 see also ghetto
Engel, Lieutenant Colonel Siegfried, 123
Enriquez, Federigo, 29
"Entwicklungsroman", 168
Erdely, Nicola, 33
Essere ebrei in Italia, 213
Essere ebreo, 213
Ethiopia, 26
Etruscans, 188
European Court of Human Rights, 123
Explaining Hitler, 219

Fadigati, Athos, 194, 195
Fargion, Liliana Picciotto, 213
Farinacci, Roberto, 137, 138
Fascism, 48, 66, n80, 92, 93, 119, 120-122, 128, 133, 134, 139, 141, 143, 144, 149, 161, 166, 167, 168, 180, 181, 185, 200, 202, 203, 210, 226, 227; anti-fascism, 28, 121, 122, 138, 141, 147, 160, 192, 205, 227, 229; Racial Laws, 102, 139; Nazi Alliance; post-fascist National Alliance, 122, 117; Grand Council, 133; Movement, 133, 137, 138; Laws, 161
Fascist Regime, 27, 32, 79, 120, 121, 128, 136, 139, 201, 220; Fall of, 29 see also Mussolini, Benito
Feltre, Bernardino da, 20
Feltrinelli, 216

Ferand, Clairemont, 40
Ferdinand, Viceroy Don de Acugna, 53
Fermi, Enrico, 145
Ferramonti camp, 33
Ferramonti, La Vita e Gli Uomini del piú Grande Campo D'internamento fascista, n37
Festa, 83; Festa dei Giudei, 86, 87, 89-93
Feste dell'Unità, 221
Fini, Gianfranco, 120-122
Finzi, Aldo, 144
Finzi-Continis, 188, 189, 191-193, 218
First Kiss, The, n235, 237
First Republic, 80
Flaccus, Valerius, 39
Flavius, Joseph, 17
Flick, Giovanni Maria, 123
Florence, ghetto 8; Medici Family, 20
Florida, Baroness de la, 87
Franciscan Missionaries, Sister Esther of the, 180
French, 51
French Girls of Killini, 237-239
French Revolution, 22
Freud, 28, 186, 190, 193
Foà, Carlo, 144
Foà, Vittorio, 146
Folklore, 3, 4, 11, 23 see also ghetto
Formiggini, 27
Fosse Ardeatine, Le, see also Ardeatine caves
Fourth Lateran Council, 41
Fulbright grant, 239
Futurist Movement, 120

Gabriel Magino, di Meir, 15
"Gagliardetti", 157
Garibaldi, Giuseppe, 23, 107, 202
Gaius, 20
Gailieo, 49
Gattopardo, Il, 65, 66

INDEX

Geneva Convention, 229
Genocide, 33, 65, 218
Gentile, Emilio, 136
Gerarchia, 144
German, occupation, 10, 29, 134; printing, 20; refugees, 26; persecution of Jews, 30, 228; Germany 48, 124, 137, 157, 161, 163, 199; accomplices, 118, 160; military, 119; Federal Police, 123; Nazism, 139
Gerusalemme Liberata, 191
"gesia", 67, 68
Gestapo, 119, 124
Ghetto, 1, 42, 45, 45, 48, 100, 107, 129, 158, 159, 207; 1st Ghetto, 1; Ghetto Vecchio, 2, 4, 6-8, 10; Ghetto Nuovo, 2, 7; Nuovissimo, 3, 7; folklore, 3, 4, 11; physical conditions, 5, 8, 20,22; symbolism, 10; renaming to Ctr dell'Unione, 10; holiday, 10; negative attitude toward, 9; location 9; Florence, 8; effect of encyclical, 22; Feb 17th, 23, Rome ghetto, 24, n35, n36, 117, 222; Jewish, 155
Ghetto di Roma, Il, n35, n36
Ghirlandina tower, 27
Giachini, Paolo, 123
Giardino dei Finzi-Contini,Il 185, 188
Gigliotti, Giovanni, n35
Gilbert, Martin, 177
Ginsberg, Asher, 149
Ginzburg, Leone, 28, 163, n173
Ginzburg, Natalia, 163-165, 167-173, n173
Giovanni, Giovanni di, 69-72, 74, n80, n81
Girgenti, Fra Matteo da, 69
Giustini Family, 129
Giustizia e Libertà, 146
Gobetti, Piero, 121
Golden Book of Italian Poetry,The, n234

Goldhagen, Daniel, 119, n125, 135
Goldman, Cesare, 143
Gold-Rimmed Eye-Glasses, The, see Occhiali D'oro
Gramasci, Antonio, 121
Granada, 59
Grand Canal, 9; palazzi, 9
Grand Inquisitor Torquemada, 52
Great War, 143
Greeks, 51
Green Party, 120
Gregorian calendar, 107
Gregorius Magnus, pontificate of, 67
Gregory the Great, 18
Guelfo Zamboni, 128

Ham, Achad, see Ginsberg, Asher
Haman, 91
Hass, Karl, 123
Hauteville, Constance of, 56
Hebrew, 20, 23, 39, 45, 46, 61, 132, 180; Commission, 182
Hecht, Warren, 231
Henry VI, 56
Herzer, Ivo of America, 127, 129
Herzog of Palestine, Chief Rabbi Isaac, 183
HIAS, 199
"*Historikerstreit",* 122
History of Ester, 46
Hitler, Adolf, 33, 117, 122, 128, 129, 137-139, 157, 158, 199
Hitler's Willing Executioners, 119, 135
Holiday, Sukkot, 10; Yom Kippur, 25; Sabbath, 40; New Year, 41, 45; Purim, 46, 68, 90, 91; Christian, 69; Easter, 83, 84, 86, 90, 91; Simchat Thorà, 107
Holocaust, 10, 32, 34, 49, 65, 122, 127, 130, 139, 155, 177, 178, 182, 186-188
Holy Father, 182

Holy See, 36, 41, 182
Holy Week, 84, 91, 93
Hopwood Writing Awards, 231
Horace, 17, 131
Horned Moses in Medieval Art and Thought, The, n95
Hudal, Bishop Alois, 118

Iberian Peninsula, 53
If this is a Man, 32; see also Levi, Primo
Ingrille, Franco, 88, n94, n95
Innocent II, 19
Inquisition, 20, 71, 72, 88, 89, 210; death of Reubeni, 21; Holy Office, 21; *see also Pope Paul III*
Institute of Jewish Culture, 52
Interlandi, Telesio, 138
International College of St. Alessio Falconieri of the Servants of Mary, 31
International Red Cross, 179
Internment Camps, 128, 228, 237; Canadian, 231
"*Interviews with Mussolini*", 26
Introduction to Atlas of the Holocaust, 177
Invisible Cities, 225, n233
"Irredentismo", *142*
Islam, civilization, 20; spirtual form of, 92
Israel, 10, 32, 49, 108, 142, 143, 149, 183, 213, 214, 221; Dubnov, historian, 17
Israel, 150
Italian Communication Media Award, 239
Italian Constitution, n80; Minister of Justice, 123; Occupation Zone, 34; Parliament, 136; Navy, 208; literature, 213
Italian Folktales, 230, n235

Italy, of Savoy, 79; post-unification, 112, 186, 217; Republic of, 118, 230
Italians and the Holocaust, The 128, 134

Jacono, Titta Lo, 52, 54, 58, n62, n63
Jarach, Vera Vigevani, 36
Jerusaleum, 16, 102, 114, 150; liberation, 21
Jesuit, 157
Jesurum, Stefano, 213, 221
Jesus Christ, 48, 92; Crucifixation of, 85, 87, 91, 92
Jewish, community, 9, 31, 75, 97, 98, 99, 102, 119, 127, 130, 144, 145, 148, 151, 185, 200, 214, 215, 218;Diaspora, 17; relations w/Christians, 18, 19, 30, 58, 67, 113, 114, 131, 161, 178; relations with Muslims, 40; relations with Arabs, 55; burning of doctrines, 19; writers, 20, 25; physicians, 20,21, 25; journalist, 26; effect of encyclical, 22; abuses, 22, 26, 200; as Roman citizens, 23, 24, 160, 179; Sicilian, 51, 54, 69; schools, 27, 28; persecution, 30; Brigade, 33; Testament, 111; Fascism, 135; ghetto, 155; anti-, 177, 217; Dutch, 177; integration, 193; Venetian, 226
Jews Abhor Continence, The, n80
Jewish Statue, 36
Jewish Youth Congress in Leghorn, 146
Jews and the Mediterranean Economy 10th-15th Centuries, n63
Josef, King of Tribe of Reuben, 21
Josz, Geo, 186
Judaeis, Sicut, 18
Judaic Salem, 54, n62, n63
Judaism, 18, 31, 44, 49, 56, 178, 215; Roman, 22; famous philosophers, 28

INDEX

Judges of the Magna Curia the Masters of the Royal Patrimony, 53
Julius Caesar, 16; rival Pompey, 16; murder, 16
Jump, The, 238
Jung, Guido, 144

Kabbalah, 100
Kaess, Lieutenant Otto, 123
Kafka, 28
Kappler, Herbert, 117, 118
Katz, Robert, n124, n125
Keeler, William Cardinal of Baltimore, 178
Kesslering, Field Marshal, 202
King Alfonso, 68
Kingdom of Italy, 26; *see also Albertine Statue*
Kingdom of Spain, 52, 53, 70-72, 77
King Ferdinand of Spain, 52, 53, 60, n62, 70-72, 77
King Ferrante of Naples, 60
King Roger II, 56
King, Mackenzie, 229, 238
King Martin I, 68, 69
Korherr, Richard, 136
Kustenland, 43

LaLumia, Isidoro, n62, 65, 66, 68, 69, 71, 72, 76, 77, 79, 80, n81
Lager, 213, 215, 216, 219
Lampedusa, Tomasi di, 58, 65
Language, dialect vs. standard, 9, 215; latin, hebrew, 20, 25, 26; Spanish, 25, Italian-hebrew dictionary, 33; finzi-continico, 189
Lateran Accords, 137
Latif, Rabbi Isaac ben Meir, 102
Latin America, 27
Latin Council, 41
Lattes, Dante, 149, 217
League of Nations, 146, 148-149

Lea, Henry Charles, n95
Leggi Razziali, see *Racial Laws*
Leggi Razziali, Le, n153
Leghorn, 20, 43
Leone da Modena, House of Study of, 6
Lepre, Aurelio, n125
Lessico Famigliare, 163
Leti, Giuseppe, 107
Levai, Jeno, 183
Levantine Synagogue, 8; in cities, 9; activities of religious life 9
Levi, Carlo, 28, 32, 98, 103, 146, n175, 217, 222
Levi, David, 44, 110, 112
Levi, Lia, 214
Levi, Primo, 32, 214-217, 220
Libro della Memoria, Il, 213
Life Magazine, 181
Loggia (Via della Loggia), 102
Lombardi alla Prima Crociata, I, 24
Lombardo, Dr. Maria, n130
Lombardo – Venetian Kingdom, 43
Louis XI, 68
Loyola, Ignatius of, 21
Luce, Dr., 203
Ludwig, Emil, 26
Luna, Conte di, 24
Luther, Martin, monk, 21
Maccabee, Judas, 15
Maccoby, Haym, 219
Madonna, 85
Mafia, Miriam, n173
Mafia, 80, 205
Maghen, David, 33
Magino, Gabriel di Meir, 15, n35,
Magna Graecia, 39
Malnate, Giuseppe, 192
Mangione, Salvatore, 86, n94-n96
Manifesto of 1925, 146
Manifesto on Race, 133, 227
Mantino, Jacob, 21
"March on Rome", 117, 144, 145; *see also Mussolini*
Maria, Benedetto, 33

Marxist, 28, 220; doctrine, 220
Mary, 85
Massacro delle Fosse Ardeatine, Il, n124
Mattatia, Joseph of, 17; *see also Flavius, Joseph*
Matteotti, Giacomo, 121, 144
Mazzara, 69
Mazzini, Giuseppe, 45
Medici, family, 20
Meir, Golda, 183
Melfi Charter of 1231, 54, 56, n62
Mellinkoff, Ruth, n95
Memories of a crepuscular community;Ancona, 100
Messiah, 114
Michaelis, Meir, 134
Michigan Residential College, 231
Michigan University, 231
Middle Ages, 18, 19, 41, 42, 54, 86, 91, 217
Mignone, Mario B., 39
Mila, Massimo 28, 36, 101, n105
Milano, Attilio, 15, n35, n62, n104, n106
Military Tribunal, 119
Minister of Corporations, 120
Minister of Education, 120
Ministry of Foreign Affairs, 34
Ministry of the Interior, 144, 200
Mio Marito, n175
"Mirabilia Urbis," 16
Miti dell'impero e della razza nell'Italia degli anni '30, I, 138
"Mizvot", 111
Modigliani, Enrico, 180
Modigliani, Franco, 32;
Mojtabai, A.G., 232
Momigliano, Attilio, 111
Moncada, Tommaso, 53
Mondadori Editore, 214, 217
Mondolfo, Abramo Giuseppe, 108
Monferini, Enzo, 27
Montanelli, Indro, 119

Monte, Crescenzo Del, n36
Monte di Pietà, 21-22; *see also Pope Paul III*
Monti, Augusto di Turin, 28
Moors, 52
Moravia, Alberto, 217, 222
Mordechai, Issac of, 20
Mortara case, 23
Mortara, Neomi Levi, 149
Moscato, Carlo, 101
Moses, 109, 111, 112
Moslem, 78; domination, 67
Mosse, George, 135
Muslims, 21
Mussolini, Alessandro, 121
Mussolini and the Jews(1978), 134
Mussolini, Arnaldo, 136
Mussolini, Benito, *(duce),* 26, 46, 86, 92, 93, 117, 120, 121, 128, 133-139, 141, 144-146, 150, 156, 163, 202, 228

Nabucco, 24
Napoleon, 3, 23
Naselli, C., n94
Nathan, Ernesto, 45
Nathan, Dr. Joseph, 182
Nathan of Jechiel, of the House of Anav, 19; *see Aruch*
National Alliance, 120
National Conference of Catholic Bishops, 178
National Endowment for the Arts grant, 239
Nazarene, 17
Nazi, 30, 34, n80, 103, 118, 124, 129, 130-132, 134, 157, 171, 177, 185; Germany, 33, 127, 135, 179-182; Revolution, 178
Nelvil, Lord Oswald, 97-99
Nero, 17
New Orleans Jazz Band, 201
New Yorker, The, 225, 240

INDEX

New York Times, The, 178, 218, 232
Noble Prize Winners, 32
Normans, 51, 55
Nostra Bandiera, La, 150, n153
Nuovi Sonetti Giudaico-Romaneschi", 36
Nuremberg Trial, The, 123, 182

Occhiali d'oro, Gli, 185, 187, 188, 190, 192-194
Oecumenical Council, 41
Opere et caritate, 177
Orlandi, Sister Lelia, 181
Osride, 112
Ottoman, n35; Empire, 20
Ovazza, Ernesto, 149, 150
Ovazza, Ettore, 144, 147, 150

Pacifici, Emanuele, 180
Pagan, 18
Palazzo Barberini, n37
Palazzo Salviati, 30 *see also Tiber River*
Panzieri, Rabbi David, 111
Palestine, 27, n36, 39, 47, 60, 108, 148-150, 221, 222; soldiers, 32
Papal Nuncio, 31
Papal States, 19
Papacy, 39, 42
Parlata, La, n36
Parliament in 1921, 146
Parma, University of, 161
Partisan, 118, 123; Resistance, 119, 123
Partito Nazionale Fascista, 145
Passover Seder, 10, 91; foods, mazzah, calle del forno 10
Pavese, Cesare, 28, n36, n175
Pedretti, Sig., 202
Pegna, Antonio de la 77
Peretti, *see Sixtus V*
Perlasca, Giorgio, 128
Pertini, Sandro, 121

Pessach, 222
Pezzana, Angelo, 213
Philo, 17
Phoenicians, 51
Piattelli, Rabbi Aldo, 131, 132
Piazza, Bruno, 216
Piazza, campo, 3
Piazza San Marco, 2, 9
Pierloni, 19; *see Benedictus*
Piccole virtù, Le, n173
Piperno, Giorgio, 28, n36
Pitigliano, 155, 157, 160, 161
Pitre, Giuseppe, 83, 84, n94, n95
Podestà, 163
Poesie, 239
Pogroms, 218
Poliakov, Léon, 34, n36, n37
Pomp and Sustenance, n63
Pompey, 16, 55
Pontecorvo, Giuliana, 147
Ponte Tresa, 147
Pontificial Commission, 177
Pontius Pilate, 86
Pope, 15, 18, 111, 118, 129; papal temporal power, 23
Pope Alexander VI, 20, 60
Pope Clement VIII
Pope Benedict XIII, 40
Pope Boniface VIII, 20
Pope Boniface IX, 40
Pope Jean XXIII, 48
Pope Jean Paul II, 48, 49
Pope John Paul II, 131, 178, 181
Pope John XXIII, 31; *see also the Rome Synagogue*
Pope Leo X, 21
Pope Martin V, 21
Pope Nicholas IV, 20
Pope Pacelli, see Pope Pius XII
Pope Paul III, 21
Pope Paul IV, 15, 21, 22, 42, 99; *see also Reubeni*
Pope Pietro, 19
Pope Pius IV, 42

Pope Pius V, 97, 99
Pope Pius VI 22; *see also French Revolution*
Pope Pius XI, 30
Pope Pius XII, 30, 48, 117, 157, 158, 160, 177-182
Pope Sergius VI, 67
Pope Sixtus V, 15
Pope Urbano II, 40
Porta Pia, 111
Porto, Bruno di , n114
Postel, Guillaume, 100
Pratolini, Vasco, 214
"Presa di Roma", 109, 111, 114
Preti, Luigi, 138
Preziosi, Giovanni, 138
Priebke, Erich, 117-119, 123, 124; trial, n125, 222
Prisoners Of War, 229
Protestants, 209, 210, 226
Puccini, Mario, 97, 99-103, n105, n106
Pucci, Sister Maria, 181
Pulga, Luciano, 194
Purim, 45

Queen Isabella of Spain, 52, 53, 70-72, 77
Quest'anno a Gerusalemme, 213
Questione Romana, *see Roman Question*
Quistelli, Agostino, 124

Raccontalo ai tuoi figli, 213
Racial Laws, 102, 120, 128, 141, 147, 148, 151, 160, 163, 167; see *also Fascism*
Racist Manifesto, 26
RAI (Radiotelevisione Italiana), 32
Raphael, David 72, 73
Rassegna mensile d'Israel, n36
Ravenna, Leone, 143

Red Bank, *see also Banco Rosso*
Red Cross, 182, 238
Redentore, Cristo, n94
Refugio precario – Gli esuli in Italia dal 1933 al 1945, n37
Relations between Romans & Jews, 16; other communities, 16; Jews and Christians, 18, 19
Religion of Nation, The, 112
Religion, criticisms, Horace, 17; Tacitus, 17
Religious Festivals in Sicily, 86
Religious Teachers of Filippini, 181
"Regnum", 53
Reign of the Holy, 111
Renaissance, 20
Resistance, 121, 123; anti-fascist, 122
Reubeni, David, 21; *see also Inquistion*
Revere, Giuseppe, 110, 112-114, n115
Rheinisch, Giovanna Sullam, 3
Ribbentrop, Herr von, 178
Ribbentrop, Joachim von, 178
Righteous Enemy, 127
Rinaldi, Riccardo, n114
Rio di Canareggio, 4
Risorgimento, 23, 32, n35, 44, 45, 110, 112, 141, 149, 185, 193, 217
Rochlitz, Imre, 127
Roman Empire, 17, 40
Roman Curia, 21
Romano, Immanuel, 20
Roman Proconsul Crassus, 55
Roman Question, 109, 110, 112
Roman Republic, 23, 40;
Rome, of the Counter Reformation, 15; as Italian state, 23, 110, 222; School,the, 27; bombing of, 29; Vicarate, 31; Synagogue, 30; Romans, 51; Berlin Axis, 134, 139; University of, 180, 239
Rosenbaum, Ron, 219
Rosenberg, Rabbi Haym, 100, n104
Rosselli, Carlo, 122, n125, 146, 151

INDEX

Rosselli, Nello, 146, 151
Roth, Cecil, 3, 88, n95, n104, n105, n152, 158, n162
Royal Council, 76
Royal Edict, 77
Royal Institute of Foreign Affairs, 122
Royal Majesty, 78
Run to the Waterfall, 238
Russian Revolution, 143
Rutelli, Francesco, 120

Saba, Umberto, 217, 222
Sabbath, 40; *see also* holidays
Sacerdoti, Susanna, 101
Saewecke, Theodor, 123
Saint Anthony, 88
Saint Basil, Church of, 16
Saint Francis, 101
Saint Helene Island, 229
Saint Mary Major, Basilica of, 15
Saint Peter, 157
Salonicco, 61
Sanbenito, 88, 89
San Ciriaco Cathedral, 98, 103
San Fratello, 83, 86, 87, 92, 93
Santayana, George, 156
Sardinia, Kingdom of, 43; deportation of Jews, 16
Sarfatti, Margherita, 134, 137, 144, n152, n153
Savonarola, 49
Scazzocchio, Umberto, 142
Schindler, Oscar, 179
Schindler's List, 127
Schreiber, Captain Gerhard, 119
Sciascia, Leonardo, 86, 87, n94, n95
Scola, n35
Scritti in memoria di Enzo Sereni, 36
Second Armed Division, 33
Second Temple, 17
Second Vatican Council, 31; *see also* Pope John XXIII

Segre, Cesare, n173
Segre, Dan, 112, 145
Segre, Emanuel, 149
Sejanus, 16
Semitism, anti, 49, 53, 70, 90, 128, 133-135, 138, 139, 157-159, 164, 173, 196, 217; philo, 172
Se questo è un uomo, 215, 216
Serbo-Croatian, 102
Sereni, Ada, 214
Sereni, Emilio, 148
Sereni, Enzo, 149
Sergente nella neve, Il, 216
Sestieri, Lea Scazzocchio, 36
Seta, Alessandro Della, n35
Seta, Fabio Della, 36, 208, 214
Seta, Ugo Della, n35
Settuna, Joseph, 76
Seutonius, 17
Shelah, Menachem of Israel, 127
Shema Israel, 180
Shoa, 160, 182, 214, 216, 219, 220, 230
Sicily, 20; Kingdom of, 58
Silenzio dei vivi, 214
Simetti, Mary Taylor, n63
Sinigaglia, Davide, 100
Sinigaglia, Oscar, 143
Sistema Periodico, Il, 216
SLM, 52
Smith, Denis Mack, 69
Smolensky, Eleonora Maria, 36
Social classes, Jewish Community, 10
Socialist Party, 146
Society of Jesus, 21; *see also* Council of Trent, Pope Paul III
Soft Core, The, 228
Solaia a Malafresca, 226, 227, 230
Sommersi e i salvati,I, 216
Sonetti postumi giudaico-romaneschi e romaneschi, 56
Sordi, Italo, 87
Sound of the Cicadas, The, 226, n233, n234

Spain, 20, 25; kingdom of, 71; monarchs of, 79
Spanish Edict of 1492, the 71, 72, 76
Spengler, Oswald, 136
Spielberg, Steven 117, 127
Spinoza, 28
Spizzichino, Giulia, 123
Springer, Elia, 214
Staël, Madame de, 97, 98, n104, n105
Starace, Achille, 137
Starobinsky, Jean, 215
Steinberg, Jonathon, n37, 134
Stein, Edith, 178
Stern, Mario Rigoni, 216
Stille, Alessandro, 135, n153
Storia degli Ebrei d'Italia, La, n35
Storia degli Ebrei in Italia, La, n62
Storie degli Ebrei Italiani sotto il fascismo, 134
Storie Siciliane, 65, 80, n81
Strada che va in città, Tutti i nostri ieri, La, 163, 164, 167, 169, n173, n175
Stream, The, 239
Sukkot, 10; sukkah, 10
Sulla parlata giudaico-romensca, 36
Sultans, 20
Surnames, Massima & Sabella Families, 16; Delli Mansi, Almansi, Umani, Piatelli, Levi & Coen, 16, Alceste, Alexander, Aeschylus and Clytemnestra, 25
Swiss University of Freibourg, 29
Synagogue, 7, 10, 39, 45, 46, 55, 59, 61, 207; Levantine, 8; torah scrolls, 7; of Rome, 25, n35, n36, 48, 67, 68
Syriac Dynasty of the Seleucides, 15

Tabet, Duccio, 146
Tacitus, 17
Talese, Gay, 218
Talmud, 19; studies of, 45, 108
Tante voci, una storia – Italiani ebrei in Argentina, 36

Tartar Lands, 21
Taucci, Fr. Raffaello, 31
Tedeschi, Rabbi Isaac Raffaele, 100
Terracina, Umberto, 148
Tesio, Giovanni, n173
Testament, Old 109, 113; New, 113
Tevere, Il, 138
Throne of Peter, 15; Sixtus V 15
Tiber Afire, The, 25, 27, 32, 36
Tiber River, 30
Tiberius, 16; Regime of, 16
Ticknor, George, 97, n103
Titus, Roman Emperor, 131
Toaff, Rabbi Elio, 31, 119, 131, 146, n152, n153, 181, 213
Tornimparte, 166, 167
Torquemada, 70
Trasselli, Carmelo, n63
Tregua, La, 216
Treves, Claudio, 146, 150
Trovatore, Il, 24
Tudela, Benjamin of, 56
Tunisia, 33
Tutti i nostri ieri, 167, 169, 170, n173, n175

Ulysses, 191
Una Bambina e basta, 214
Una Lapide in via Mazzini, 186
Union of Jewish Communities, 123
Ustachi, 127

Vaccari, Mayor Stefano, 130
Vatican, 30, 33, 36, 48, 58, 118, 137, 156, 157, 160, 177, 179, 180; Concordat w/Third Reich, 157; War documents, 182
Vatican Secretary of State, 30
Venice, 1; as Venetian state, 2; Venetian Jews, 1-3, 4, 5, 7 see also Rheinisch, Giovannina Sullam
Vecchio, Gina del, 100

INDEX 253

Veneto, Vittorio, 150; Liceo, 204
Verdi, Giuseppe, 24
Vessillo Israelitico, Il, 142, 143, 148, n152, n153
Via Rasella, n125
Vivante, Arturo, 225, 229, 231-236, 239, 240
Vivante, Leone, n233
Vivante, Paolo, n233
Voghera, Battlefield of, 44

Waldenses, 44
Wallenberg, Raoul, 127, 179
Washington Post, 225
Weberian Approach, 74
We Remember: A Reflection on the Shoah, 177
Wiesel, Elie, 155, 182
Women, 83; Women's Organization, 9; A.d.e.i, 9
World Council of Churches, 179

World War, I, 8, 97, 128, 133, 141, 142, 148, 151, n152, 159, 160, 199-200; post-war, 33, 167
World War II, 66, n80, 121, 122, 124, 127, 146, 152, 156, 157, 182, 193, 220, 225, 229, 230, 232; post-war, 121,

"Yeshibot", 100
Yours is a Precious Witness: Memoirs of Jews and Catholics in Wartime Italy, 180

Zevi, Tullia, 123
Zion, 27
Zionist, n36, 101, 137, 141, 142, 147-149; organization, 100; London Conference (1919), 146; anti, 150
Zionist Rassegna Mensile di Israel, 148, n153
Zuccotti, Susan, 128, 134, n162